Eagle's Wings

Comprehensive Handbook
of

Phonics

for
Spelling, Reading, and Writing

by

Susan Mortimer
and
Betty Smith

Soaring into higher learning . . .
Eagle's Wings
Educational Materials

P.O. Box 502
Duncan, OK 73534
www.EaglesWingsED.com

Special thanks to: ***Faith and Dick Blight, Tom Blight, Ron Smith, Greg Mortimer, and our children for their help in this project.***

Revised 1991, 1996, 2001

ISBN: 1-931292-07-8

TABLE OF CONTENTS

Introduction: What this handbook is all about.

Unit 1. Focus On: Teaching Eagle's Wings Phonics.

Gives various options and directions for using this handbook as a teaching aid or resource manual. Detailed directions for using as an independent phonics program.

Unit 2. Focus On: Consonants with Short Vowels and Silent 'e'.

Covers consonants, double consonants ['cliffs(z)'] with short vowels or with a single long vowel and silent 'e'.

Unit 3. Focus On: Vowels. Covers all the vowel sounds but short vowels.

Unit 4. Focus On: Ends of Words and Silent 'e' Helping Consonants.

Covers consonants that change their spelling at ends of words ['cliffs(z)'] and silent 'e's special relationship to consonants.

Unit 5. Focus On: Suffixes.

To double or not to double—adding suffixes.

Unit 6. Focus On: Letter Studies.

Studies function of various letters in words.

Unit 7. Focus On: Meaning.

Studies on prefixes, suffixes, root meanings, homonyms, synonyms, antonyms, heteronyms, and contractions.

Unit 8. Focus On: Penmanship, Writing, and Book Reports.

Provides poems and detailed directions for teaching formation of numbers, manuscript and cursive letters, creative writing concepts and exercises, including forms for 'clustering' and book report ideas.

Unit 9. Focus On: Activities. Games and activities for learning.

Eagle's Wings
Comprehensive Handbook
of
Phonics
for
Spelling, Reading, and Writing

Now that you have ***Eagle's Wings Comprehensive Handbook of Phonics for Spelling, Reading, and Writing***, you need to spend some time becoming familiar with it. It is packed full of exciting and helpful material!

The first section in this book consists of words lists. They have been six years in the making—compiling, organizing and making them practical and useful. Each chart contains from 200 to 600 words. These word lists are not intended to intimidate or overwhelm you. They are intended to give you a sense of security by giving you the whole picture of a particular word pattern. For example, knowing that there are only 19 common independent words with 'igh' builds an inner confidence . You will not be always wondering when another 'igh' word will "attack".

These charts are to be used progressively and are to be read as graphs. Because each new chart adds one concept, they can be effectively used for spelling purposes. And the order of the charts will help you as a teacher to present the information in a logical, step by step sequence. **Does all this seem a little overwhelming?** If you can picture this program as a building project, it may help you better understand what is happening. The first units are like the nuts and bolts of a creation. If they are not strong and properly placed, anything built with them will not hold up well. Once they are mastered, in an orderly fashion, they can be used to create anything imaginable. And that is the ultimate goal of our program—to help you give your students the tools and materials they need to communicate effectively, whether in reading or writing. By taking time now to learn the structure of the WORD, they will gain ultimate freedom of expression.

The first unit is **Focus On: Teaching Eagle's Wings Phonics**. If you are using this handbook as a teaching program, please study this unit for the correct study sequence as well as valuable teaching tips. The charts are to be used in the sequence given and mastered before continuing on to the next one, except where noted. The basic procedure for teaching each chart consists of reading and discussing the description of what is happening (which will be the write-up across from the chart) and then reading, marking, and spelling the words on the chart. There are flash cards at the very end of the book to be used to teach the phonics sounds ("Tell-a-Phone" cards), and reading pages that introduce multi-syllable words and sight words (pages 191-194). Although this book provides many resources to help in this process, the "meat" of the program is contained in the word lists. There is also valuable information on what to do if you are experiencing problems with your student. Feel free to use as much or as little of the teaching directions as you find helpful with your particular student.

Unit Two, **Focus On: Consonants with Short Vowels and Silent 'e'**, covers the sounds and spelling of the short vowels and a single vowel made long with silent 'e'. It also introduces when and which consonants double at the ends of words ('ck', 'll','ff', 'ss', 'zz'), blends—beginning and ending ('bl', 'br', 'cl', 'cr', and so forth), digraphs, ('sh', 'ch', 'th', and so forth) and silent 'e' helping 'g' and 'v' ('dge', 'ge', 've').

The next unit, **Focus On: Vowels**, continues with all vowel combinations except short vowels. Long vowels, ('ai', 'ea', 'igh', 'oa', etc.), diphthongs ('ou', 'oi', 'ow', 'oy'), vowels with 'r' ('ur', 'ar', 'or', 'ir', and so forth) plus any other vowel combinations or sounds.

Unit Four is **Focus On: Ends of Words and Silent 'e' Helping Consonants ['Cliffs(z)]**. At ends of words, there are consonants that often double or have a silent 'e' with them: Following short vowels ('ck', 'll', 'ff', 'ss', 'zz', 'tch', 'dge', 've'), following long vowels, ('ce', 'se', 'ze', 'ge', 'ch', 've'), and in multi-syllables ('le', 'ic', 'que', 'gue', and so forth).

The next section, Unit Five, is **Focus On: Suffixes**. This section deals with syllables and adding suffixes. It also covers how and when to double consonants (diner, dinner), and how to spell words with a long 'e' sound.

Unit Six is **Focus On: Letter Studies**. In this section, we look at many letters and try to see how they function in all positions within a word. This helps give a better understanding of why words are spelled the way they are. By teaching your students the unique characteristics of each letter, they will be able to have a better grasp of spelling than if it was approached it in a random fashion.

Unit Seven, **Focus On: Meaning**, is the last unit in the first section. Included in this unit are homonyms, antonyms, heteronyms. Also, charts on prefixes, suffixes and roots will give a clearer picture of where the English words originated and open up a whole new world of ideas. It will help tie words and ideas together in a way that will give a new meaning and interest in English. Marva Collins, a teacher who started a school in the inner city of Chicago, Illinois, introduced her students to new words and their meanings on a daily basis. The results were amazing! English is a rich language, and building a large vocabulary will help your students achieve more effective communication skills.

Unit Eight, **Focus On: Penmanship, Creative Writing, and Book Reports**, brings us to the point of why we study phonics at all—to use those skills in becoming a creative writer. Penmanship studies give directions for teaching both manuscript (printing) and cursive styles of writing. Then, many concepts and practical exercises are presented for developing skills in creative writing. A "First Story" form asks questions to help you pull stories out of reluctant or inexperienced writers. The "Letter Form" will forever eliminate letters limited to, "Dear Tom, How are you? I am fine. Love, Joey." There are other helps for the more advanced student to organize his thoughts on paper. Finally, a list of 50 ways for students to tell about a book will make book reports more exciting and discerning.

Next, Unit Nine, **Focus On: Activities**, a section with games and activities, gives you numerous ideas to make the charts more usable and to give variety to the serious business of learning to read and spell. Finding a few "old faithfuls", that is, games that work well for you and your particular students, will increase your effectiveness. There are also pages for reading and spelling practice. Spending a few minutes of daily practice with pages 191-194 will greatly improve reading speed, fluency, and comprehension.

Make sure you are familiar with the section, **Focus On: "Fun Forms"**, many of which are helps taken from the ***Alphabet Island Phonics*** program. It is good to know what is in this section so you can use the material that fits in with each lesson. You may copy these pages for use only with your immediate students. Some of the topics included are poems and pictures for learning all the words with '-ough/-augh', '-ail' vs. -ale', military words (many of which, thanks to the French, don't sound at all the way they are spelled—"colonel", "sergeant" and so forth).

To give your beginning student a head start in reading, take advantage of the "**Tell-a-Phone**" cards (on pages 219-226). Information on the backs of these flash cards gives you spelling tips as well as directions for making the correct sound.

You will also want to use "**Eagle's Wings 600 Sight Words**" (on pages 171-172 and in column form on pages 193-194) right from the beginning. This was designed to give you, at your finger-tips, the majority of words that are used in what we write and read. Just for fun, take a magazine article and underline all the words you find that are on the chart. You'll be surprised! Beginning students should first learn to recognize these words instantly without having to sound them out and learn to spell them later on. For young writers, this page gives a freedom to write more fluently and at the same time, reinforces the habit of good spelling by teaching them to look up words they don't know. For adults who are poor spellers, this list can provide a quick desk reference, helping their written material to be received with respect and not dismissed or ignored because of spelling errors.

This book is a treasure house of information. There is so much you won't want to miss. Spend time with it, get to know it. And it will help you to be the teacher you always wanted to be—confident, clever, and, more often than not, correct.

Tell me more about Eagle's Wings Phonics.

Q: What is Phonics and why is it important?
A: Phonics is the study of sounds, the sounds that form the words of language. Each sound is called a "phone". (Hence the reason for the name of our phonetic sound cards: "Tell-a-phone"—literally tell a phone!) There are two main approaches to phonics: phonics directed toward reading and phonics directed toward spelling. Eagle's Wings gives consideration to both approaches.

Q: What is the difference between spelling and reading?
A: Spelling (or encoding) is the process of putting written symbols together into words. Reading (or decoding) is the process of interpreting those written symbols and figuring out what the word is. Reading with meaning (or comprehension) is the process of understanding the meaning of what is read. All of these processes are necessary for effective communication, and all involve different skills. Therefore, it is important to be sensitive to a student's progress in each area in order to be able to effectively direct their learning activities.

Q: What are phonics rules?
A: A phonics rule is a description of a pattern that is observed in the way words with similar characteristics are spelled. What constitutes a rule is determined by (1) the data (or in this case, the word lists) being examined, and (2) by the observers of that data. We feel that it is important to know if a rule holds true for five words or five hundred. By giving you complete word charts, we allow you to see the patterns, enabling you to judge for yourself whether or not a rule is valid. For example, in our observation of the patterns, we were able to tie together 56 isolated "rules" from other programs and describe them with two basic rules. We have based our rules on the following concepts:

Eagle's Wings rules are based on the following concepts:

1. The consonant following the vowel dictates the sound the vowel makes and its spelling. [This concept helps to explain silent or doubled consonants.] The letters most affecting the vowels are 'l', 'n', 'r', and 'w'.
2. Several consonants and all vowels [designated as 'cliffs(z) letters'] change their spellings at ends of words.
3. Silent 'e' helps both vowels and consonants.
4. For a rule to be valid, words that break the rule must be accounted for and limited in number.

Q: How did you get your word lists?
A: Instead of relying on existing word lists, we independently collected raw data from many sources (including several types of dictionaries). These words were sorted, examined for patterns, and then cross-referenced using a 130,000 word spell dictionary computer program, WORDFIND, by Wayne Holder.

Q: When your lists say "complete list", why do numbers vary from other books on the number of words?
A: There are two main reasons for the number differences. The first reason is that no obscure or obscene words and few proper names are included. These words do not help us to see the predominant patterns and serve only to confuse the issue. We feel that this would have made the book less useful. The second reason the word counts may differ is that we have not included variations on the same word—"earthy", "earthly", "unearth", and so forth.

Q: How do you decide what words to include?
A: In a way it is difficult to judge which words might be obscure. We have made every attempt to include every wholesome and familiar word we find. Words that are specific to a trade or specialty might be very commonplace to someone familiar with that area but completely unknown to another person of the same age. If a word is not familiar to you, look it up and see if you wish to learn it! By the same token, if we have excluded a word that you wish we

hadn't, feel free to write it in and use it as if we had. A word of caution, however: Make sure you know what pattern is being dealt with. For example, if you look on the list of words covering the long 'o' sound, (Chart 18) you will see that "cow" is not listed even though other '-ow' words are there. "Cow" is not an obscure or obscene word—it merely does not say the /ō / sound. You will find the word with the list of /ou/ sounds (Chart 25).

Q: What is the difference between "complete lists" and "entire lists"?
A: Many of our charts deal only with words containing a designated number of syllables. The complete list, therefore, would be all the words that follow that particular pattern. However, when a certain spelling is rare, the "entire list" will be used, indicating that the list includes each and every word with that spelling, regardless of the number of syllables.

Q: Why does *Eagle's Wings Phonics Handbook* have different symbols for marking words?
A: A few symbols are the same or related to traditional markings. The reason for the variations and the new symbols is so that students can **ACCOUNT** for every letter used. The symbols help to show the function of each letter in the word. This will develop a **REASONING** capability that would not be possible with more traditional markings. A complete list of these symbols is on pages 12-13. However, each symbol will also be introduced later, as it is needed.

Q: Why are there fewer vowel sounds and symbols listed in *Eagle's Wings Phonics Handbook*?
A: Vowel symbols vary from dictionary to dictionary. Some have more while others have several spellings grouped into a single sound. This is because phonics is not an exact science. Several dictionaries agree with this handbook that the vowel sound for the 'a' in "car" is the same sound as the short 'o' in "lot". Other dictionaries also agree that the vowel in an unaccented syllable (sometimes also known as a schwa) is the same sound as a short 'u'.

Q: What are the words in parenthesis following another word?
A: There are a couple types of words that are put into parenthesis. The most common use of the parenthesized word is to give the homonym of the word being focused upon. If the word has a homonym in an adjoining column, the homonyms will be connected by thin lines. Occasionally, a parenthesized word may be used to contrast a vowel sound [shack (shake)] or to give a short definition [deer (animal); dear (beloved)].

Q: What do I need to know to understand the charts?
A: Each chart is labeled with a brief description of what it contains. Headings across the top row of the chart break the information down into manageable sections. Headings along the left side of the chart show further divisions. The words in the body of the chart are to be read as a graph. On the page opposite the chart is a written description of the phonics pattern shown in the chart.

Q: How do you alphabetize your word lists?
A: For the most part, the lists follow generally accepted rules for alphabetizing, arranging them according to the first letter, then second, and so forth. In lists that include single- and multi-syllable words, the single-syllable words may be alphabetized together, followed by the multi-syllable words. In cases where it seemed appropriate, the words were alphabetized by what was next to the letters under consideration. For example, these words are ordered first by what follows the 'a', and secondly by what precedes the 'a'. This procedure allows us to see more clearly which letters affect a particular vowel sound, and which do not.

clan bland brand gland grand clang

Q: What significance is attached to bold or underlined letters?
A: In most cases, the bold letters are used to call attention to a particular pattern. The underlined letters are primarily used to mark an "exceptional spelling", that is, a spelling that does not follow the expected pattern [t<u>wo</u>, y<u>ou</u>, fl<u>u</u>, sh<u>oe</u>].

Q: What is the distinction between the letters enclosed in slash marks and the letters with single quotation marks?
A: The letters of the alphabet are written with single quotation marks ('e', 'g', and so forth) and are to be read as the letter name. The phonetic sounds are enclosed in slash marks, followed by a word containing the sound to help the teacher recall what the sound is (/j/ "jolly", /b/ "boy", and so forth). These letters are to be read as the sound, not the letter names, and the word in double quotation marks is there as a reminder and not to be read aloud.

Q: Do you include the definitions for all the words?
A: Brief definitions are included for a few words, such as the page on homonyms. For the most part, students will be able to develop their dictionary skills by using a dictionary to look up the meaning and syllable division of their assigned spelling words. Ideas for using the dictionary are included in Unit Nine.

Q: How is *Eagle's Wings Phonics Handbook* meant to be used?
A: The Handbook may be used as a reference manual or as a phonics/spelling/reading program. The sequence of the charts is designed to be used for teaching. **Each chart builds on the preceding charts and only one new concept is added with each new chart.** In this way, the charts may be used as a phonics/spelling/reading program, since the words and rules are given in a progressive and systematic sequence. Directions for teaching from this book are given in Unit One, **Focus on: Teaching Eagle's Wings Phonics**. Numerous activities and helps are included in this handbook as well.

Q: How can I locate a particular word or sound?
A: There are two ways you can look up a word. First isolate the part of the word you are interested in: Is it the blend at the beginning of the word? The vowel? The silent letter? Now look at the Table of Contents to see which chart deals with this. If you cannot find it there, check it out on the Eagle's Wings Comprehensive Chart of Consonants (page 14) or Eagle's Wings Comprehensive Chart of Vowels (page 16). Locate the chart and number and look it up.

Q: How do I get started?
A: To get an overview of what you will be covering in this book, spend some time looking over pages 14-18. Studying these charts will give you a clearer picture of where you are heading from the very beginning. These charts summarize virtually everything that happens with English consonants and vowels. Looking over these charts will also give you practice in reading the charts as graphs, which will help you when you start using the rest of the charts in this book. After you have a general understanding of the consonant and vowel charts, move to Unit One, paying particular attention to page 24, where you will find a basic lesson plan that can be adapted to each chart as well as to your individual pupil's needs. Unit One, **Focus on Teaching Eagle's Wings Phonics**, gives you vital information that is not found elsewhere. However, some items will not be introduced until necessary. Now, take a deep breath and jump right in!

Eagle's Wings Symbols

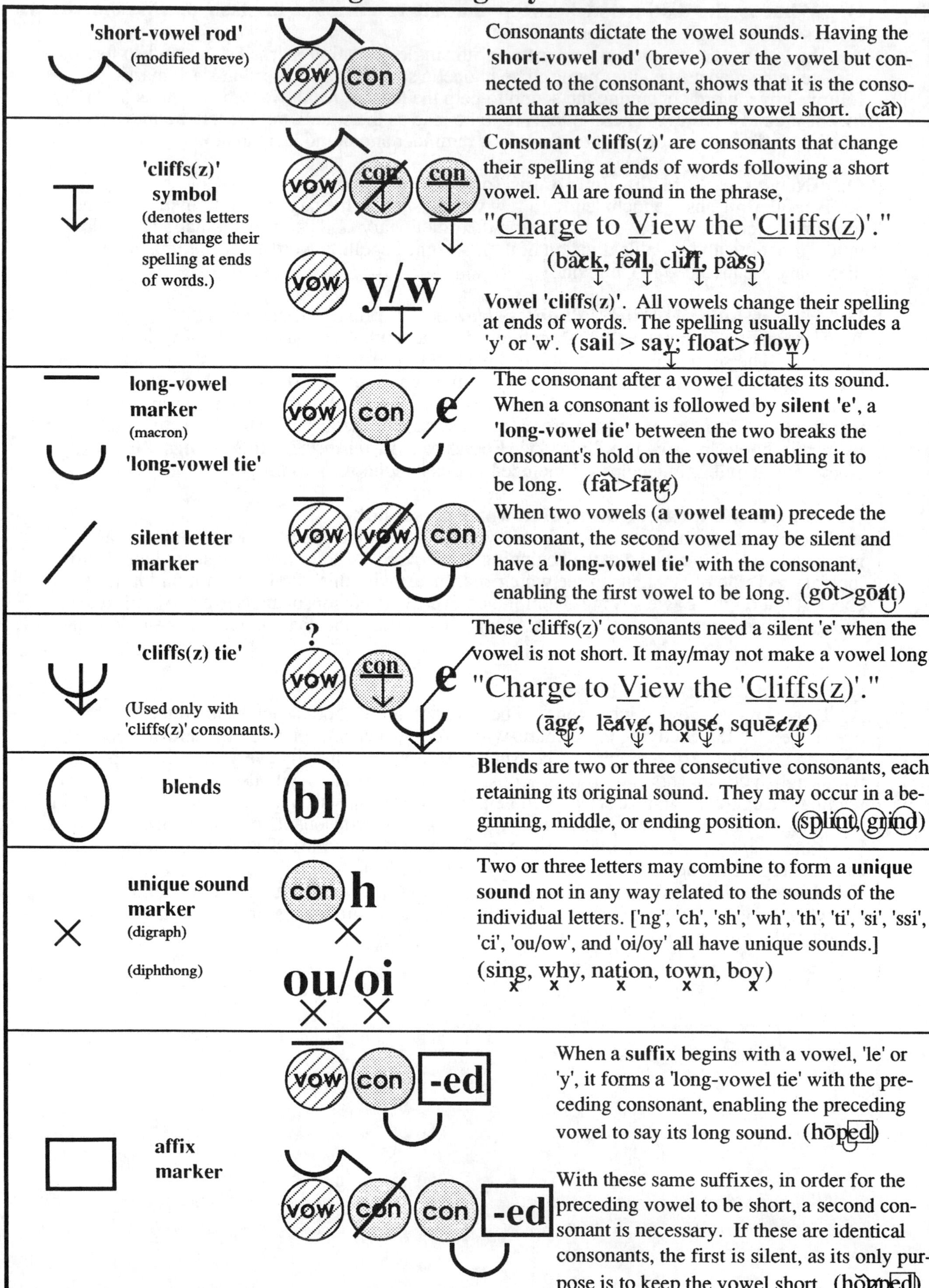
'short-vowel rod'
(modified breve)
vow
con
Consonants dictate the vowel sounds. Having the 'short-vowel rod' (breve) over the vowel but connected to the consonant, shows that it is the consonant that makes the preceding vowel short. (căt)
'cliffs(z)' symbol
(denotes letters that change their spelling at ends of words.)
vow
con
con
y/w
Consonant 'cliffs(z)' are consonants that change their spelling at ends of words following a short vowel. All are found in the phrase,
"Charge to View the 'Cliffs(z)'."
(back, fell, cliff, pass)
Vowel 'cliffs(z)'. All vowels change their spelling at ends of words. The spelling usually includes a 'y' or 'w'. (sail > say; float> flow)
long-vowel marker
(macron)
'long-vowel tie'
vow
con
e
The consonant after a vowel dictates its sound. When a consonant is followed by silent 'e', a 'long-vowel tie' between the two breaks the consonant's hold on the vowel enabling it to be long. (făt>fāte)
silent letter marker
vow
vow
con
When two vowels (a vowel team) precede the consonant, the second vowel may be silent and have a 'long-vowel tie' with the consonant, enabling the first vowel to be long. (gŏt>gōat)
'cliffs(z) tie'
(Used only with 'cliffs(z)' consonants.)
?
vow
con
e
These 'cliffs(z)' consonants need a silent 'e' when the vowel is not short. It may/may not make a vowel long.
"Charge to View the 'Cliffs(z)'."
(āge, lēave, house, squēeze)
blends
bl
Blends are two or three consecutive consonants, each retaining its original sound. They may occur in a beginning, middle, or ending position. (splint, grind)
unique sound marker
(digraph)
(diphthong)
con
h
ou/oi
Two or three letters may combine to form a unique sound not in any way related to the sounds of the individual letters. ['ng', 'ch', 'sh', 'wh', 'th', 'ti', 'si', 'ssi', 'ci', 'ou/ow', and 'oi/oy' all have unique sounds.]
(sing, why, nation, town, boy)
affix marker
vow
con
-ed
When a suffix begins with a vowel, 'le' or 'y', it forms a 'long-vowel tie' with the preceding consonant, enabling the preceding vowel to say its long sound. (hōped)
vow
con
con
-ed
With these same suffixes, in order for the preceding vowel to be short, a second consonant is necessary. If these are identical consonants, the first is silent, as its only purpose is to keep the vowel short. (hŏpped)

Eagle's Wings Symbols (continued)

✏	**'Everyday Words'** (sight words) ✏ **and**	**'Everyday Words'** are the most often used words. In written material, these words make up the majority of the text. Instant recognition of these words will make a reader more fluent. (and, at, can, it, not, that, ask)
*	**'Everyday Bloopers'** (rule-breaking sight words) ***the**	**'Everyday Bloopers'** are commonly used words that break the rules. The more often a word is used, the more likely it is to be "misspelled" or not follow the rules. What has happened is that a "short-hand" has developed for frequently used words and normal patterns are disregarded. (are, the, is, of, these, whose)
☆	☆ ☆ **l / n**	The letters, 'l' and 'n' affect the spellings and sounds of vowels differently than any other consonants, except for 'r'. Visualizing 'l' and 'n' with a star will set them apart as unique. This will help reinforce the concept that they can change the rules. (bal̊d, blin̊d)
←	← **r**	The letter 'r' affects the vowel sound that precedes it more than other consonants do. This is indicated by the arrow pointing to the left. (car, burn, fern, sir, corn)
↔	↔ **w**	The only consonant that affects the vowel on either side of it is 'w'. This is indicated by an arrow pointing both directions. It is also a 'cliffs(z) vowel' that helps vowels at ends of words. (want, cow, law)
a/o (with u under)	**Additional vowel markers**	The vowels 'a' and 'o' have an additional sound which is closely related to the short 'u' and is marked with a small 'u' under the letter. (about, love)
å		The letter 'a' also has a sound which is closely related to the short 'o' sound and is marked with a small 'o' over the letter. (åll, wånt, får)
ü / oo		The letter 'u' can have the sound of 'oo'. This is marked with a small 'oo' over the 'u', /ü/. (tüne—moon)
🖳	**Computer checked**	Word lists marked with the **computer checked** symbol have been cross-checked with WORDFIND, a 130,000 word spell dictionary program by Wayne Holder, and include all the **wholesome** and **familiar** words following a particular pattern.

Understanding these new symbols, markings, and basic concepts will make it easy to **REASON** out the spelling of almost any word and account for every letter used.

Eagle's Wings Comprehensive Chart of Consonants

Consonant Sounds: Consistent Spelling ① Chart 1, 51

Sound/Spelling	
/b/	boy
/d/	dad
/h/	hop
/m/[1]	mat
/n/[1]	not
/p/	pat
/r/[1]	ran
/t/	top
/w/[2]	wet
/y/[2]	yes Chart 70

'Cliffs(z) Consonants': "Charge to View the Cliffs(z)!"

Varied spellings:

②	Chart	At beginnings	Chart	At ends of words [Cliffs(z)] ③ Following a short vowel.		Chart	Not following a short vowel	
/k/[3]	51/59	cat; kit; chord	30/38	-ck/-c	back; picnic	38	-k/-que	bank; opaque
/l/	51	lot	30/31	-ll[5]	tell; awful	36	-l/-le	sail; apple
/f/[1]	51 58	fan; photo	30/31 39	-ff/-ph (-ffs)[6]	cliff; graph (cliffs)	7/31 39	-f/-gh (-ves)[4]	leaf; tough (leaves)
/s/[1;3]	51	sat; city	30/31	-ss[7]	pass	32-34	-ce/-se[7]	dance; house
/z/	51	zoo; xylophone	30	-zz	fizz	32-34	-se/-ze	cheese; sneeze
/ch/[4]	57	cheese	39	-tch	catch	39	-ch	each
/j/[3]	51/61	jam; gem	37/62	-dge	judge	37/62	-ge	hinge
/g/[3]	61	got; guitar	37/38 62	-g/-gue	bag catalogue	38	-gue	vague
/v/	51.63	vine	37/38 63	-ve[8]	have	37/38 63	-ve[8]	sleeve

[1] See "Silent Consonants", below. [2]'w' and 'y' act as consonants only at the beginning of syllables.
[3]/k/= c & /s/= s>a,o,u, & consonants; /k/= k & /s/= c & s>e,i,y. Generally: /g/= g & /j/= j>a,o,u, & consonants; /j/=g & /g/=gu>e,i,y.
[4]See "Blends". [5]'all'=/ål/,"tall"; 'oll'=/ōl/,"toll". [6]To pluralize words ending in 'ff', add 's'. To pluralize a word ending in a single 'f' or 'fe', change to 'ves'. [7]A single 's' or 'es' is used for plurals, possesives, and tense. [8]'ove'=/uv/, /üv/, /ov/, /ōv/ ('u' is never next to a 'v'.)

Beginning Blends Chart 4, 52, 53, 54 ④

'-l'	'-r'	'-w'	's-'
bl black	br brag		sc scab
cl clam	cr crab		sk skid;school
	dr drag	dw dwarf	sm smog
fl flag	fr frog		sn snap
gl glad	gr grin		sp span
pl plan	pr prim		st stop
	tr trap	tw twig	spl splash
		/kw/[1] quote choir	scr scrap spr sprig
sl slam		sw swing	str strap squ[1] squid

Ending Blends[3] Chart 6, 7, 8 ④

'-t'	'-d'	'-p'	'-k'
-ct act			
-ft gift			
		-mp camp	
-nt bent	-nd bend		-nk[4] bank
-pt wept			
-st mast		-sp gasp	-sk mask
-xt next			
-lt belt	-ld held	-lp help	-lk milk
			/ks/[2] mix;licks[3]

[1]'qu' = /kw/ ; 'qua'=/kwŏ/ [2]'x' = /ks/ [3]Adding 's' to a word will make a consonant blend with the consonant preceding it; cat/cats. [4]'nk' = /ngk/

Digraphs (unique sounds) ⑤

	Chart	Beginning	Chart	Medial	Chart	Final
/ch/	8/55	cheese;cello	46/57	picture;question	9/57	catch;each
/sh/	8 55 57	shh!;shut chandelier	49 57	caption;mission physician;pension conscious	9 56	fish
/zh/			46/ 48/58	vision;pleasure	57	garage
/th/	8/55	think			9/56	path
/th/	8/55	that	56	other	9/56	loathe
/hw/	8/55	when				
-/ng/			6/8	bank; anchor	6/8	sing;tongue

Silent Consonants Chart 71 ⑥

lf=/f/ calf	ps=/s/ psychiatrist
sle=/l/ aisle	sc=/s/ scene
chm=/m/ drachm	st=/s/ castle
gm=/m/ phlegm	sw=/s/ sword
lm=/m/ palm	bt=/t/ debt
mb=/m/ comb	rh=/r/ rhythm
gn=/n/ gnat, sign	wr=/r/ wren
kn=/n/ knee	dj=/j/ adjacent
mn=/n/ mnemonic	lk=/k/ walk
pn=/n/ pneumonia	gh=/ / sigh (Chart 58)
	h=/ / exhibit, hour

Consonants

If you can understand and apply the comprehensive charts on consonants and vowels, you are a long way toward better understanding the English language!

Consonants: Twenty-one letters of the alphabet are consonants, five are vowels. Two of the consonants, 'y' and 'w' function as both vowels and consonants. They are only consonants at the beginning of a syllable or in a consonant blend. (yard, win, swim)

① **Consistent Consonants:** Of the consonant sounds, only ten have consistent spellings. For example, a /b/ sound anywhere in a word will be spelled with a 'b', and a /d/ sound will be a 'd'. The /n/ has numerous variations ('gn, 'kn', 'mn', 'pn'); however these are rare and considered the exception.

② **Several Sounds:** A few consonant sounds change their spelling at the beginnings of syllables. 'C' has no sound that is uniquely its own, but it follows a consistent pattern: 'c' says /s/, "**city**" before 'i', 'e' and 'y', and /k/ ,"**cat**" elsewhere. 'G' also has two sounds but is not as predictable. Generally 'g' says /j/, '**gem**', before 'i', 'e', and 'y' if there is a single vowel followed by a single consonant. It says /g/, "**goat**", elsewhere. 'Gu' is commonly used to keep the /g/ before 'i', 'e', and 'y', "**guitar**". For a more complete discussion of 'g', see Charts 61 and 62. /f/ can be spelled with 'f', 'gh' or 'ph', but there are a relatively few number of words that use the 'ph', "**photograph**" or 'gh', "**tough**".

③ **'Cliffs(z)' or Ends of Words:** Certain consonants and all vowels change their spellings at ends of words. The most common vowel spellings at ends of words have a 'y' or 'w' in them (**say**, happy, **sky**, **boy**, **few**, **cow**, **low**, **law**). The consonants that change their spelling are underlined in the phrase, "Charge to view the cliffs(z)." The following rule will aid in remembering the spellings and when they occur. The examples beside it clearly show that the silent 'e' is used to help the consonant. The silent 'e' may or may not help the vowel. With 'ce' and 'dge/ge', the silent 'e' dictates which of the two sounds the **consonant** is to say.

Ends of Words:	Examples:
At ends of words when by a short vowel	
Use 'ck', double 'l', 'f', 's', 'z'.	—băck, fĭll, clĭff, frĭzz
Use 't' with 'ch', 'd' with 'ge',	—bătch, fŭdge
But always have 'e' with 'v'.	—hăve
At ends of words when not by a short vowel	
'c', 's', and 'z' always need an 'e'.	—rejoice, mouse, frēéze
No 't' with 'ch', no 'd' with 'ge',	—ēách, cāge
But always have 'e' with 'v'.	—sāve

Multi-syllable words can end with '-ic' saying the /k/ sound, "plast**ic**". Not following a short vowel sound, the /k/ sound can be 'que', "uni**que**". Use an 'le', "app**le**" when the /l/ sound is at the end of the word as a syllable without another vowel. Following a long vowel, 'gue', "va**gue**" is needed for a /g/ sound since 'ge' would say /j/, "ca**ge**". Also, when a word ends with 'fe' or a single 'f', the 'f' often changes to 'ves' when it is pluralized (leaf, leaves).

④ **Consonant Blends:** Blends are sounds made by two or more consonants that can be broken down into the individual parts. If a blend is sustained, you will end up saying the final sound of the blend. There are not endless variations of blends. At beginnings of words, blends are only made with a consonant followed by 'r', 'l', and 'w', or with 's' preceding a consonant. Ending blends are with 't', 'd', 'p', or 'k'. When 's' is added to a word, it forms a blend with the final consonant (cat > cats). 'l' and 'n' blends following a vowel tend to change the vowel sounds (blind, child, colt, bald). The consonant sounds we spell with 'x' and 'qu' are really blends. The sound of 'x' is /ks/, "fo**x**" and 'qu' is /kw/, "**qu**ick".

⑤ **Digraphs:** Digraphs are unique sounds that are not related to either of the letters that make them. Most digraphs are a consonant plus 'h'. In the middle of words, the /ch/ sound can be spelled with a 't' before a 'u', "cap**t**ure"; '-tion', '-ssion' and '-cian' all say /shŭn/. A vowel before '-sion' usually makes it say /zhŭn/, "televi**sion**". The 'ch' sound at ends of words following a short vowel (or in compound words containing these words) is spelled 'tch', "pa**tch**". Elsewhere it is 'ch', "ea**ch**".

⑥ **Silent consonants:** There are several sets of consonants in which one is silent. Not many words use them. The entire lists for all of them are on Chart 71.

Eagle's Wings Comprehensive Chart of Vowels

Short Vowels Unit 2, 5	ă	ĕ	ĭ	ŏ		ŭ	o͝o
Key Words ①	apple	echo	inch	on		up	good book
Hand Symbols ①	(hand round like apple)	(cup hand to mouth)	(put finger/ thumb an inch apart)	(turn switch on with finger)		(point up)	
Single Syllable vow con ②	sad	set	big	hop		fun	oo – d good oo – k book
Multi-Syllable 2 consonants before vowels, 'le', or 'y' ④ Unit 5	sadder	settle	bigger	hopping		funny	
'Cliffs(z)' ⑤	sack	sell	cliff	boss		fuzz	
/ŭr/= ⑧ Chart 28, 44, 66		er fern	ir girl	(w)or worm		ur curl	
Other ⑨		ea head Chart 13	y gym	↕ contrast		a banana Ch. 23, 24 o love	u put
Long /other Vowels Charts 11-25	ā	ē	ī	å ↔ contrast	ō	ū/ü	ou/oi
Silent 'e' vow con e ③	cape	It takes two vowels to make a long 'e' for Silent 'e' rarely helps an 'e'.	hike style		cope	/ū/ cute /ü/ lute	
-l ☆ **-n** ☆ Chart 64-65 ⑦	ai – l nail ai – n pain	ie–ld field	i – ld child i – nd kind	a – ll tall a – ld bald a – lt malt awn lawn	o – ll toll o – ld bold o – lt molt own grown		ow – l owl ow – n town
Double vowels ⑥	ai – l mail ai – n rain ai – t bait ai – d paid	ee feel ea heat ie – ld yield ie – f brief ie – ve believe ie – ge siege (c)ei receive		au fraud Chart 27	oa boat	oo moon	ou ouch oi oil
r Chart 29, 67, 68 ⑧	air hair are care ear bear	ear fear eer steer	ire fire	ar car cart	or- corn -ore more oor poor oar soar (w)ar warm	ure cure	our flour ower flower
Multi-Syllable Unit 4 ④	taping	eagle	diving flying	collar ('all' becomes 'oll')	pony	super	outer boiling
Cliffs(z) Con ⑤	maze	cheese	slice	sauce	nose	huge/snooze	house/choice
'Cliffs(z)' ⑨ **Word end** – y/w	-ay say	-y baby	-y shy	-aw law	-ow follow arrow	-ew few	-oy toy
other		-ee/ea see/sea	-ie (rare) pie		-o go	-ue (rare) blue	-ow cow
Other spellings ⑨ – -gh	eigh eight		igh high	augh taught ough ought	ough dough	ough through	ough bough
	eign/ é / ey reign/ café / they	-ie brownie -i Indian	ign sign	(w)a want (qu)a squat	-oe hoe eau beau	ui suit	©1989 S.M.

Vowels

① **Short Vowels and Long Vowels:** Each vowel has two main sounds; long and short. The long sound is the name of the vowel, with the exception of 'u' which has two sounds, /ü/, "flute" (the same sound as /o͞o/, "boot"), and /ū/ or /yü/, "cute". The short vowel sounds are not related in any way to the name of the vowel; therefore, a key word is helpful to reinforce the short vowel sounds. Hand symbols are an excellent tool to use in learning short vowels. If the hand symbol is learned properly, a student stuck on the short vowel sound in a word can quickly be prompted by simply seeing the hand symbol.

② **Short Vowels (Single Syllable):** A vowel is consistently short in a one-syllable word of a (c)vc (consonant-vowel-consonant) pattern, when one of the final consonants is 'b', 'd', 'g', 'm', 'n', 'p', or 't'. (See Chart 1.) To help reinforce the fact that it is the consonant following the vowel which dictates that the vowel is short, we have devised the 'short-vowel rod', which is the breve with a line that extends to the consonant.

tăp băd sĭt tŏp hŭb

③ **Long Vowels with Silent 'e' (Single Syllable):** Rule: **Silent 'e' helps most vowels to be long, but it takes two vowels to make a long 'e' for silent 'e' rarely helps an 'e'.** We have developed a symbol called a 'long-vowel tie'. The consonant must either make the vowel preceding it short with a 'short-vowel rod' or have a 'long-vowel tie' with another letter ('le', 'y', or a vowel). This 'long-vowel tie' allows the preceding vowel to be long. In this case, the 'long-vowel tie' is with the silent 'e'. Long 'e' is not represented here. Generally two vowels, 'ee', 'ea', 'ie', or 'ei' are needed to make a long 'e' sound.

Short:	căp	fĕd	rĭd	hŏp	cŭt
Long:	cāpe	*	rīde	hōpe	cūte

*("feed"—It takes two vowels to make a long 'e'.)

④ **Multi-syllable:** In multi-syllable words where the second syllable begins with a short vowel, '-le', or '-y', the consonant preceding it connects with the vowel, '-le', or '-y' by a 'long-vowel tie', enabling the vowel before the consonant to be long. In order to make a short vowel, another consonant must be added.

Short:	tăpping	pĕbble	tĭnny	hŏpping	sŭpper
Long:	tāping	*	tīny	hōping	sūper

*("feeble"—It takes two vowels to make a long 'e'.)

⑤ **'Cliffs(z)' Consonants:** In words that end in the letter sounds underlined in the phrase, "Charge to view the 'cliffs(z)' ", the spelling changes. In general, directly following a short vowel in a one-syllable word, we use 'ck', 'll', 'ff', 'ss', 'zz', 'tch', 'dge', and 've'. In words where these letters do not directly follow a short vowel, 'ce', 'se', 'ze', 'le' ('le' applies only to multi-syllables), 'ge', 'gue', 've', and 'ch' are commonly used. The silent 'e' is there specifically to help the 'cliffs(z)' consonant and may or may not help the vowel. When silent 'e' is with one of the 'cliffs(z)' consonants, a new symbol—'cliffs(z) tie', a 'long-vowel tie' with an arrow through it, shows that the silent 'e' is there for the consonant and may or may not help the vowel. It may help 'a', 'i', 'u' and 'o'. However, when we use two vowels ('ee', 'ea', 'ie', 'ei', 'au', 'ou', 'oi'), the silent 'e' is still needed for these consonants and not for the vowels. Also the silent 'e' is needed when one of the 'cliffs(z)' consonants follows another consonant, as in "hinge".

Short:	băck	tĕll	stĭff	bŏss	fŭzz
Short:	hăve	ĕtch	mĭss	lŏg	fŭdge
Long:	bēhāve	ēach	mīce	rōgue	hūge
Others:	bēlieve	ĭnch	house		hĭnge

⑥ **Double Vowels:** When two vowels are used in the middle of a word, one vowel, usually the second, is silent but is needed to make a 'long-vowel tie' with the consonant, allowing the first vowel to be long. The diphthongs 'oi', 'ou', 'oo', and 'au' are exceptions because they combine to form a unique sound.

Short:	răn	bĕd	fĭt	cŏt	mŭd
Long:	rāin	bēad	*	cōat	mōod

*('i' has no commonly used vowel combinations in root words and 'ie' = /ī/ in only 7 independent words.)

⑦ **L/N:** The letters 'l' and 'n' affect the vowels more than any other consonants. 'Ai' is used in front of 'l' and 'n' except for homonyms (mail/male). 'I' is long with the blends 'ld' and 'nd'. 'O' and 'a' change sounds with 'l' blends and may have a 'w' before an 'n'. 'Ou' changes to 'ow' in front of 'l' and 'n' if they are not in a blend.

l☆	trāil	fīeld	chīld	tōll/bōld/mōlt	tål, båld, målt	owl
n☆	trāin		kīnd	mōwn	lawn	town

⑧ **R:** 'R' changes many of the vowel sounds. In accented syllables 'er', 'ir', 'ur', and (w)'or', say /ŭr/. The spelling of these words must be memorized, as the only predictable spelling for the /ŭr/ sound is 'or' following a 'w', as in "world". In unaccented syllables a single vowel with an 'r' usually says /ŭr/.

Accented Syll.	/ŭr/	fern	girl	worm	curl (occur)
Unaccented Syll.	/ŭr/	dollar	paper	doctor	

With the long vowels, more than one vowel is needed except for 'or' in the middle of a word,"corn" and '(w)ar', "warm". Elsewhere, 'ar' says /år/, "car".

Long Vowel:

hair, care, bear	fear, steer	fire	corn, more, poor, soar,(w)arm	cure

⑨ **Vowel 'Cliffs(z)':** At ends of words we rarely have a vowel by itself. For short vowels sounds, 'a' says the /ŭ/ sound at ends of words, "banana" and 'aw' says the /ŏ/ or /å/ sound, "law".
For long vowels sounds, the majority of the spellings have a 'y' or a 'w'. 'ow' is used for both the /ou/ sound, "cow" and the /ō/ sound, "low". We use 'ow' for the /ō/ sound at ends of words following 'l' or 'r', "follow", "arrow". Elsewhere we usually use an 'o', "tomato".

	ā	ē	ī	ō	ōo	å	ou	oi
y/w ↓	say	baby	shy	low	few	law	cow	boy
gh	sleigh		high	though	through	taught	bough	
Other	café	see/sea brownie	pie	go hoe	moo blue			

UNIT 1

FOCUS ON:
TEACHING EAGLE'S WINGS PHONICS

Unit One is your guide to actually putting this handbook into use. There are several approaches to using the book. It may be used as a supplement to any other phonics program, it may be used according to the guidelines and format in the teacher's manual that follows, or it may be used simply for spelling words from each chart. The material can be adapted to custom fit any student.

If you are using this handbook as a teaching program, please study this unit for the correct study sequence as well as valuable teaching tips. The charts are to be used in the sequence given and mastered before continuing on to the next one, except where noted. The basic procedure for teaching each chart consists of reading and discussing the description of what is happening (which will be the write-up across from the chart) and then reading, marking, and spelling the words on the chart. There are flash cards at the very end of the book to be used to teach the phonics sounds ("**Tell-a-phone**" cards, pages 219-226), and reading pages that introduce multi-syllable words and sight words (pages 191-194).

If you are teaching a **remedial** or **intermediate** student, read this section carefully.
1. Spend a month to six months (or even longer) teaching all the words on the *Eagle's Wings 600 Sight Words* list (pp. 172, 193-194). Have the student memorize them first as **sight words** (that is being able to recognize them instantly without having to sound them out). Then have him learn to spell them all. Since this makes up the majority of the most used words in the English language, knowing them, no matter how long it takes, will be well worth the time and effort.

2. Every third week, it would be good to give **dictation**. Pick a paragraph from a book the student can read. Read it aloud as the student writes it down. Help with the structural aspects, indenting for paragraphs, capitals at beginning of sentences, punctuation marks and so forth. Have him spell the words he missed five times. Repeat the same paragraph three times during the week. This will help in several ways. It will help him learn the structural aspects of sentences and paragraphs (grammar). It will review words he all ready knows and introduce challenging new words he might not be exposed to for awhile. This will help you assess what he needs to learn next. For example, if the dictation paragraph has the word "nation" and he has no idea how to spell it, your next spelling unit could be on all the words with /shŭn/ (page118).

3. While you work with spelling, also use the section on **Creative Writing** (pages 165-184). Have your student write at least one polished paper a week. Being able to use spelling to express his thoughts on paper should be one of your main goals. Each student should have a copy of the *Eagle's Wings 600 Sight Words* list in front of him. This will help him focus on the creative process while still spelling correctly.

4. The final step is to have a systematic approach to spelling. **In Unit 1: Focus on Teaching, look over the Basic Teaching Procedure** (page 24)**.** This can be used for lesson planning. Begin by explaining the pattern from a given chart. Then select 20-30 spelling words. If the student understands the pattern, move on to the exceptions, and when those are mastered, to the next chart. Do not feel overwhelmed . If you have been through ***Alphabet Island Phonics***, the student knows more than you think he does. **You have already covered up to ROUND TWO** (page 39) with ***Alphabet Island Phonics***. Now you will review what was studied and teach the exceptions and longer words. Would it help to know most spelling books teach under twenty words a week? There are as many words in three or four charts as most students study in a year. If you go at a steady pace, you can easily and thoroughly cover what your student needs.

Trouble Shooting for Spelling, Reading and Writing

Problem: How do I use this Handbook with other phonics programs?
Solution: ***Eagle's Wings Comprehensive Handbook of Phonics*** can complement and expand any phonics, spelling, or reading program. For example, you studied blends, and your student did not get enough practice to be proficient. Look up blends in the **Table of Contents** (Charts 4-7). Then you can read how to teach these charts in Unit 1: **Focus on Teaching Eagle's Wings Phonics** and give the student more practice in hearing, reading and spelling with blends. Another unique feature of the Handbook is the ease in looking up specific words, such as words with 'ough'. The **Table of Contents** (and **Eagle's Wings Comprehensive Chart of Vowels**) show that this is found on Chart 58. This chart will have all the words with 'ough' categorized under the correct sounds, plus it will refer you to a 'help' in the Fun Form section (page 213) to help the student learn these words. This Handbook will give you confidence as a teacher, because you will have examples available at your fingertips for whatever you are teaching in another program.

Problem: My child wants to read above his spelling level. He is bored with simple books.
Solution: That is great! Reading levels are, for the most part, above spelling levels. In order to help with this problem, use the "**Tell-a-Phone**" cards (pages 219-226). These are flash cards with the phonemes (or the letter sounds) which are the building parts of words. They are primarily designed to get your child reading a little sooner by introducing new sounds or letter combinations that have not yet been introduced for spelling purposes. Your child does not need to know lengthy rules to work with these. He needs to know that when he sees certain letters together they make a certain sound. **When the flash cards have multiple sounds (such as the 'a'), do not introduce more than one sound at a time**. Work with these cards regularly and independently of the spelling phonics.

Problem: How can I help my student be a successful speller?
Solution: Do not try to "trick" student. Exaggerate the sounds. Tell how many letters are in the word. Tell him to be careful if the word is tricky. Do what you need to in order to make sure your student is successful. Good spelling is a habit and the more times a word is spelled right, the better his good-spelling habit will be.

Problem: My student refuses to write. He just bursts into tears and won't write a word.
Solution: Start off with dictation. Use any book at or below his reading level. Let him have his **Eagle's Wings 600 Sight Words** (page 172) handy. Give him only a few words at a time. Tell him when to indent for a paragraph, if there is a capital letter, a comma, a quotation mark, or period. This is a wonderful exercise to quickly learn writing skills and punctuation. Use it often. Another step to get him going is to teach him to 'cluster'. (There are forms to get started ☛ See pages 178, 180, 181.) Take the time to cluster with the student of any age who has trouble expressing his thoughts. Write more complete sentences for the younger student, and only words or thought fragments for the older ones. Keep probing for more until you feel they have enough information to get them started with their writing. Ask questions like: "Tell me more." "What else?" "What happened next?" "Describe it." "How did it make you feel?" "What colors, smells, or sounds were there?" When these ideas are all down on paper, show your student how to put them into paragraphs. You'll both be amazed at the quality of work that can be accomplished with this technique.

Problem: "They" say my son is doing OK, but I feel there is a problem. He just isn't reading as well as he should be.
Solution: The problem could be one of several things. 1) Are you expecting too much? It could be that he is right on schedule for his age and ability. 2) Does he know only 'sight words' and is unable to "attack" a new word? Then he probably needs to develop phonics skills. 3) Does he not know any 'sight words' and has to sound out every word? A 'sight word' means knowing a word so well that it is instantly recognized without having to sound it out. If this is the problem, using the **Eagle's Wings Sight Words for Reading** (pages 193-194) will make a marked improvement in his reading.

Problem: I know my child is smart—he can take a lawn mower apart and put it back together—but can't read. What is wrong?
Solution: A person with a wide variation in ability between one type of task and another may be likely to have some learning disability. Schools are required to test for these and to give appropriate instruction. Sometimes it will take a persistent parent to insure that the child gets the help he needs. A child cannot fight for himself. You must fight for him.

Problem: I want to help my child with reading but he won't let me. What can I do?
Solution: Hire a teenage neighbor to listen to him read. A teenager with gentle ways who gives encouragement can do wonders. In classrooms, teachers have brought in older students to do the very same thing with their students who needed an extra one-on-one help. This has been very successful.

Problem: I have an older student. How do I go about teaching remedial spelling?
Solution: Start at the beginning of this handbook with the Eagle's Wings Symbols (pages 12-13) for marking sounds. Discuss each one. Work through the charts in the order suggested in Unit 1 (pages 25-39). Begin working on each new chart by discussing the pattern it covers. One way to do this is to select random words from the chart and ask your student to sort them in logical groups. (This is an "inductive" method of teaching.) Ask him to compare his observations of this chart to previous charts. Then select at least 20-30 spelling words. You may also use the "I Can Read and Spell" pages that go with the charts. (See pages 191-192.) These are multi-syllable words and will give the older student a greater sense of accomplishment. Exaggerate the sounds and discuss the correct spelling immediately. If the student understands the pattern, move on to the exceptions, and when those are mastered, to the next chart. Use the **Eagle's Wings 600 Sight Words** (page 172) concurrently for spelling. Discuss each word—how it sounds, and if it does not follow the rules, which letters do not. Unit 7, **Focus On: Meaning**, will also be very helpful with an older student or a student who is learning English as a second language. Every third week, it would be good to give dictation. (See directions for this procedure and other valuable information on page 19.)

Problem: I am tutoring someone who is learning English as a second language. What can I use to help her?
Solution: English as a second language presents special challenges to teachers. The Handbook is especially valuable in these cases because of its systematic approach to the English language. For example, each concept builds on the next in logical sequence. And the vowel charts will be especially helpful to those learning English as a second language, because they deal with all the ways which a vowel can be spelled and yet still say the same sound. (For example, Chart 11 on long 'a' sounds shows that 'eigh', 'ay', and 'ai' all say /ā /.) Unit 7, **Focus On: Meaning**, will also be very helpful with a student who is learning English as a second language. Follow the directions given in the solution for teaching an older student and proceed at a rate which is challenging yet achievable for your student. Don't forget to use the "Tell-a-Phone" cards for regular review of the sounds of each letter or letter combination.

Problem: I am a secretary and I can't spell. You don't know the humiliation I feel. I can't even spell simple words!
Solution: A quick help is to glue and laminate a copy of **Eagle's Wings 600 Sight Words** (page 172) onto one side of a paper folder. On the other side, glue a sheet of lined paper, but do not laminate it. Sit down with a good friend who is a good speller. Ask your friend to help you write down all the words that have been giving you problems. These are usually ones that occur on a regular basis. Write these word in alphabetical order on the lined paper. Be sure to include that ones that particularly pertain to the business or school you are working for. When new problem words come up, look them up (with your friend again if necessary) and add them to your list. Keep the folder handy for a quick personalized spelling reference.

Reading vs. Spelling Skills

In order to be a good reader and speller, a unique interaction between many skills is needed. There is the need to first be able to hear the specific sound parts and then to be able to recognize the written symbol for those sounds. Also needed, is the ability to take the sounds apart and then to put them back together into a word that has meaning. [A third factor, not dealt with at this time is the ability to understand the written word (comprehension).]

Consequently, there are two types of phonics needed for effective mastery of the written language. One is needed for reading (decoding) and one for spelling (encoding). Let us give an example of what we mean by showing the difference in the rules used for each.
A reading rule says:

"When two vowels go walking,
The first one does the talking and says his name."

This rule means that if we see the words "bait" or "beat'" or "boat", the first vowel is long and the second one is silent. This type of general rule will help speed up the reading process but does not help in the spelling of words with these type of vowel teams. The reading rule gives no clue to which vowels form a vowel team or where they will be used in specific words.

A spelling rule on the other hand says,

"Use 'ow' before 'l' and 'n'
Whenever they are not in a blend."

This rule tells us that we are to use 'ow' for the vowel team with 'l' and 'n' and in addition that they must not be in a blend. We would be able to spell "owl", "town", and "round" correctly, because of the information given in the rule. However, knowing the sounds 'ow' makes would be enough for reading purposes.

For reading, the rules can be quite general, but for spelling purposes, the rules must be very specific.

Reading and spelling skills develop at different rates and are some what independent of each other. The following two examples demonstrate that reading and spelling skills must be worked on separately. They are not one and the same. One student, an eight year old boy, had taught himself to read with little instruction. He was limited by his parents to reading only one "Hardy Boys" book a day, which took him only an hour to finish. Even though he was an accomplished reader, absolutely none of his reading skills transferred over to his spelling. He was at a total loss to write even the simplest of words. He was able to "decode" (read) and comprehend, but not to "encode" (spell).

Another student knew each sound and its symbol and in any given word, she could isolate the sounds and write them down. If the word was spelled phonetically, she would be able to spell it correctly. However, because of memory difficulties, she was not able to read back the words she had just written. She had difficulty retrieving ("decoding") but had no problem spelling ("encoding").

Most of this book is directed to teaching the phonics rules for spelling. But this approach alone can slow down the reading process. Students need to know the expected sounds of letters and letter combinations. In order to accomplish this, a section has been included to develop reading skills as well. Most students will be able to and want to read above their spelling ability. This is good. Work with the student on two levels—one in reading and one in spelling.

There are two main things that may be holding a student back in reading or writing: 1. Not having basic phonics skills. 2. Not knowing basic 'sight' words. The two go hand in hand. If a student only knows words by sight and not how words are put together, he may have difficulty figuring out how to read or spell words. If the student knows only the phonics rules, he will be slowed down in reading time and comprehension if every word must be sounded out. Since in reading and writing certain words show up hundreds of times in one text, it is important that these words are known by 'sight' without having to spend time laboriously sounding them out each time they are encountered. To help with this problem, we have developed Eagle's Wings 600 Sight Words. You will see a big jump in a student's reading and spelling ability by spending just a few minutes every day working on these words.

Phonics alone is of little value to the average person. It is merely a tool which assists in achieving the ultimate purpose of any reading program—communication both written and oral. By giving your students the building blocks they need to achieve this, you can open up a wonderful world of literature, creative writing, business and personal communication and the ability to find out about almost anything that can be written down.

Informal Scope and Sequence

Kindergarten: For Kindergarten, you will be using only a few pages in the handbook. However, these pages will provide the firm foundation your student needs to get a good start in reading and spelling. Pages 165-168 teach how to form each letter and number. Chart 51 provides lists of words for the initial sound of each letter of the alphabet, as well as two sounds each for the vowels, 'c', and 'g'. The "Tell-a-Phone" cards are flash cards to review the isolated sounds (or phonemes) of 'a' to 'z'. And page 196* can be photo-copied to use as an exercise for matching the "Tell-a-Phone" cards (pages 219-222) to the picture beginning with that letter. Put a paper clip on pages you use to help you find them easily.

When the alphabet is mastered, your student is ready for the next step—being able to spell any two- or three-letter short-vowel word on Chart 1 (page 42-43). All of this can take a year or more, depending on your particular student. [Directions are included in this unit for how to teach Kindergarten. If you would like more direction on a daily basis, ***Alphabet Island Phonics Level 1 (Kindergarten)*** is a program (designed to dovetail with ***Eagle's Wings Comprehensive Handbook of Phonics***) which provides step-by-step instruction for teachers, student workbook, music tapes, and more.]

*Fun Form Page 196 Words: ant, boat, candle, duck, Eskimo, fish, goat, horse, Indian, jar, kite, leaf, monkey, needle, octopus, porcupine, quilt, raccoon, sewing machine, tepee, umbrella, violin, web, fox (the few words beginning with 'x' say /z/, "xylophone"), yoyo, zebra.

First Grade: Your first grade student needs to review all that is covered in Kindergarten. The time for this will vary depending on the student's experience and ability. First grade will cover the first ten charts. Each chart should take from one to three weeks. Your student will be learning greater proficiency in handwriting and will be able to spell: Three letter words. Words ending in 'ck', 'll', 'ff', 'ss', and 'zz'. Words with long vowels made with silent 'e. Words with beginning and ending blends. Words with beginning and ending digraphs. And words ending in 'dge', 'ge', and 've'. Your student will also learn to read and say all of the 70 phonemes ("Tell-a-Phone" cards, pages 219-226) and know 300 sight words.

There are numerous games and fun forms in the back of the Handbook, along with the "Tell-a-Phone" cards and Eagle's Wings 600 **Sight Words** (page 171-172). Photo-copy a copy of the Sight Words for each student to use for their writing time. For **handwriting practice**, tape record (three times in a row) each of the formation poems on pages 166-168. Turn on the tape and have your student write his letters along with the poems.

Second Grade/Third Grade: Your student will be able to read and spell: One-syllable words with any vowel combination (such as—'ai', 'ay', 'eigh', 'ea', 'ee', 'ie', 'igh', 'oa', 'ow', 'oo', 'ew', 'ue', 'oi', 'oy', 'ou', 'ow', 'all', 'oll', 'aw', 'au', 'ur', 'er', 'ir', 'ear', 'wor', 'are', 'eer', 'ore', 'oar', 'oo', 'our', and so forth.)

For second grade and third grade, your student will need to review everything from Kindergarten through the previous grade. This will take a few weeks to a few months, depending on the student's experience and ability. You may wish to introduce cursive writing during this time (pages 169-170).

The focus of phonics and spelling for second and third grade is Unit 3. Each chart will take from three to six weeks to cover. You will use **only the charts with one-syllable words** in Unit 3 (this is Round ONE). There are numerous games and Fun Forms included in the back of the Handbook along with the "Tell-a-Phone" cards and Eagle's Wings 600 Sight Words (page 172). Photo-copy one for each student to use in their daily writing. For part of the handwriting practice, write sentences on the blackboard to copy, or have student copy sentences from a favorite book.

Fourth Grade and up: The basics of phonics have been covered in Kindergarten through third grade. At this point, your student needs to be adding new words for reading, vocabulary and spelling. Follow the procedure listed in Round TWO.

[Again, further directions are included in this unit. If you would like more direction on a daily basis, ***Alphabet Island Phonics Level 2*** is a program (designed to dovetail with **Unit 1, 2, 3 and 4** of ***Eagle's Wings Comprehensive Handbook of Phonics***) which provides step-by-step instruction for teachers, student workbooks, music tapes, and more.]

Basic Teaching Procedure

Below are general guidelines to be followed for teaching each new concept or chart.

Teacher Procedure	Student Check List
PREPARATION: In preparation for the lesson, the teacher needs to become familiar with the rule and chart to be studied. Look over it and examine the words for patterns that need to be pointed out to the student. Prepare games or flash cards. (3 x 5 cards work well for flash cards of "Everyday Words" and "Everyday Bloopers".) Some preparation needs to be done ahead of time, but while the teacher is making last minute preparations, the student may practice handwriting.	❑ I practiced handwriting.
PHONETIC SOUNDS: The "Tell-a-Phone" cards are used primarily to develop reading skills. The student is to see letters and learn to quickly identify the probable sounds. Hold the card up with the letter facing the student and say the isolated sound of each phoneme. The back of the card gives words that will help the teacher isolate the sound—these words are not to be read aloud. When cards have multiple sounds, such as 'a', introduce only one sound at a time. The student will repeat the sound. For review, the student should be able to quickly say the sounds of "Tell-a-Phone" cards he has studied. Gradually add new sounds.	❑ I can say my phonemes.
INTRODUCE: Read and/or explain rule (pattern) and chart to student. If the concept is complex, make it "bite-size". Demonstrate how to mark the sample words, using the examples given in the write-up.	❑ I can say the rule.
KINESTHETIC AND AUDITORY ACTIVITY: Practice the rule in isolation. Use the charts to read words out loud. Have student listen for the specific detail being covered and respond when he hears it—usually with flash cards, games, or on blackboard.	❑ I can use the rule. ❑ I can hear it in words.
READING SKILLS: Have student memorize sight words. Use flash cards, charts, or "Read and Spell" pages. Use any book the student is interested in and let them read the words they know as you read the rest. Also, use the games included in Unit 9.	❑ I can read words with it.
SPELLING SKILLS: Use games from Unit 9. Give 15-20 spelling words daily. Use words from the chart being studied and review previously studied charts. You may give the spelling words: 1. Changing one letter at a time— bad - bid - hid - had - sad 2. Randomly— dad - mom - cat - sun - mud	❑ I can spell with it.
VOCABULARY BUILDER: Use Unit 7 with intermediate student to build vocabulary/comprehension. Introduce 1-3 new words or concepts daily. Write the word on the blackboard and "take it apart", showing how the word is put together. Talk about the meaning of the word. Have student paraphrase meaning of word and/or use it in a sentence.	❑ I increased my vocabulary.
"EVERYDAY BLOOPERS" (on Charts) & SIGHT WORDS (Page 193-194): These words can be put on 3 x 5 cards. Study for instant recognition of some or all, focusing on reading not spelling.	❑ I know sight words.
WRITING SKILLS: Practice writing daily. Have student keep a diary. Dictate sentences, using words that the student has studied. (For example. **"Come here," said Chris.** The teacher would dictate: Quotation marks capital letter come here comma quotation marks said capital letter Chris period.) Write poems, short stories and letters. Unit 8 is full of ideas and exercises for developing writing skills.	❑ I have written today.

KINDERGARTEN: (The alphabet: a-z) Procedure	Student Check List
FORMATION (Handwriting): Use "Formation Poems" (pages 166-167, Numbers-165) to teach the formation of each lower case letter: 1. In the air with full arm movement. 2. On the blackboard, between two lines painted 12 inches apart. 3. On wide lined paper.	❑ I can form my letters.
RECOGNITION: A. Learn the capital letters and be able to associate each with its corresponding lower case letter. (Page 168) B. Use "Tell-a-Phone" cards (a-z only) and have student be able to point to any letter that is named. (Connecting name with symbol of letter.) C. Have student be able to name any card that is pointed to. (Connecting symbol with name of letter.)	❑ A. I can name my capital letters. ❑ B. I can name my lower-case letters. ❑ C. I can recognize my letters.
ALPHABETIZING: Alphabetize letter cards daily. (Only up to the last letter that has been studied to that point.)	❑ I can alphabetize my letters.
PHONEMES: Use the "Tell-a-Phone" cards to teach the phonetic sound of each letter and two sounds for 'a', 'e', 'i', 'o', 'u', 'c', 'g', and 's'. (Key words are on the back of each card.) Isolate the sound. (Do not say the key word. Make sure each phone is clear and not tainted by a vowel sound. Don't say 'duh' for the /d/ sound, but /d/ as final sound in "dad".)	❑ I can say my phonemes.
AUDITORY DISCRIMINATION: Practice hearing the sound of a letter as it is studied. Have student hold up the correct "Tell-a-Phone" card as you read words beginning with various letters. (Chart 51, p. 123)	❑ I can hear my letters.

Special Note: Learn when to use 'c' or 'k', 'c' or 's' and 'g' or 'j'. Use page 197 and the following directions.

A. Make 3x5 cards of 'a', 'o', 'u' on blue paper and of 'i', 'e', 'y' on pink paper, and 'c' on white.

B. Show the picture of 'Clever C' (page 197) and tell student that 'c' is so clever he can make two sounds and always knows when to say them. With the 'boys' (blue cards) 'a', 'o', 'u', he says /k/, as in "kangaroo". Next to the 'girls' (pink cards) 'i', 'e', and 'y', he says /s/, as in "silly".

C. Place the white 'c' card on the table. Put a vowel card next to it and have student tell what sound 'c' makes. Practice with all the cards several times.

Repeat the procedure for 'g'. At this stage, the student does not need to know the full rule for 'g', but only needs to be able to function with 'g' = /g/ with 'o', 'a', and 'u', and 'g' = /j/ with 'i', 'e', and 'y'.

CHART 1: (2-3 Letter, Short-Vowel Words) Procedure	Student Check List
PREPARATION: In preparation for the lesson, the teacher needs to become familiar with the write-up on page 42. Make flash cards on 3x5 cards with words from Chart 1 (page 43) for reading. Some preparation needs to be done ahead of time, but while the teacher is making last minute preparations, the student may practice handwriting, listening to tape of formation poems.	❑ I practiced handwriting
PHONETIC SOUNDS: Review "Tell-a-Phone" cards 'a' to 'z'.	❑ I can say my phonemes.
INTRODUCTION: Explain that you will be putting letters together to make words. Tell the student that he will only be working with the short vowel sounds for awhile. On the blackboard, demonstrate the markings and symbols using the sample word.	❑ I can find my words and hear them.
KINESTHETIC ACTIVITY: Use most of the games in Unit 9 .	❑ I can work with my words.
READING SKILLS: Teach the cards in word families ('-at': "cat", "fat", "sat", "mat", and so forth) using the following sequence: (Note: 'i' and 'e' are the hardest to differentiate between, so they should be taught as far apart in the sequence as possible.) Make up poems with each word family if desired, having student read the words he is learning. 1. All the words with /ă / first. 2. All the words with /ĭ /. 3. All the words with /ŭ /. 4. All the words with /ŏ /. 5. All the words with /ĕ /.	❑ I can read my words.
SPELLING SKILLS: Give 10-20 spelling words a day (include review words), having student write the words on the blackboard, on wide-lined paper, or with "Tell-a-Phone" Cards. Give spelling lists by: 1. Changing the vowel — bad - bed - bud - bid 2. Changing the beginning consonant— bid - hid - did - kid - lid - rid 3. Changing the ending consonant— pan - pat - pad 4. Changing one letter at a time— bad - bid - hid - had - sad 5. Randomly— dad - mom - kid - cat - sun - mud	❑ I can spell my words.

CHART 2: **('Cliffs[z]') Teacher Procedure**	**Student Check List**
PREPARATION: Study write-up on page 44. Take out "Tell-a-Phone" cards a-z. Write "Everyday Words" and "Bloopers" on 3x5 cards.	❑ I practiced handwriting.
PHONETIC SOUNDS: Review the "Tell-a-Phone" cards 'a' to 'z'.	❑ I can say my phonemes.
INTRODUCE: Explain the concept of 'Cliffs(z)', using the write-up on page 44. Write the word 'cliffs(z)' on the blackboard as it appears in the write-up. These are the letters that change their spellings at ends of words. Show how they change their spelling following a short vowel.	❑ I can say the rule.
KINESTHETIC ACTIVITY: Take the "Tell-a-Phone" cards (a-z, excluding vowels, 'y', 'v', 'j', 'q', and 'w'). Have the student hold up one finger if the consonant can be by itself at ends of words following a short vowel. Hold up two fingers if the consonant needs a helper. (c, l, f, s, and z need helpers)	❑ I can use the rule.
READING SKILLS: Review "Everyday Words". Learn new ones. "Read and Spell" page 191 (use rows marked Chart 1 and Chart 2).	❑ I can read words with it.
SPELLING SKILLS: Give 15-20 spelling words daily. Use words from Chart 2, page 191, and review Chart 1. Mark words with symbols.	❑ I can spell with it.
VOCABULARY BUILDER: Use Unit 7 only for an intermediate level student to build vocabulary. Introduce 1-3 new words or concepts.	❑ I increased my vocabulary.
"EVERYDAY BLOOPERS" (Chart 2) & SIGHT WORDS (Page 193): Study for instant recognition of some or all.	❑ I know sight words.
WRITING SKILLS: Practice writing daily. (Use Unit 8)	❑ I have written today.

CHART 3: **(Long vowels/silent 'e') Teacher Procedure**	**Student Check List**
PREPARATION: Study write-up on page 46. Get out 'e' card. Write "Everyday Words" and "Bloopers" on 3x5 cards.	❑ I practiced handwriting.
PHONETIC SOUNDS: Review the "Tell-a-Phone" cards 'a' to 'z'.	❑ I can say my phonemes.
INTRODUCE: Explain silent 'e', using the write-up on page 46. Go over each rule and demonstrate how to mark sample words on blackboard.	❑ I can say the rule
KINESTHETIC AND AUDITORY ACTIVITIES: Practice with silent 'e' card. Read words randomly from Chart 3 and have student hold up silent 'e' if the vowel says its long sound (which is its name). The words in parenthesis have short vowel sounds, the words with silent 'e' have the long vowel sound. Remember, long 'u' has two sounds: /ü/, "tune", and /ū /, "cute".	❑ I can use the rule. ❑ I can hear it in words.
READING SKILLS: Review "Everyday Words. Learn new ones. "Read and Spell" page 191. (Words for Charts 1-3)	❑ I can read words with it.
SPELLING SKILLS: Give 15-20 spelling words daily. Use words from Chart 3 and review previous charts. Mark words with symbols.	❑ I can spell with it.
VOCABULARY BUILDER: Use Unit 7 only for an intermediate level student to build vocabulary. Introduce 1-3 new words or concepts.	❑ I increased my vocabulary.
"EVERYDAY BLOOPERS" (Chart 3) & SIGHT WORDS (Page 193): Study for instant recognition of some or all.	❑ I know sight words.
WRITING SKILLS: Practice writing daily. (Use Unit 8)	❑ I have written today.

CHART 4: **(Beginning Blends: r, l, w, & s) Procedure**		**Student Check List**
A	**PREPARATION:** Study write-up on page 48. Take out 'r', 'l' cards. Write "Everyday Words" and "Bloopers" on 3x5 cards.	❑ I practiced handwriting.
	INTRODUCE: Explain blends, using the write-up on page 48. Demonstrate how to mark sample words on blackboard.	❑ I can tell about blends.
	KINESTHETIC AND AUDITORY ACTIVITY: Practice hearing blends with 'r' and 'l' only. Use Chart 4 or 52 for words to read aloud to student. Have student hold up 'r' or 'l' card as these words are read, according to which letter is in blend.	❑ I can use the rule. ❑ I can hear it in words.
	SPELLING SKILLS: Give 15-20 spelling words daily. Use words with blends with 'l' and 'r' from Chart 4 and review previous charts. Mark words with symbols.	❑ I can spell with it.
B	**PREPARATION:** Study write-up on page 48.	❑ I practiced handwriting.
	INTRODUCE: Explain blends, using the write-up on page 48. Demonstrate how to mark sample words on blackboard.	❑ I can tell about blends.
	KINESTHETIC AND AUDITORY ACTIVITY: Practice hearing blends with 's' only. Have student write what consonants go with 's' to form a blend as you read the words aloud from Chart 53 or Chart 4.	❑ I can use the rule. ❑ I can hear it in words.
	SPELLING SKILLS: Give 15-20 spelling words daily. Use words with blends with 's' from Chart 4 and review previous charts. Mark words with symbols.	❑ I can spell with it.
C	**PREPARATION:** Take out "Tell-a-Phone" cards 'l', 'r', 'w', and 'qu'.	❑ I practiced handwriting.
	INTRODUCE: Explain blends, using the write-up on page 48. Demonstrate how to mark sample words on blackboard.	❑ I can tell about blends.
	KINESTHETIC AND AUDITORY ACTIVITY: Practice hearing blends with 'l', 'r', 'w' or 'qu'. Note that the 'qu' sound is /kw/. Have student hold up the card of the letters that blend as you read the words aloud from Chart 52, 54 or Chart 4.	❑ I can use the rule. ❑ I can hear it in words.
	SPELLING SKILLS: Give 15-20 spelling words daily. Use words from Chart 4 and review previous charts. Mark words with symbols.	❑ I can spell with it.

DAILY ACTIVITY	
PHONETIC SOUNDS: Review the "Tell-a-Phone" cards 'a' to 'z'.	❑ I can say my phonemes.
READING SKILLS: Review "Everyday Words". Learn new ones. "Read and Spell" page 191. (Words for Charts 1-4)	❑ I can read words with blends.
VOCABULARY BUILDER: Use Unit 7 only for an intermediate level student to build vocabulary. Introduce 1-3 new words or concepts.	❑ I increased my vocabulary.
"EVERYDAY BLOOPERS" (Chart 4) & SIGHT WORDS (Page 193): Study for instant recognition of some or all.	❑ I know sight words.
WRITING SKILLS: Practice writing daily. (Use Unit 8)	❑ I have written today.

CHART 5: (Blends and 'cliffs[z]') Teacher Procedure	Student Check List
PREPARATION: Study write-up on page 50. Write "Everyday Words" and "Bloopers" on 3x5 cards.	❑ I practiced handwriting.
PHONETIC SOUNDS: Review the "Tell-a-Phone" cards studied. Daily introduce a new vowel combination ("Tell-a-Phone" page 223).	❑ I can say my phonemes.
INTRODUCE: Review 'cliffs[z]', blends, and silent 'e'. Demonstrate how to mark sample words on blackboard.	❑ I can tell about them.
READING SKILLS: Review "Everyday Words". Learn new ones. "Read and Spell" page 191. (Words to go with Charts 1-5)	❑ I can read words with them.
SPELLING SKILLS: Give 15-20 spelling words daily. Use Chart 5, page 191, and review previous charts. Mark words with symbols.	❑ I can spell with them.
VOCABULARY BUILDER: Use Unit 7 only for an intermediate level student to build vocabulary. Introduce 1-3 new words or concepts.	❑ I increased my vocabulary.
"EVERYDAY BLOOPERS" (Chart 5) & SIGHT WORDS (Page 193): Study for instant recognition of some or all.	❑ I know sight words.
WRITING SKILLS: Practice writing daily. (Use Unit 8)	❑ I have written today.

CHART 6: (Ending Blends) Teacher Procedure	Student Check List
PREPARATION: Study write-up on page 52. Write "Everyday Words" and "Bloopers" on 3x5 cards.	❑ I practiced handwriting.
PHONETIC SOUNDS: Review the "Tell-a-Phone" cards, add 'ng'.	❑ I can say my phonemes.
INTRODUCE: Explain ending blends, using the write-up on page 52. Demonstrate how to mark sample words on blackboard.	❑ I can tell about blends.
KINESTHETIC AND AUDITORY ACTIVITY: Have student write ending blends or 'ng' as you read words from Chart 6.	❑ I can use the rule. ❑ I can hear it.
READING SKILLS: Review "Everyday Words". Learn new ones. "Read and Spell" page 191. (Words for Charts 1-6)	❑ I can read words with it.
SPELLING SKILLS: Give 15-20 spelling words daily. Use words from Chart 6 and review previous charts. Mark words with symbols.	❑ I can spell with it.
VOCABULARY BUILDER: Use Unit 7 only for an intermediate level student to build vocabulary. Introduce 1-3 new words or concepts.	❑ I increased my vocabulary.
"EVERYDAY BLOOPERS" (Chart 6) & SIGHT WORDS (Page 193): Study for instant recognition of some or all	❑ I know sight words.
WRITING SKILLS: Practice writing daily. (Use Unit 8)	❑ I have written today.

CHART 7: **(Beginning/Ending Blends) Procedure**	**Student Check List**
PREPARATION: Study write-up on page 54 Write "Everyday Words" and "Bloopers" on 3x5 cards.	❑ I practiced handwriting.
PHONETIC SOUNDS: Review the "Tell-a-Phone" cards, add new vowel combinations daily.	❑ I can say my phonemes.
INTRODUCE: Review blends, using the write-up on page 54. Demonstrate how to mark sample words on blackboard.	❑ I can tell about blends.
KINESTHETIC AND AUDITORY ACTIVITY: Have student write beginning or ending blend as you read words from Chart 7.	❑ I can use the rule. ❑ I can hear it.
READING SKILLS: Review "Everyday Words". Learn new ones. "Read and Spell" page 191. (Words for Charts 1-7)	❑ I can read words with it.
SPELLING SKILLS: Give 15-20 spelling words daily. Use words from Chart 7 and review previous charts. Mark words with symbols.	❑ I can spell with it.
VOCABULARY BUILDER: Use Unit 7 only for an intermediate level student to build vocabulary. Introduce 1-3 new words or concepts.	❑ I increased my vocabulary.
"EVERYDAY BLOOPERS" (Chart 7) & SIGHT WORDS (Page 193): Study for instant recognition of some or all	❑ I know sight words.
WRITING SKILLS: Practice writing daily. (Use Unit 8)	❑ I have written today.

CHART 8: **(Beginning 'h' Digraphs) Teacher Procedure**	**Student Check List**
PREPARATION: Study write-up on page 56. Write "Everyday Words" and "Bloopers" on 3x5 cards.	❑ I practiced handwriting.
PHONETIC SOUNDS: Review the "Tell-a-Phone" cards, add 'h' digraphs—'sh', 'ch', 'th', and 'wh'.	❑ I can say my phonemes.
INTRODUCE: Explain digraphs, using the write-up on page 56. Demonstrate how to mark sample words on blackboard.	❑ I can tell about digraphs.
KINESTHETIC AND AUDITORY ACTIVITY: Take out "Tell-a-Phone" cards: 'sh', 'ch', 'th', 'wh'. Have student practice sounds and hand symbols of 'h' digraphs. Practice distinguishing between 'sh' and 'ch' by holding up correct card as you read the 'sh' and 'ch' words from Chart 8 or Chart 55. Then repeat with 'th' and 'wh'.	❑ I can use the rule. ❑ I can hear it.
READING SKILLS: Review "Everyday Words". Learn new ones. "Read and Spell" page 191. (Words for Charts 1-8)	❑ I can read words with it.
SPELLING SKILLS: Give 15-20 spelling words daily. Use words from Chart 8 and review previous charts. Mark words with symbols.	❑ I can spell with it.
VOCABULARY BUILDER: Use Unit 7 only for an intermediate level student to build vocabulary. Introduce 1-3 new words or concepts.	❑ I increased my vocabulary.
"EVERYDAY BLOOPERS" (Chart 5) & SIGHT WORDS (Page 193): Study for instant recognition of some or all.	❑ I know sight words.
WRITING SKILLS: Practice writing daily. (Use Unit 8)	❑ I have written today.

CHART 9: **(Ending Digraphs) Teacher Procedure**	**Student Check List**
PREPARATION: Study write-up on page 56. Write "Everyday Words" and "Bloopers" on 3x5 cards.	❑ I practiced handwriting.
PHONETIC SOUNDS: Review the "Tell-a-Phone" cards, add 'tch'.	❑ I can say my phonemes.
INTRODUCE: Explain ending digraphs, using the write-up on page 56. Demonstrate how to mark sample words on blackboard. Emphasize that /ch/ is spelled /tch/ when it directly follows a short vowel, "pitch". It is 'ch', "pinch", elsewhere.	❑ I can tell about digraphs.
KINESTHETIC AND AUDITORY ACTIVITY: Take out "Tell-a-Phone" cards: 'ch', 'sh', 'th', 'tch'. Have student hold up cards as you read words from Chart 9.	❑ I can use the rule. ❑ I can hear it.
READING SKILLS: Review "Everyday Words". Learn new ones. "Read and Spell" page 191-192. (Words for Charts 1-9)	❑ I can read words with it.
SPELLING SKILLS: Give 15-20 spelling words daily. Use words from Chart 9 and review previous charts. Mark words with symbols.	❑ I can spell with it.
VOCABULARY BUILDER: Use Unit 7 only for an intermediate level student to build vocabulary. Introduce 1-3 new words or concepts.	❑ I increased my vocabulary.
"EVERYDAY BLOOPERS" (Chart 9) & SIGHT WORDS (Page 193): Study for instant recognition of some or all.	❑ I know sight words.
WRITING SKILLS: Practice writing daily. (Use Unit 8)	❑ I have written today.

CHART 40, 41, 42: **(Adding -ing/-s/-ed) Procedure**	**Student Check List**
PREPARATION: Study write-up on page 108. Write "Everyday Words" and "Bloopers" on 3x5 cards.	❑ I practiced handwriting.
PHONETIC SOUNDS: Review the "Tell-a-Phone" cards, add daily.	❑ I can say my phonemes.
INTRODUCE: Introduce the ending '-ing'. Explain from write-up on page 108. Demonstrate how to mark sample words on blackboard. (Repeat with '-s', and then with '-ed', each on different days.)	❑ I can tell about '-ing', '-s', and '-ed'.
KINESTHETIC AND AUDITORY ACTIVITY: Have student write the base word you say on the blackboard and then rewrite it, adding the suffix being studied. Talk about when the consonant needs to be doubled. (run—running; sit—sits; pat—patted)	❑ I can use the rule. ❑ I can hear it.
READING SKILLS: Review "Everyday Words". Learn new ones.	❑ I can read words with it.
SPELLING SKILLS: Give 15-20 spelling words daily. Use words from Chart 40, 41, 42 and pages 193,194. Mark words with symbols.	❑ I can spell with it.
VOCABULARY BUILDER: Use Unit 7 only for an intermediate level student to build vocabulary. Introduce 1-3 new words or concepts.	❑ I increased my vocabulary.
SIGHT WORDS (Page 193): Study for instant recognition of some or all.	❑ I know sight words.
WRITING SKILLS: Practice writing daily. (Use Unit 8)	❑ I have written today.

	CHART 10: (Final /j/, /g/, and /v/) Teacher Procedure	**Student Check List**
A	**PREPARATION:** Study write-up on page 59. Make a 3x5 card with 'dge' on one side and 'ge' on the other. Write "Everyday Words" and "Bloopers" on 3x5 cards.	❑ I practiced handwriting.
	INTRODUCE: Go over write-up on page 59 and demonstrate how to mark sample words on blackboard. Explain that 'j' will never be found alone at ends of words. The 'j' is replaced with 'dge' following a short vowel and 'ge' elsewhere.	❑ I can tell where to use 'ge', 'dge' and 'j'.
	KINESTHETIC AND AUDITORY ACTIVITY: Have student hold up the 'dge' side of card if the /j/ sound directly follows a short vowel and the 'ge' side elsewhere. Use words from Chart 10.	❑ I can use the rule. ❑ I can hear it.
B	**PREPARATION:** Study write-up on page 59.	❑ I practiced handwriting.
	INTRODUCE: Go over write-up on page 59 and demonstrate how to mark sample words on blackboard. Explain that 'v will never be found alone at ends of words. The 'v' always needs an 'e' whether the vowel is long or short. There are no 'uve' words. Instead 'ove' is used.	❑ I can tell about 've'.
	KINESTHETIC AND AUDITORY ACTIVITY: Have student spell words on blackboard as you read from Chart 10.	❑ I can use the rule. ❑ I can hear it.
	DAILY ACTIVITIES	
	PHONETIC SOUNDS: Review the "Tell-a-Phone" cards, add 'dge', 'ge'.	❑ I can say my phonemes.
	READING SKILLS: Review "Everyday Words". Learn new ones. "Read and Spell" pages 191-192.	❑ I can read words with it.
	SPELLING SKILLS: Give 15-20 spelling words daily. Use words from Chart 10 and review previous charts. Mark words with symbols.	❑ I can spell with it.
	VOCABULARY BUILDER: Use Unit 7 only for an intermediate level student to build vocabulary. Introduce 1-3 new words or concepts.	❑ I increased my vocabulary.
	"EVERYDAY BLOOPERS" (Chart 10) & SIGHT WORDS (Page 193): Study for instant recognition of some or all.	❑ I know sight words.
	WRITING SKILLS: Practice writing daily. (Use Unit 8)	❑ I have written today.

CHART 11: (Long 'a') Teacher Procedure (Round ONE)		**Student Check List**
A	**PREPARATION:** Study write-up on page 62. Make a 3 x 5 card with 'a_e' on the front and 'ay' on the back.	❑ I practiced handwriting.
	INTRODUCE: Memorize "What Makes a Long 'a'?" Go over rule and demonstrate how to mark sample words on blackboard.	❑ I can say the rule.
	ACTIVITY: Work with 'a_e' versus '-ay'. Read words from Chart 11, columns ① and ④. Have student hold up 'a_e' if the long 'a' sound is in the middle of the word, and 'ay' if at the end.	❑ I can use the rule.
	SPELLING: Give 15-20 words from columns ① and ④.	❑ I can spell with it.
B	**PREPARATION:** Study write-up on p. 62. Photo-copy p. 199. Write "Everyday Words" and "Bloopers" on 3x5 cards.	❑ I practiced handwriting.
	INTRODUCE: Study 'ail' and 'ale'. Review rule and markings.	❑ I can say the rule.
	ACTIVITY: Memorize poem on page 199.	❑ I can use the rule.
	SPELLING: Use words with 'ail' and 'ale' from column ②. Also include words from columns ① and ④.	❑ I can spell with it.
C	**PREPARATION:** Study write-up on page 62. Photo-copy page 200.	❑ I practiced handwriting.
	INTRODUCE: Study 'ain' and 'ane'. Review rule and markings.	❑ I can say the rule.
	ACTIVITY: Memorize poem on page 200.	❑ I can use the rule.
	SPELLING: Use words with 'ain' and 'ane' from column ②. Also include words from columns ① and ④.	❑ I can spell with it.
D	**PREPARATION:** Study write-up on page 62. Photo-copy page 201.	❑ I practiced handwriting.
	INTRODUCE: Study 'aid' and 'ade'. Review rule and markings.	❑ I can say the rule.
	ACTIVITY: Memorize poem on page 201.	❑ I can use the rule.
	SPELLING: Use words with 'aid' and 'ade' from column ②. Also include words from columns ① and ④.	❑ I can spell with it.
E Optional	**PREPARATION:** Study write-up on page 62. Photo-copy page 198.	❑ I practiced handwriting.
	INTRODUCE: Study 'eigh' and 'é'. Review rule.	❑ I can say the rule.
	ACTIVITY: Memorize poems of 'eigh' and 'é' on 198.	❑ I can use the rule.
	SPELLING: Use words with 'eigh' column ④. Also include words from columns ①, ②, and ④.	❑ I can spell with it.
DAILY ACTIVITIES		
PHONETIC SOUNDS: Review the "Tell-a-Phone" cards, add daily.		❑ I can say my phonemes.
READING SKILLS: Review "Everyday Words". Learn new ones.		❑ I can read words with it.
VOCABULARY BUILDER: Use Unit 7, ***Focus On: Meaning*** for words to build vocabulary. Introduce 1-3 new words or concepts.		❑ I increased my vocabulary.
"EVERYDAY BLOOPERS" (Chart 11) & SIGHT WORDS (Page 194): Study for instant recognition of some or all.		❑ I know sight words.
WRITING SKILLS: Practice writing daily. (Use Unit 8)		❑ I have written today.

CHART 13: **(Long 'e') Teacher Procedure (Round ONE)**		**Student Check List**
A	**PREPARATION:** Study write-up on page 66. Photo-copy pages 202-204.	❑ I practiced handwriting.
	INTRODUCE: Memorize "What Makes a Long 'e'?" poem. Work with 'ee' words.	❑ I can say the rule.
	ACTIVITY: Work with pages 202,203. Be accountable for only one row at a time. Then review 'ee' and 'ea' homonyms with page 204.	❑ I can use the rule.
	SPELLING: Give 15-20 words from Chart 13. Use only 'ee' words that have been studied and any 'ea'=/ē / word.	❑ I can spell with it.
B	**PREPARATION:** Study write-up on page 66. Make a card with 'ie' on one side and 'cei' on the other side. Write "Everyday Words" and "Bloopers" on 3x5 cards.	❑ I practiced handwriting.
	INTRODUCE: Work with 'ie' and 'cei' words. Note that most 'ie' words are followed by 'l', 'd', 'f' or 've'. Review rule and markings.	❑ I can say the rule.
	ACTIVITY: Read words with 'ie' or 'cei' in them and have student hold up the correct side of the card.	❑ I can use the rule.
	SPELLING: Use words with 'ail' and 'ale' from column ②. Also include words from columns ① and ④.	❑ I can spell with it.
C	**PREPARATION:** Study write-up on page 66.	❑ I practiced handwriting.
	INTRODUCE: Work with 'ea' = /ĕ / words.	❑ I can say the rule.
	ACTIVITY: Write words from column ⑤ on the blackboard with 'ea' saying both long and short 'e'. Have student read the words, trying both the long and short 'e' and deciding which is correct.	❑ I can use the rule.
	SPELLING: Use only "Everyday Words" for spelling test.	❑ I can spell with it.
DAILY ACTIVITIES		
PHONETIC SOUNDS: Review the "Tell-a-Phone" cards, add daily.		❑ I can say my phonemes.
READING SKILLS: Review "Everyday Words". Learn new ones.		❑ I can read words with it.
VOCABULARY BUILDER: Use Unit 7, ***Focus On: Meaning*** for words to build vocabulary. Introduce 1-3 new words or concepts.		❑ I increased my vocabulary.
"EVERYDAY BLOOPERS" (Chart 13) & SIGHT WORDS (Page 194): Study for instant recognition of some or all.		❑ I know sight words.
WRITING SKILLS: Practice writing daily. (Use Unit 8)		❑ I have written today.

CHART 16: **(Long 'i') Teacher Procedure (Round ONE)**		**Student Check List**
A	**PREPARATION:** Study write-up on page 70. Make a 3x5 card with 'i_e' on one side and 'y' on the other.	❑ I practiced handwriting.
	INTRODUCE: Memorize "What Makes a Long 'i'?" poem. Contrast 'i_e' with '-y' words.	❑ I can say the rule.
	ACTIVITY: Have student hold up the correct side of the card as you read words from Chart 16, columns ① and ②.	❑ I can use the rule.
	SPELLING: Give 15-20 words from Chart 16, columns ① and ②.	❑ I can spell with it.
B	**PREPARATION:** Study write-up on page 70. Write "Everyday Words" and "Bloopers" on 3x5 cards.	❑ I practiced handwriting.
	INTRODUCE: Work with long 'i' with 'ld' and 'nd'. Review rule and markings.	❑ I can say the rule.
	ACTIVITY: Write words randomly on blackboard from Chart 64, Row 3 ('i' row). Have student tell which 'i' is long and which is short (only the 'i' with 'ld' and 'nd' is long).	❑ I can use the rule.
	SPELLING: Give 15-20 spelling words daily from Chart 64, Row 3 ('i' row). Mark words with symbols.	❑ I can spell with it.
C	**PREPARATION:** Study write-up on page 70. Photo-copy page 205.	❑ I practiced handwriting.
	INTRODUCE: Work with 'igh' words.	❑ I can say the rule.
	ACTIVITY: Memorize poem on page 205.	❑ I can use the rule.
	SPELLING: Give 15-20 spelling words daily from Chart 16.	❑ I can spell with it.
DAILY ACTIVITIES		
PHONETIC SOUNDS: Review the "Tell-a-Phone" cards, add daily.		❑ I can say my phonemes.
READING SKILLS: Review "Everyday Words". Learn new ones.		❑ I can read words with it.
VOCABULARY BUILDER: Use Unit 7, ***Focus On: Meaning*** for words to build vocabulary. Introduce 1-3 new words or concepts.		❑ I increased my vocabulary.
"EVERYDAY BLOOPERS" (Chart 16) & SIGHT WORDS (Page 194): Study for instant recognition of some or all.		❑ I know sight words.
WRITING SKILLS: Practice writing daily. (Use Unit 8)		❑ I have written today.

	CHART 18: **(Long 'o') Procedure (Round ONE)**	**Student Check List**
A	**PREPARATION:** Study write-up on page 74. Make 3x5 cards of "Everyday Words" and "Bloopers". Photo-copy p. 206.	❑ I practiced handwriting.
	INTRODUCE: Memorize "What Makes a Long 'o'?" Go over rule and demonstrate how to mark sample words on blackboard.	
	ACTIVITY: Work with 'oa' words. Study page 206 of 'oa' words, and memorize a few at a time.	
	SPELLING: Give 15-20 words daily of 'oa' and 'o_e' words.	❑ I can spell it.
B	**PREPARATION:** Study write-up on page 74 for Chart 20. Make a 3x5 card with 'o' on one side and 'ow' on the other.	❑ I practiced handwriting.
	INTRODUCE: Study 'ow' and 'o' at ends of words. Review rule and markings. Following 'l' or 'r' we use 'ow'. There are a few more '-ow' words that must be memorized and only a few single-syllable '-o' words that also must be memorized.	❑ I can say the rule.
	ACTIVITY: Read words from Chart 20 and have student hold up 'ow' when after 'l' or 'r', and 'o' elsewhere. (Don't use exceptions.)	❑ I can use the rule.
	SPELLING: Review from Chart 18.	
C	**PREPARATION:** Study write-up on page 74.	❑ I practiced handwriting.
	INTRODUCE: Study 'ol-', 'ole', and 'oal'.	
	ACTIVITY: Have student memorize words from Chart 18.	
	SPELLING: Use 'ol', 'ole', and 'oal' words as well as review.	❑ I can spell it.
D	**PREPARATION:** Study write-up on page 74.	❑ I practiced handwriting.
	INTRODUCE: Study 'one', 'oan', and 'own' words.	
	ACTIVITY: Have student memorize words from Chart 18.	
	SPELLING: Use 'one', 'oan', and 'own' words & review words.	❑ I can spell it.
E	**PREPARATION:** Study write-up on page 74. Take out "Tell-a-Phone" cards 'or' and 'ore'.	❑ I practiced handwriting.
	INTRODUCE: Study 'or' versus 'ore'. We use 'or' in the middle of a word, and 'ore' at the end.	❑ I can say the rule.
	ACTIVITY: Read words from ②; have student hold up 'or' or 'ore'.	❑ I can use the rule.
	SPELLING: Use words from Chart 18.	❑ I can spell it.
	DAILY ACTIVITIES	
	PHONETIC SOUNDS: Review the "Tell-a-Phone" cards, add daily.	❑ I can say my phonemes.
	READING SKILLS: Review "Everyday Words". Learn new ones.	❑ I can read words with it.
	VOCABULARY BUILDER: Use Unit 7, ***Focus On: Meaning*** for words to build vocabulary. Introduce 1-3 new words or concepts.	❑ I increased my vocabulary.
	"EVERYDAY BLOOPERS" (Chart 18) & SIGHT WORDS (Page 194): Study for instant recognition of some or all.	❑ I know sight words.
	WRITING SKILLS: Practice writing daily. (Use Unit 8)	❑ I have written today.

CHART 21: **(Long 'u') Procedure (Round ONE)**		**Student Check List**
A	**PREPARATION:** Study write-up on page 78. Make a 3x5 card with o͞o on one side and o͝o on the other.	❑ I practiced handwriting.
	INTRODUCE: Study the sounds of 'oo'. When followed by a 'd' or 'k', 'oo' says, o͝o . ("good book")	❑ I can say the rule.
	ACTIVITY: Have student hold up the correct side of the 'oo' card as you read words from Chart 21, columns ④ and ②.	❑ I can use the rule.
	SPELLING: Give 15-20 words from Chart 21, columns ④ and ②. Review words from previous charts.	❑ I can spell with it.
B	**PREPARATION:** Study write-up on p. 78. Write "Everyday Words" and "Bloopers" on 3x5 cards. Photo-copy page 208.	❑ I practiced handwriting.
	INTRODUCE: "Memorize What Makes a Long 'u'?" Review rule and markings.	❑ I can say the rule.
	ACTIVITY: Learn page 208 for 'u_e' words.	❑ I can use the rule.
	SPELLING: Give 15-20 spelling words studied daily from Chart 21. Mark words with symbols.	❑ I can spell with it.
C	**PREPARATION:** Study write-up on page 78. Photo-copy page 198.	❑ I practiced handwriting.
	INTRODUCE: Work with exceptions.	❑ I can say the rule.
	ACTIVITY: Memorize "The Camping Trip" and "I Would" on page 198.	❑ I can use the rule.
	SPELLING: Give 15-20 spelling words daily from Chart 21. Include review words from previous charts.	❑ I can spell with it.
DAILY ACTIVITIES		
PHONETIC SOUNDS: Review the "Tell-a-Phone" cards, add daily.		❑ I can say my phonemes.
READING SKILLS: Review "Everyday Words". Learn new ones.		❑ I can read words with it.
VOCABULARY BUILDER: Use Unit 7, ***Focus On: Meaning*** for words to build vocabulary. Introduce 1-3 new words or concepts.		❑ I increased my vocabulary.
"EVERYDAY BLOOPERS" (Chart 21) & SIGHT WORDS (Page 194): Study for instant recognition of some or all.		❑ I know sight words.
WRITING SKILLS: Practice writing daily. (Use Unit 8)		❑ I have written today.

CHART 23: **('a' in unaccented syllables) Procedure**	**Student Check List**
PREPARATION: Study write-up on page 82. Make a 3x5 card with $\overset{a}{u}$ on one side and 'u' on the other.	❑ I practiced handwriting.
PHONETIC SOUNDS: Review the "Tell-a-Phone" cards, add daily.	❑ I can say my phonemes.
INTRODUCE: Introduce 'up' and 'un' versus initial 'a'.	❑ I can tell the rule.
KINESTHETIC AND AUDITORY ACTIVITY: Have student hold up the correct side of the card as you read 'up' and 'un' and initial 'a' words from Chart 23.	❑ I can use the rule. ❑ I can hear it.
READING SKILLS: Read final 'a' words on Chart 23.	❑ I can read words with it.
VOCABULARY BUILDER: Use Unit 7, ***Focus On: Meaning*** for words to build vocabulary. Introduce 1-3 new words or concepts.	❑ I increased my vocabulary.
SIGHT WORDS (Page 194): Study for instant recognition.	❑ I know sight words.
WRITING SKILLS: Practice writing daily. (Use Unit 8)	❑ I have written today.

CHART 25: **(oi/oy and ou/ow) Teacher Procedure**		**Student Check List**
A	**PREPARATION:** Study write-up on page 86. Make a 3x5 card with 'oi' on one side and 'oy' on the other. Write "Everyday Words" and "Bloopers" on 3x5 cards.	❑ I practiced handwriting.
	INTRODUCE: Go over write-up on page 86 of 'oi' and 'oy', and demonstrate how to mark sample words on blackboard.	❑ I can say the rule.
	KINESTHETIC AND AUDITORY ACTIVITY: Have student hold up the 'oy' side of card if the /oi/ sound is at the end of the word, and 'oi' elsewhere.	❑ I can use the rule. ❑ I can hear it.
B	**PREPARATION:** Study write-up on page 86. Make a 3x5 card with 'ou' on one side and 'ow' on the other.	❑ I practiced handwriting.
	INTRODUCE: Go over write-up on page 86 of 'ou and 'ow', and demonstrate how to mark sample words on blackboard.	❑ I can say the rule.
	KINESTHETIC AND AUDITORY ACTIVITY: Have student hold up the 'ow' side of card if the /ou/ sound is at the end of the word or in front of 'l' and 'n' (but not if they are in a blend), and 'ou' elsewhere.	❑ I can use the rule. ❑ I can hear it.
DAILY ACTIVITIES		
PHONETIC SOUNDS: Review the "Tell-a-Phone" cards, add daily.		❑ I can say my phonemes.
READING SKILLS: Review "Everyday Words". Learn new ones. "Read and Spell" pages 191-192.		❑ I can read words with it.
SPELLING SKILLS: Use only one-syllable words on Chart 23 and review previous charts. Mark words with symbols.		❑ I can spell with it.
VOCABULARY BUILDER: Use Unit 7, ***Focus On: Meaning*** for words to build vocabulary. Introduce 1-3 new words or concepts.		❑ I increased my vocabulary.
"EVERYDAY BLOOPERS" (Chart 25) & SIGHT WORDS (Page 194): Study for instant recognition of some or all.		❑ I know sight words.
WRITING SKILLS: Practice writing daily. (Use Unit 8)		❑ I have written today.

At this point in the learning sequence, it is important and extremely helpful for the student to be able to visualize what is going on by having the actual charts in front of him. Therefore, each student will need a personal copy of ***Eagle's Wings Comprehensive Handbook of Phonics.*** You will direct the order of study and discuss the write-ups of each chart prior to the student's independent study of the words. You will then be testing the student over his assigned words. The suggested order of study is listed for each chart.

CHART 26: Comparison of 'o' and 'a'. Memorize "More about 'o' and 'a'."

A. 'o' and 'a' with 'l' and 'r'.
B. 'wa', 'wo', 'war', and 'wor'. You may use the following poem if desired:

'WOR'

The work of one word brought the world into being
From the one by whom we live, move and have our seeing,
And from the best to the worst, from the worm to the sod
We all have our worth in the eyes of God.

C. 'ough'/'augh'. Use page 213
D. Ends of words—'aw' and 'ow'.

CHART 28: One-syllable words with /ŭr/.

A. 'ir' words. Use page 209. Give spelling from columns 4 and 5.
B. 'ur' words. Use page 210. Give spelling from columns 1, 4, and 5.
C. Memorize 'er' words. Give spelling from columns 1, 2, 4, and 5.
D. Memorize 'ear' words. You may use the following poem if desired:

'EAR'

If you search to the ends of the earth you will learn
To earn the pearl of wisdom should be something you yearn
So search for it early and keep looking late
And if you heed what you've heard you will truly be great.

CHART 29: One-syllable words with /r/.

Preparation: Photo-copy page 211-212, so that 212 is on the back of the paper. You may use card stock or laminate a lighter weight paper. Have student match up the spelling with the pictures of the sounds. Further directions are on the Form.

A. Study columns 1 and 2 for spelling tests.
B. Study columns 3 for spelling tests.
C. Study columns 4 and 5 for spelling tests.
D. Study columns 6, 7, and 8 for spelling tests.

CHART 30: One-syllable 'Cliffs(z)'.

This is a review of 'cliffs(z)'. See directions for Chart 2 and review with student.

CHART 32: Silent 'e' in One-syllable words with 'c', 's', and 'z'.

A. Study 'se' in contrast with 'ze'.
B. Study 'ce' in contrast with 'se'

CHART 36: Silent 'e' in Multi-syllable words with 'l'.

A. Study patterns of words with 'le'.
B. Point out 'ee'/'ea' words.

CHART 38: Silent 'e' with 'g' and 'v'.

Preparation: Study write-up on page 102.

A. Study 'ge' and review 'g'.
B. Study 've'.

Round TWO

The student is now ready to move on to Round TWO. In this section, the general procedure will be as follows. Also, spend several weeks memorizing sight words from p. 172, 193-4.

Review Chart	**Memorize:** Words not learned in Round ONE. **Spelling Test:** Over these words.
New Chart	**Introduction:** Study write-up with chart. It will give insight on what to teach about that chart.
	Memorize: Give portions or complete lists depending on student's ability.
	Practice: Spell words daily, correct misspelled words and spell these 5 times each.
	Spelling Test or Spelling Bee: Give test at end of week or end of study.

Suggested Order of Study

New Chart	Review Chart
48-49	
12	Chart 11 and 'Cliffs(z)'
14, 15	Chart 13 and 'Cliffs(z)'
17	Chart 16 and 'Cliffs(z)'
19-20	Chart 18 and 'Cliffs(z)'
22	Chart 21 and 'Cliffs(z)'
23	
24	
25	All Words
27	Chart 26
54	Chart 26
31	Chart 30
33	Chart 32
34	Chart 32
35	Chart 36
46-47	Chart 44-45
64	
65	
38	Chart 37
61	Page 197
62	Chart 37
63	Chart 37
69	Chart 26
50	Chart 49
52	Chart 4
53	Chart 4
55	Chart 8
56	Chart 9 and 39
57	Chart 48 and 49
58	Page 198, 205, 213
59	Chart 38
60	Page 197
66	Chart 28
67	Chart 29
68	Chart 29
70	
71	Page 214, 215, 216

UNIT 2

FOCUS ON:
CONSONANTS WITH SHORT VOWELS AND SILENT 'E'

Unit Two covers the sounds and spelling of the **short vowels** and of a single vowel made long with **silent 'e'**. It also introduces when and which **consonants double** at the ends of words ('ck', 'll','ff', 'ss', 'zz'), **blends**—beginning and ending ('bl', 'br', 'cl', 'cr', etc.), **digraphs**, ('sh', 'ch', 'th', etc.) and silent 'e' helping 'g' and 'v' ('dge', 'ge', 've'). Before beginning this unit, a student should have a command of the alphabet, including the formation and sound of each letter. (See Unit One for further teaching instructions.)

Chart		Beginning				Vowel		Ending			
#	Topic	One Syl.	Single Beg. Cons.	Beg. Blend	Beg. Digraph	Single Short Vowel	Single Long Vowel w/ Silent 'e'	Single End Cons.	Two Cons. One Sound	End Blend	End Digraph
1	2-3 Letter	✔	Intro.			Intro.		Intro.			
2	'Cliffs(z)'	✔	✔			✔			Intro.		
3	Silent 'e'	✔	✔			✔	Intro.	✔			
4	Beginning Blends	✔		Intro.		✔	✔	✔			
5	Beg Blends 'Cliffs(z) Silent 'e'	✔		✔		✔	✔	✔	✔		
6	Ending Blends	✔	✔			✔				Intro.	ng
7	Beg./End. Blends	✔		✔		✔				✔	ng
8	Beginning Digraphs	✔			Intro.	✔	✔	✔	✔	✔	ng
9	Ending Digraphs	✔	✔	✔	✔	✔					Intro.
10	dge/ge/ve	✔	✔	✔	✔	✔	✔	Intro. dge, ge, ve			

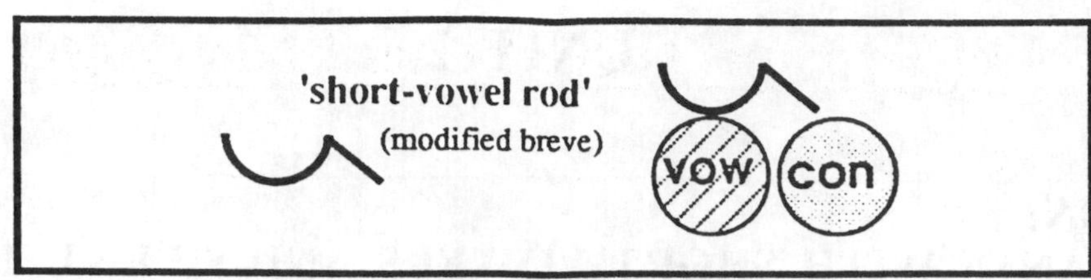
'short-vowel rod'
(modified breve)
vow
con

căt

Two and Three-Letter Short-Vowel Words: This chart of over 250 words is the complete list of words with a consonant—short vowel—consonant pattern [(c)v̆c]. What became evident in researching these words was that out of the 21 consonants in the alphabet, only eight consonants were found in the final position of the (c)v̆c pattern. These were 'b', 'd', 'g', 'm', 'n', 'p', 't' and 'x'. The importance of this finding is that these are the only consonants that make a vowel short while, at the same time, do not change their spelling at the end of a word. For instance, "bad"-/băd/, "bag"-/băg/, "ban"-/băn/, "bat"-/băt/ all end with one of those eight consonants. All the other consonants either change their spelling and/or affect the vowel sound, as in these words: "ball"-/bål/, "bar"-/bår/, "bass"-/băs/, "back"-/băk/, "badge"-/băj/. Each of these words only have three sounds, and yet have more than one letter for the final consonant sound and/or do not have a short-vowel sound.

Since it is the consonant following the vowel that dictates the sound the vowel makes, Eagle's Wings has developed the 'short-vowel rod'. This symbol, which is a breve with a line extending to the consonant, helps reinforce this concept: **When after one vowel is one consonant, or two, the vowel will be short, it's true.**

As you glance over the word lists, several words may pop out as missing—common words such as: "is", "as", "yes", "us", and "if". By turning to the next word list, entitled "**One-Syllable Cliffs(z)**", these words can be plainly seen to be exceptions. All should have two final consonants. These words, along with all the asterisked words found under the list of exceptions, are what we have coined as 'Everyday Bloopers'. 'Everyday Bloopers' are commonly used words that break the rules. Notice that the 'Everyday Words' are commonly used words that follow the rules.

Since the /k/, /s/, /g/, and /j/ sounds can be spelled in different ways, make sure the student has a good grasp of those sounds along with their most likely spelling. All the words marked with a number one fall into that category. Use those words (over 40 in all) to practice the following concept. Here are the rules for deciding which letter to use at **beginnings of syllables**. (Note that 'c' and 's' over lap and there is no way to predict which to use when an /s/ sound is followed by 'e', 'i' or 'y'. These words must be memorized. ☛ See page 197)

c = /s/ s = /s/ k = /k/	**with i e y**	**c = /k/ s = /s/**	**with a o u consonant**
g = /j/	**with i e y**	**g = /g/ j = /j/**	**with a o u consonant ee** (2 vowels) **(v)tt** (i, e, or y and 2 consonants)

Memorize:

✏ 'Everyday Words'			
bad	ran	did	on
dad	at	big	top
mad	sat	him	got
sad	red	in	hot
am	ten	it	lot
an	let	sit	not
can	met	six	fun
man	yet	mom	run
		but	up

*'Everyday Bloopers'	
*add	*one
*been	*said
*get	
*come	
*some	
*son	
*done	
*gone	
*none	

Entire List of Two and Three-Letter Short-Vowel Words

	ă	ĕ	ĭ	ŏ	ŭ
b	[1]cab nab dab tab gab jab	web	bib fib rib	bob rob [1]cob [1]sob [1]job mob	[1]cub pub dub rub hub [1]sub nub tub
d	bad had [1]sad [1]cad lad dad mad fad pad	bed wed fed led red	bid lid did mid hid rid [1]kid	[1]cod rod God [1]sod nod pod	bud [1]cud dud mud
g	bag rag [1]gag [1]sag lag tag nag	beg [1]keg leg peg	big wig dig fig pig rig	bog log [1]cog [1]jog dog fog hog	bug lug dug mug hug rug [1]jug tug
m	am jam dam ram ham yam	gem hem	dim him rim	mom tom	bum mum gum rum hum sum
n	an man van ban pan [1]can ran fan tan	den ten hen yen men pen	in gin tin bin kin win din pin fin [1]sin	on [1]con	bun pun fun run gun [1]sun nun
p	[1]cap rap [1]gap [1]sap lap tap map yap nap zap	pep	dip rip hip [1]sip lip tip nip yip pip zip	[1]cop pop hop [1]sop lop top mop	up [1]cup pup [1]sup
t	at mat bat pat [1]cat [1]sat fat rat hat vat	bet pet let [1]set met wet net yet vet	it lit bit [1]sit fit wit hit [1]kit	[1]cot lot dot not [1]got pot hot rot [1]jot tot	but [1]jut [1]cut nut [1]gut rut hut
x	ax lax tax	vex	fix mix [1]six	ox lox box pox fox	
	Exception *add gnat wrap [2]wag [2]wan [2]wax	**Exception** debt ebb egg *[1]get [1]jet knit *said	**Exception** inn [1]gig gym [1]jig mitt	**Exception** odd *[1]gone knob knot	**Exception** *[1]come *done mutt numb *none——(nun) *[1]son——(sun) *[1]some—(sum) ton won——*one

Computer checked. *'Everyday Bloopers': Must be memorized.

[1]**At beginnings of syllables:** Use 'k' for /k/ and 'c' or 's' for /s/ before 'e', 'i' or 'y'. (Memorize these.) Use 'c' for /k/ and 's' for /s/ elsewhere. Generally, use 'gu' for /g/ and 'g' for /j/ before 'e', 'i' or 'y'. Use 'g' for /g/ and 'j' for /j/ elsewhere. [2]'wa' usually says/wå/, "want".

Chart 1

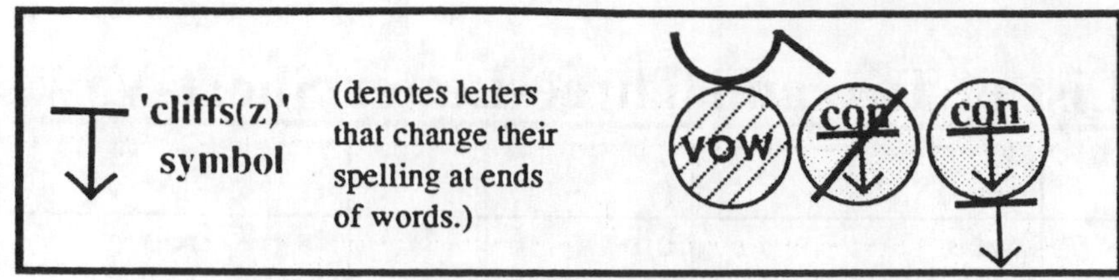
'cliffs(z)' symbol
(denotes letters that change their spelling at ends of words.)
VOW
con
con

tĕll

'Cliffs(z)': Following Short Vowels at Ends of Words: Many letters have consistent spellings anywhere in a word. Other letters change their spellings at ends of words. Consequently it is important to know which letters change and which do not. Certain consonants and all the vowels change their spellings at ends of words. This chart deals with the words that have a single consonant and a short vowel followed by two consonants that make a single consonant sound, (c) v̆ c ȼ. Following a short vowel, the consonants that double at ends of words to make a single consonant sound are found in the word "cliffs(z)". The 'cliffs(z)' symbol indicates that the extra consonant is not heard but is needed at ends of words for the consonant. The following analogy may be helpful to understand and remember this concept.

Cliffs(z) Story:

> When letters get together to form words, the last letter is by a 'cliff'. And as with people, some are afraid to be there and others are not. Although many letters do not mind being at the end of a word, some letters will not be there at all and others will be there only if another letter is with them. All the vowels are afraid of the 'cliffs' and usually have a 'y' or 'w' to help them. The key phrase, "Charge to view the 'cliffs(z)'" contains the consonants that are afraid of ends of words.

Following Short Vowels at Ends of Words:

c /k/>ck "back"

l /l/>ll "fell"*

i (All vowels change their spelling at ends of words.)

ff /f/>ff "off"

s /s/>ss "pass"

z /z/>zz "fizz"

*['all' says /ål/, "ball", and 'oll' says /ōl/ "poll", and is studied in detail on Charts 64, 65.]

Under the exceptions are many commonly used words or 'Everyday Bloopers' that must be memorized—"if", "of", "yes", "plus", "us", "is", "as", "was", and "has". These are exceptions because they should, but do not, have double consonants at the end.

The complete list of consonants that change their spelling at ends of words are underlined in the phrase, "Charge to view the cliffs(z)." It is important to note that these consonants usually have a silent 'e' with them when not directly following a short vowel ("house", "hinge", "apple", "snooze", "sleeve", and so forth). In these words, the silent 'e' is there for the consonant and may or may not help the vowel. The concept of 'cliffs(z)' will be greatly expanded in further charts (Unit 4.)

Memorize:

'Everyday Words'		
back	fill	less
fell	till	miss
tell	will	
well	off	
yell	pass	

*'Everyday Bloopers'		
*half	*yes	*of
*as	*if	*guess
*has	*his	*full
*was	*is	*pull
*says	*does	*us

Complete List of One-Syllable, Short-Vowel 'Cliffs(z)' (no blends)

☑	ck ↧	ll ↧	ff ↧	ss ↧	zz ↧
ă	back hack jack lack pack rack sack tack	'all' = /ål/		bass lass mass pass sass	jazz razz
ĕ	deck peck neck	bell [1]jell cell sell dell tell fell well hell yell		less mess	
ĭ	hick kick lick nick pick rick sick tick wick	bill sill dill till fill will hill ill kill mill pill		hiss kiss miss	fizz
ŏ	cock dock hock lock mock rock sock	'oll' = /ōl/	off	boss loss moss toss	
ŭ	buck duck luck muck puck suck tuck	cull dull gull hull lull mull null	buff cuff huff puff muff	cuss fuss muss	buzz fuzz
	Exception yak	**Exception** [1]gill nil doll bull *full *pull	**Exception** calf *half laugh cough rough tough *if *of	**Exception** gas alas *yes *[1]guess bus pus *plus *us	**Exception** *as *has *says *was *his *is *does

☑ Computer checked. *'Everyday Bloopers': Must be memorized. [1] 'g'=/g/ > 'e', 'i' or 'y' plus two consonants.

Chart 2

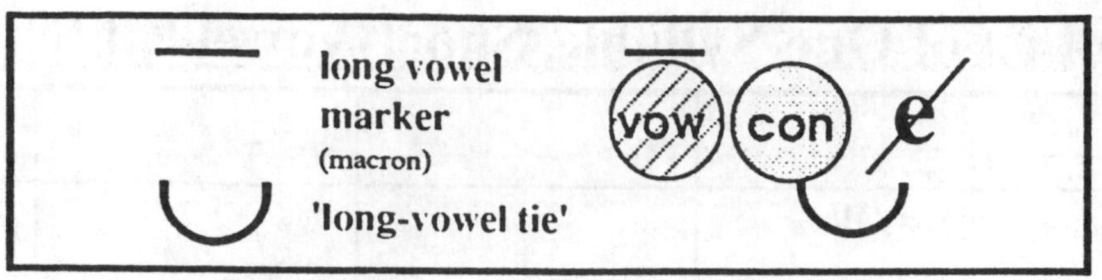
long vowel
marker
(macron)
'long-vowel tie'
vow
con
e

Silent 'e' in One-Syllable Words:

Rule①: Silent 'e' helps most vowels to be long.
②: It takes two vowels to make a long 'e',
For Silent 'e' rarely helps an 'e'.

măd māde

① Silent 'e' at the end of a word can help a vowel in the middle of the word to be long. To symbolize what is happening, we use a symbol which we call a 'long-vowel tie'. This shows that the silent 'e' has a 'long-vowel tie' with the consonant, enabling the preceding vowel to be long. The words in parenthesis are included to show the contrast of a short vowel without a silent 'e'.

② There are very few one-syllable words that have an 'e' made long with the aid of a silent 'e'. If the student understands that it usually takes two vowels to make a long 'e', many spelling errors would be eliminated (f<u>ee</u>d, m<u>ea</u>t, <u>ea</u>gle). This concept will be further discussed on Chart 13.

Remember, the long 'u' has two sounds; a /ü/ ,"dude", and a /ū/ or /yü/,"cute". The bold letters in this chart have the /ū/, "cute", sound.

Included in the lower portion of this chart are the 'cliffs(z)' consonants (k, l, f, s, z, g, v) since these consonants frequently change sounds or affect the vowel spelling or sound. **Only the words that are predictable in their spellings are included at this point.** The 'r' words are not included here, for 'r' also affects the vowel sounds and spelling.

Another interesting occurrence is that the /k/ sound following a short vowel in a one-syllable word is spelled 'ck'. Following a long vowel it is often a 'k'-silent 'e'. 'K' never makes a vowel short. In multi-syllable words, 'c' and 'que' are often used to make a /k/, "picni<u>c</u>" sound at the end of a word. (See Chart 59 and 60.)

Memorize:

✏ 'Everyday Words'			
made	name	save	hide
make	same	like	wide
sake	ate	time	home
take	date	line	hope
came	gave	mine	note

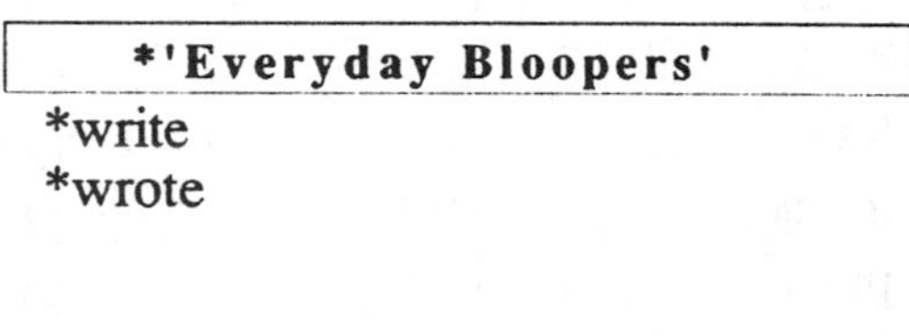

*'Everyday Bloopers'
*write
*wrote

Complete List of One-Syllable Words with Silent 'e' (no blends or 'r')

☑	ā__e̸	ē__e̸	ī__e̸	ō__e̸	ū__e̸ ü__e̸
b	babe	It takes		lobe robe (rob)	cube (cub) tube (tub)
d	bade (bad) wade fade (fad) jade made (mad)	two vowels to make a long	bide (bid) side hide (hid) tide ride (rid) wide Exception: [1]guide	bode node (nod) code (cod) ode mode (mod) rode (rod) lode	dude (dud) rude
m	came lame dame (dam) name fame same game tame	'e' For Silent 'e'	dime (dim) lime mime time	dome home	fume
n	cane (can) sane lane vane (van) mane (man) wane (wan) pane (pan)	rarely helps an 'e'.	dine (din) nine fine (fin) pine (pin) line vine mine wine (win)	bone zone cone (con) lone tone	dune tune
p	ape cape (cap) gape (gap) nape (nap) tape (tap)		pipe (pip) ripe (rip) wipe	cope (cop) nope dope pope (pop) hope (hop) rope lope (lop) mope (mop)	dupe
t	ate (at) hate(hat) bate (bat) late date mate(mat) fate (fat) rate(rat) gate		bite (bit) site (sit) cite kite (kit) mite Exception: *write	dote (dot) tote (tot) mote vote note (not) rote (rot) Exception: *wrote	cute (cut) jute (jut) lute mute
			Predictable 'Cliffs(z)' ↧		
f	safe		fife life wife		
k	bake (back) rake (rack) cake sake (sack) fake take (tack) lake (lack) wake make		bike mike dike pike (pick) hike (hick) like (lick)	coke (cock) joke (jock) poke (pock) woke yoke	duke (duck)
l ↧	ale male bale pale dale sale gale tale hale		bile (bill) rile file (fill) tile (till) mile (mill) vile pile (pill) wile (will)	dole role hole sole mole pole	mule rule
v ↧	cave rave gave save pave wave		dive jive five live hive	cove rove dove (v.) wove	
s ↧	base (bass) vase case			dose	
z ↧	daze haze faze maze gaze raze		size	doze	

☑ Computer checked. *'Everyday Bloopers': Must be memorized. ↧ 'Cliffs(z)' See Unit 4. ← 'R' See Unit 3.

[1]'gu' = /g/ before 'e', 'i' or 'y'.

Chart 3

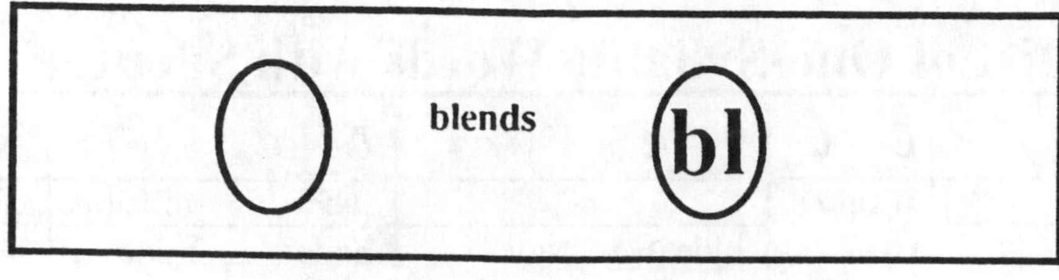
blends
bl

glăd
glāde

Beginning Blends—One-Syllable Words: Beginning consonant blends are made only with 'l', 'r', and 'w' following a consonant, and 's' preceding a consonant. A blend is two (or three) letters put together which still make their own individual sounds. (We circle these consonants to show that they are a blend.) A blend can be broken apart. When sustaining a blend, we end up saying the last letter of the blend. Try sustaining 'bl'— 'bl • l • l • l'. We end up saying an 'l'.

The blend 'qu' has the sound of /kw/, "quit", and must be practiced to put the sound with its spelling.

sk = /sk/ **sc = /s/**	**with i e y**	**sc = /sk/**	**with a o u consonant**

When the /sk/ sound is present in a blend, we must know when to use 'c' or 'k'. Use 'k', not 'c', before 'i', 'e', and 'y', since the 'c' will say /s/ with these letters. Before 'a', 'o', and 'u', use 'c', since with these letters it says /k/.

Memorize:

✏ 'Everyday Words'

plan
stop
quit
quite

***'Everyday Bloopers'**

*from
*prove

Complete List of One-Syllable Words with Beginning Blends

☑	Blends with 'l'		Blends with 'r'	
b	blab bled blip blob blot	blade blame	brad brag bran brat bred brim	brave bribe bride brine brute
c	clad clam clan clap clip clod clog clop clot club	clone clove	crab crag cram crib crop crux	crane crate crave crime crone crude
d			drab drag drug drip drop drum	drape drive drone drove
f	flag flap flat fled flex flip flit flog flop flub	flame flume flute	fret frog	frame
g	glad glen glib glob glop glum glut	glade glide globe	grab gram grid grim grin grip grit grub	grade grape grate grave grime gripe grope grove
p	plan pled plod plop plot plug plum	plane plate plume	prim prod prom prop	pride prime probe prone prude prune
t			trap trim trip trod trot	trade tribe tripe trite

Blends with 's'					
sc	scab scan scat scot	scone scope	sp	span spat sped spin spit spot spud spun	spade spine spite
scr	scrap scram scrub	scrape scribe	spl	splat split	
sk	skid skim skin skip skit		spr	sprig	
sl	slab slag slam slap slat sled slid slim slip slit slob slop slot slug slum	slate slave slide slime slope	st	stab stag stem step stop stub stud stun	state stone stove
			str	strap strip strum strut	stride strife stripe strive strode
sm	smog smug	smite smote	sw	swag swam swig swim swum	
sn	snag snap snip snob snub snug	snide snipe	squ	squib squid	
	'qu' = /kw/			'tw' = /tw/	
	quip quit	quite quote		twig twin twit	twine

Exception
[1]skate
sweat
blood
flood
plaid
*from
*prove

☑ Computer checked. *'Everyday Bloopers': Must be memorized. [1]'k' is rare with 'a', 'o', or 'u'.

Chart 4

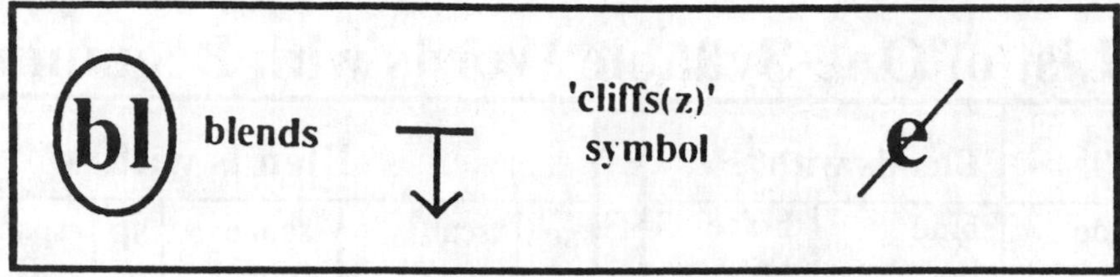
bl
blends
'cliffs(z)'
symbol
e

stack stake

Beginning Blends with Consonant 'Cliffs(z)' and Silent 'e': This chart is an expansion of two concepts—blends and 'cliffs(z)'. Blends are two (or three) consonants that blend their sounds together but still say their own sounds. We circle these consonants to show that they are a blend. Consonant 'Cliffs(z)' are the consonants in the word 'cliffs(z)', that double at ends of one-syllable words following a short vowel. With these consonants, we use a 'cliffs(z)' symbol [↧]. The words in parenthesis shows what the short-vowel word would change to by adding a silent 'e'.

Memorize:

'Everyday Words'	
black	smile
smell	spoke
spell	close
skill	cross
spill	
still	

*'Everyday Bloopers'
*plus

English

Roots

Greek
German
Latin
Old English
French

'Plane" comes from a Greek word meaning "to wander". From it we get words like "planet" (to wander in the sky) and airplane" (to wander in the air).

Beginning Blends with 'Cliffs (z)' and Silent 'e'

☑	ck ↧	ll[1] ↧	ff ↧	ss[2] ↧	zz[2] ↧
bl	black block		bluff	bless bliss	(blaze)
br	brick (brake) (broke)			brass	(braze)
cl	clack clock click cluck		cliff	class (close)	
cr	crack crock crick			crass cross	(craze)
dr	(drake)	drill		dress dross	
dw		dwell			
fl	flack flick fleck flock (flake) (fluke)		fluff	floss	
fr	frock	frill			frizz (froze)
gl				glass gloss	(glaze)
gr		grill	gruff	grass **Except:** gross	(graze)
pl	pluck			**Exception:** *plus	
pr	prick			press	(prize)
qu	quack (quake) quick	quill quell			
tr	track truck trick **Except:** trek	trill		tress truss	
tw		twill			
sc		(scale) **Except:**[3]skull	scoff scuff		
scr			scruff		
sk		skill	skiff		
sl	slack slick				
sm	smack smock (smoke)	smell (smile)			
sn	snack snuck (snake)		sniff		
sp	speck (spike) (spoke)	spell spill			
st	stack stock stick stuck (stake) (stoke)	still (stole) (stale)	staff stuff stiff	stress	
str	struck (strike) (stroke)		(strife)		
sw		swell		swiss	

☑ Computer checked. *'Everyday Bloopers': Must be memorized.

[1]For 'all' and 'oll' words see Chart 26. [2]For 'ce', 'se', and 'ze' words see Chart 32. [3]'k' is rarely used with 'a', 'o' or 'u'.

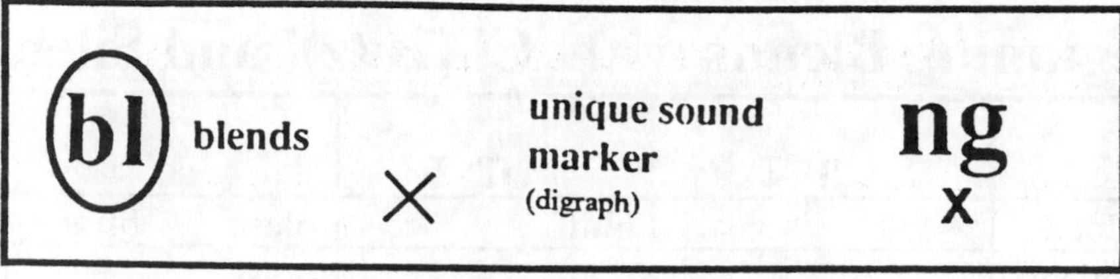
bl
blends
unique sound
marker
(digraph)
ng
x

kĕpt   săng

Ending Blends and '-ng' Digraphs (one-syllable): Ending blends, like beginning blends are two consonants that blend together but still retain their own sounds. We circle the blends to show that they go together. Most ending blends end with a 'd', 't', 'p' or 'k'. Ending blends with 'l or 'n' sometimes affect the vowel sounds. (Note: 'l' and 'n' affect vowel sounds. See Charts 64 and 65.) 'A' with an 'l' blend says /å/ "bald", 'o' with an 'l' blend says /ō/ "bold", and 'i' with 'ld' and 'nd' says /ī/ "child", "kind". These words are not included at this point.

A digraph, unlike a blend, is a unique single sound that is not related to either of the consonants sounds involved. We designate a digraph by marking an 'x' under it to show that it is a unique sound. 'Ng' is a digraph. If its sound is sustained, it remains the same and does not break down into its parts. 'Nk' is pronounced /ngk/, and may cause some confusion since it does not sound the way it is spelled.

Memorize:

✏ 'Everyday Words'				*'Everyday Bloopers'
left	sing	ask	next	*built
lift	sung	last	held	*wrong
soft	long	past	self	*[1]want
jump	cent	best	felt	*[1]guest
and	sent	test		
end	went	just		
sang	kept	must		

[1]Not "true" bloopers, as 'wa'=/wå/ and 'gu' = /g/ before 'e', 'i', or 'y'.

One-Syllable Words with Ending Blends and '-ng' (short vowels)

☑	ă	ĕ	ĭ	ŏ	ŭ
ct	act pact fact tact	sect			duct
ft	daft raft	deft left heft	gift rift lift sift	loft soft	tuft
mp	camp tamp damp lamp ramp	hemp	imp limp	pomp romp	bump lump dump pump hump rump jump sump
☆ nd	and band hand land sand	bend rend end send fend tend lend vend mend	[4]ind = /īnd/	bond fond pond	fund
[1]ng	bang rang gang sang hang tang		ding ring king sing ping wing	gong tong long song	dung rung hung sung lung
[1]nk	bank rank dank sank hank tank lank yank		kink sink link wink mink pink	bonk conk honk	bunk punk dunk sunk hunk junk
nt	ant pant rant	bent rent cent—sent dent tent lent vent pent went	dint hint lint mint tint	[4]-aunt = /ŏnt/	bunt hunt punt runt
pt	apt rapt	kept wept tempt		opt	
sk	ask mask bask task cask	desk	risk disk		dusk tusk husk musk
sp	asp rasp gasp		lisp wisp		cusp
st	cast vast fast last mast past	best rest jest test lest vest nest west pest zest	fist gist list mist	cost lost	bust rust dust gust just must
xt		next text			
ld☆	[4]ald = /åld/	held weld	[4]ild = /īld/	[4]old = /ōld/	
lf☆	[4]alf = /ăf/	elf self			
lk☆	[4]alk = /åk/	elk	milk silk	[4]olk = /ōk/	bulk sulk hulk
lp☆	[4]alp = /ălp/	help yelp kelp			gulp pulp
lt☆	[4]alt = /ålt/ [4]alm=/ålm/	belt pelt felt welt melt	hilt tilt lilt wilt silt	[4]olt = /ōlt/	cult
lm☆	waft	elm	film		
Except	wrapt	leapt knelt [2]guest scent	built jilt gilt wrist [2]guilt wring	*[3]want *wrong	monk young wrung

☑ Computer checked. *'Everyday Bloopers': Must be memorized.
[1]'ng' is a digraph—'nk' = /ngk/. [2]'gu'=/g/ before 'e', 'i' or 'y'. [3]'wa'=/wå/ [4]See Chart 64

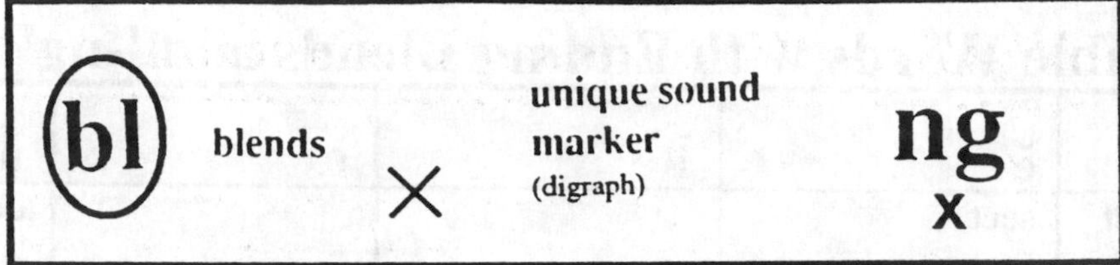
bl
blends
unique sound
marker
(digraph)
ng

stand bring

One-Syllable Words with Beginning and Ending Blends and 'ng' Digraphs. These are one-syllable words with beginning and ending blends and the 'ng' digraph. All the vowels are short with ending blends except for some with 'l' and 'n'. These have not yet been introduced. We circle the blends and use an 'x' under the 'ng' digraph.

Memorize:

✏ 'Everyday Words'			*'Everyday Bloopers'
grand	stand	bring	*front

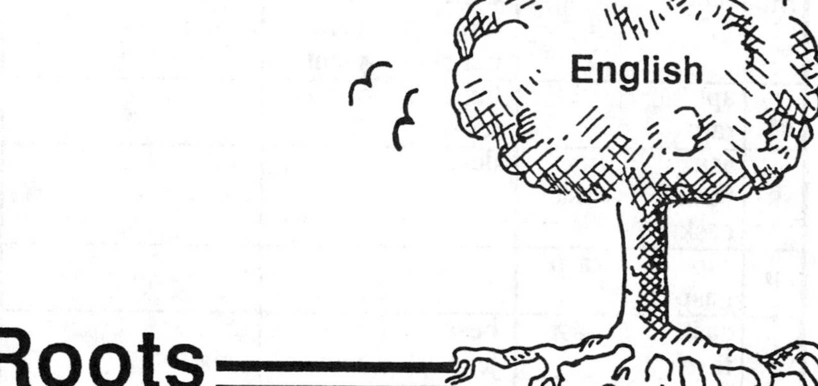
English
Greek
German
Latin
Old English
French

Roots

During the Middle Ages, in the center of every home was the fireplace, or hearth. Family life revolved around this hearth. From the hearth came light, warmth, and cooked food. The Latin word for hearth was 'focus'. And that's where we got our word "focus". For the focus of the home was the 'focus' (hearth).

One-Syllable Words with Beginning and Ending Blends (short vowels)

☑	ă	ĕ	ĭ	ŏ	ŭ
ct	tract		strict		
ft	craft graft draft	cleft	drift swift		
lt	[2]alt =/ålt/	dwelt spelt smelt	quilt stilt spilt	[2]olt =/ōlt/	
mp	clamp tramp cramp scamp stamp		blimp skimp crimp primp scrimp	stomp	clump slump frump stump grump trump plump
nd	bland grand brand stand gland strand	blend spend trend	[2]ind =/īnd/	blond	
[1]ng	clang slang sprang twang		bring spring cling sting fling string sling swing	prong strong	clung stung flung strung slung swung sprung
[1]nk	blank frank crank plank clank prank drank spank flank stank **Exception:** [3]swank		blink stink brink shrink clink drink slink		clunk slunk drunk spunk flunk stunk plunk trunk **Exception:** [4]skunk
nt	plant slant scant	spent	splint squint		blunt grunt brunt stunt **Exception:** *front
pt		crept swept slept	script **Exception:** crypt	prompt	sculpt
sk	flask		brisk frisk	frost	
sm	spasm		prism		
sp	clasp grasp		crisp		
st	blast	blest quest crest	grist twist		crust trust

☑ Computer checked.
[3]'wa'=/wå/

*'Everyday Bloopers': Must be memorized.
[4]'sk'=/sk/> 'e', 'i' or 'y' and 'sc'=/sk/> 'a', 'i', or 'u'.

[1]'ng' is a digraph—'nk'=/ngk/.

[2]See Chart 64

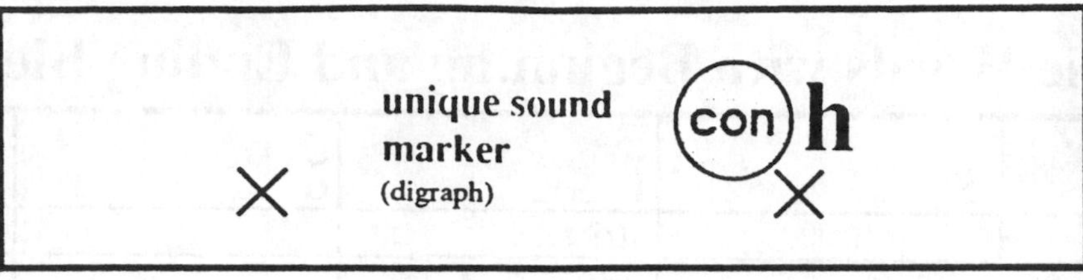
unique sound
marker
(digraph)
con
h

shāpe

One-Syllable Words with Beginning 'h' Digraphs. The majority of digraphs are with 'h'. A digraph is a sound that can be sustained and will not break down into its parts. The sound of a digraph is unrelated to the individual letters used to create it. In other words, a digraph is a unique sound that must be memorized. We mark an 'x' underneath it to show that it is a unique sound. The following hand symbols and key words will help in remembering these 'h' digraphs.

'sh' says /sh/, "shush": Put finger to mouth and say "Shhh!"
'wh' says /hw/, "what": Put finger up like a candle and blow.
'ch' says /ch/, "cheese": Put a finger on either side of mouth, smile as if posing for a picture and say "Ch-ch-cheese."
'th' says /th/, "thing", and /th/, "that": This is the only sound that is made with the tongue between the teeth. Stick your tongue out slightly and blow /th/, "thing", and then repeat with a buzz or voiced sound, /th/, "that".

✏ 'Everyday Words'

shape	that	thing	while
than	then	think	white
thank	when		

***'Everyday Bloopers'**

*shall	*this	*those
*what	*who	*whose
*the	*whom	*thus
*these	*chose	

Chart 9
Ending 'h' Digraphs

This chart show the patterns of one-syllable short-vowel words ending with 'h' digraphs. Of special note is the /ch/. At ends of words, /ch/ is spelled 'tch' when it is directly following a short vowel. The 't' is silent and is only there to make the vowel short. If the vowel is long, or the /ch/ follows a consonant, the 't' is not used.

✏ 'Everyday Words'

match	wish	with

***'Everyday Bloopers'**

*[1]watch	*both	*much
*which	*month	*such
*rich		

[1]Not a true blooper, as 'wa'=/wå/.

Complete List of Beginning 'h' Digraphs in One-Syllable Words

☑	sh	sh_ȼ	ch	ch_ȼ	th/th	th/th_ȼ	wh	wh_ȼ
One Final Cons.	shag sham shed shin ship shop shot shun shut shred shrub shrug	shade shame shape shave shine shone shrine **Exception** chute	chap chat chin chip chit chat chop chug chum	chide chime	than that them then thin thud thug throb	thine throne thrive **Exception** *the [1]theme there	wham when whet whim whip whit **Exception** *what *who *whom	whine white **Exception** where
Cliffs ↧	shack shock shell shuck shrill **Exception** *shall	shake shale	chaff check chess chill chuck	chase chafe chive choke **Exception** chose chalk	thick thrill **Exception** *this *thus	 **Exception** *[1]these *those	whiff whack whizz **Exception** *whose	whale while **Exception** *whole
Ending Blends	shaft shalt shank shelf shift shunt shrank shrink		champ chant chest chimp chink chomp chump chunk		thank theft thing think thrift thong thump		whelp whisk	

☑ Computer checked. *'Everyday Bloopers': Must be memorized. ↧ 'Cliffs(z)': See Unit 4. [1]It takes two vowels to make a long 'e'.

One-Syllable Short-Vowel Words Ending with 'h' Digraphs

sh	nch	tch	th
ash	ranch	batch	bath (bathe)
bash	bench	catch	hath
cash	inch	hatch	lath (lathe)
dash	cinch	latch	math
gash	finch	match	path
hash	pinch	patch	pith
lash	winch	fetch	with
mash	conch	etch	moth
rash	bunch	retch	
sash	hunch	ditch	depth
mesh	lunch	hitch	length
dish	munch	itch	tenth
fish	punch	pitch	fifth
wish		witch	filth
josh	**Exception**	notch	sixth
gush	wrench	hutch	width
hush		**Exception**	
mush	**lch**	[1]watch touch	**Exception**
lush	belch	wretch *such	wrath *both
rush	gulch	*rich *much	myth *month
Exception		niche	(writhe)
gnash			

With Beginning Blends

	sh	nch		tch	th
l	blush	blanch	l	blotch	cloth (clothe)
	clash	clench		clutch	sloth
	flash	clinch	r	crotch	broth
	flesh	flinch		crutch	froth
	flush		s	scotch	
	plush			scratch	smith
r	brash	branch		sketch	
	brush	brunch		squelch	
	crash	crunch		splotch	
	crush	drench		snatch	
	trash	trench		snitch	
s	shush	scrunch		stitch	
	slash	stench		stretch	
	slosh			switch	
	slush				
	smash				
	splash		th	thatch	
	squish			twitch	
	stash	quench			
	swish			**Exception**	**Exception**
th	thrash			[1]swatch	[2]truth
	thresh			*which	
	thrush				

Computer checked. *'Everyday Bloopers': Must be memorized. [1]'ua' and 'wa' = /wå/. [2]Only words with 'u'>'th'= "truth", "ruthless"

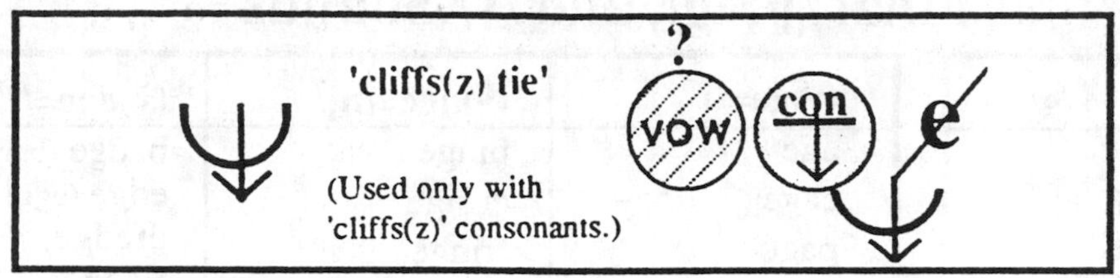

?
'cliffs(z) tie'
(Used only with 'cliffs(z)' consonants.)
vow
con
e

bădgẹ āgẹ

Chart 10
Final /j/, /g/, and /v/ Sounds.
Neither 'v' nor 'j' will ever be found alone at ends of words. The 'j' is replaced with 'dge' following a short vowel and 'ge' elsewhere. The 'd' is needed only to make the vowel short.

The 'v' always needs a silent 'e' regardless of the vowel sound. The vowel may be long or short followed by a 've'. Also, we never find a 'u' with 'v'. Any 'u' sound (/ŭ/, /ü/) will be made by an 'o'. ("love", "prove"). And "it takes two vowels to make a long 'e'" (leave, sleeve).

✏ 'Everyday Words'		
brave	live	love
save	live	move
change	lives	drove
strange	five	prove

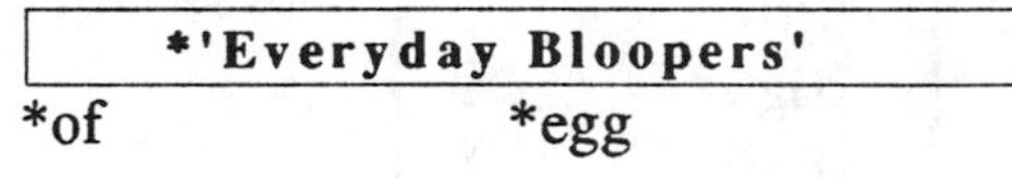

*'Everyday Bloopers'	
*of	*egg

Roots

We know what a heart is, but as part of a word, it means "strong emotion". This is where we get the words "heartache", "heartbreak", "heartily", "heartless", "hearty", "dishearten". Just think what our words might be if we considered our stomachs to be the center of our emotions!

English
Greek
German
Latin
Old English
French

Final /j/, /g/, and /v/ Sounds

(v̆)g= /g/
bag
brag
drag
flag
gag
hag
lag
nag
rag
sag
shag
snag
beg
keg
leg
peg
big
dig
fig
gig
jig
pig
sprig
swig
twig
wig
bog
clog
cog
dog
flog
fog
frog
hog
jog
log
bug
chug
dug
drug
hug
jug
lug
mug
plug
pug
rug
shrug
slug
smug
snug
thug
tug
Exception
egg

(v̆)ge=/j/	(v̆)nge=/nj/	(v̆)dge=/j/
age	binge	badge (bag)
cage	cringe	edge (egg)
page	fringe	dredge
rage (rag)	hinge	fledge
sage (sag)	singe (sing)	hedge
stage (stag)	tinge	ledge (leg)
wage (wag)	twinge	pledge
huge (hug)	lunge (lung)	sledge
gouge	plunge	wedge
		bridge
	Exception	midge
Exception	sponge	ridge (rig)
gauge (gag)		dodge
liege		lodge
siege	**ānge**	budge (bug)
	change	drudge (drug)
	mange	fudge
	range (rang)	grudge
	strange	judge (jug)
		nudge
		sludge (slug)
		smudge (smug)
		trudge
		Exception
		bulge

ove=/ŭv/	ove=/üv/	ove=/ōv/
dove (n.)	move	cove
glove	prove	clove
love		dove (v.)
shove		drove
Exception	**(v̄)ve**	grove
*of	brave	stove
	cave	strove
	crave	wove
	save	
(v̆)ve	slave	
give	wave	
live (v.)	chive	
have	dive	
	drive	
	five	
	hive	
	live (adj.)	
	lives (life)	
	strive	
	thrive	
	wives (wife)	
	Exception	
	knives (knife)	

Chart 10

UNIT 3

FOCUS ON: VOWELS

Unit Three covers all the vowel sounds and their spellings (with the exception of the short vowels which have already been studied).

Long /other Vowels (Charts 11-25)	ā	ē	ī	å ↔ (contrast)	ō	ū/ü	ou/oi
Silent 'e' (vow con e) ③	cape	It takes two vowels to make a long 'e' for Silent 'e' rarely helps an 'e'.	hike style		cope	/ū/ cute /ü/ lute	
☆ -l ☆ -n (Chart 64-65) ⑦	ai — l nail ai — n pain	ie–ld field	i — ld child i — nd kind	a — ll tall a — ld bald a — lt malt awn lawn	o — ll toll o — ld bold o — lt molt own grown		ow — l owl ow — n town
Double vowels ⑥	ai — l mail ai — n rain ai — t bait ai — d paid	ee feel ea heat ie — ld yield ie — f brief ie — ve believe ie — ge siege (c)ei receive		au fraud Chart 27	oa boat	oo moon	ou ouch oi oil
r (Chart 29, 67, 68) ⑧	air hair are care ear bear	ear fear eer steer	ire fire	ar car cart	or- corn -ore more oor poor oar soar (w)ar warm	ure cure	our flour ower flower
Multi-Syllable (Unit 4) ④	taping	eagle	diving flying	collar ('all' becomes 'oll')	pony	super	outer boiling
Cliffs(z) Con ⑤	maze	cheese	slice	sauce	nose	huge/snooze	house/choice
'Cliffs(z)' ⑨ Word end — y/w	-ay say	-y baby	-y shy	-aw law	-ow follow arrow	-ew few	-oy toy
'Cliffs(z)' ⑨ Word end — other		-ee/ea see/sea	-ie (rare) pie		-o go	-ue (rare) blue	-ow cow
Other spellings ⑨ — -gh	eigh eight		igh high	augh taught ough ought	ough dough	ough through	ough bough
Other spellings ⑨	eign/ é / ey reign/ café / they	-ie brownie	ign sign	(w)a want (qu)a squat	-oe hoe eau beau	ui suit	©1989 S.M.
/ŭr/= ⑧ (Chart 28, 44, 66)		er fern	ir girl	(w)or worm		ur curl	
Other ⑨		ea head Chart 13		↕ contrast		a banana Ch. 26 o love	u put

What makes a long 'a'?

What makes a long 'a'?	Example	
① Use 'a', silent 'e',	late	ā_e
② But use 'ai' with 'l' and 'n' That is unless it is a homonym.	tail/pain tale/pane	āi > l n t d ≠ homonym
③ There are a few 'ai's with 't' and 'd',	bait/paid	
④ At ends use 'ay', 'eigh', or accented 'é'.	say/weigh/café	āy eigh é

lāte

① There are several ways to make a long 'a' sound. In the middle of a one-syllable word or the last syllable of a multi-syllable word, the most common way is an 'a' with a silent 'e'.

tāil pāin tāle pāne

② Another spelling in the middle of a word is 'ai'. The majority of 'ai' words are with 'l' and 'n'. Many times, 'l' and 'n' affect the vowel differently than any other consonant. Putting a star above them will help reinforce the concept that 'l' and 'n' can change the rules. There are many 'a' with silent 'e' words that have 'l' and 'n' too. Most of them, however, are homonyms. Homonyms are two words that are pronounced the same but have different spellings and definitions. There are two poems to help learn these words. Homonyms with 'l': ☛ See page 199. Homonyms with 'n': ☛ See page 200.

bāit pāid

③ There are a few 'ai' words with 't' and 'd'. These can be learned with poems also. Words with 'aid': ☛ See page 201.

sāy weigh căfé

④ If a vowel sound is at the end of a word, its most common spelling is with a 'y' or 'w'. The long 'a' sound is spelled with an 'ay'. There are a few more ways to spell a long 'a' sound; 'eigh', "eight", and 'ei', "rein" are two. There are also a few words with an accented 'é', "café" and 'et', "beret" (see Chart 12). The entire list of 'eigh', 'ey' = /ā/ are on this chart. ☛ See page 198 for helps on 'é' and 'eigh' words.

Memorize:

✏ 'Everyday Words'

main	age	gave	may
made	make	save	play
ate	take	eight	say
date	came	day	stay
late	name	gray	way

***'Everyday Bloopers'**

*great	*said
*break	*says
*straight	*where
*they	*there
*their	*they're

cliffs(z)	face	place	race	space
page	change	strange	gave	save

/ā/ with 'Cliffs(z)' **(Silent 'e' is for the consonant and may or may not affect the vowel)**

'ce'=/s/		'se'=/s/	'se'=/z/	'ze'=/z/		'ge'=/j/	'nge'=/nj/	've'=/v/	
ace	race	base	braise	blaze	graze	cage	change	brave	rave
brace	space	case	praise	braze	haze	gage	mange	cave	save
face	trace	chase	raise	craze	laze	page	range	crave	slave
grace		vase	phase	daze	maze	rage	strange	gave	stave
lace			phrase	gaze		sage		grave	wave
pace				glaze		stage		nave	(waive)
place						wage		pave	

Complete List of Long 'a' One-Syllable Words

② ☑

	āi	ā_e	
☆ l	ail	ale	
	bail	bale	
	fail	dale	
	frail	gale (Gail)	
	hail	hale	
	jail	male	
	mail	pale	
	nail	sale	
	pail	scale	
	quail	shale	
	rail	stale	
	sail	tale	
	snail	vale–(veil)	
	tail	whale	
	trail		
	wail		
☆ n	brain		
	chain	cane	
	drain	crane	
	fain–(feign)	lane	
	gain	mane	
	grain	pane	
	lain	plane	
	main	sane	
	pain	vane–(vein)	
	plain	wane	
	rain-(reign)		
	slain		
	sprain		
	stain		
	strain		
	train		
	twain		
	vain		
	faint–(feint)		
	paint		
	quaint		
	saint		
	taint		
③ d	aid	bade	made
	braid	blade	shade
	laid	fade	spade
	maid	glade	trade
	paid	grade	wade
	raid	jade	
	staid	lade	
t	bait	ate(eight)	hate
	gait	bate	late
	plait	crate	mate
	strait(straight)	date	plate
	trait	fate	slate
	wait(weight)	gate	state
		grate	rate

①

	ā_e	
b	babe	
c	↧	
f	chafe	(waif)
	safe	
g	↧	
k	bake	
	cake	
	fake	
	flake	
	lake	
	make	
	quake	
	rake	
	sake	
	shake	
	snake	
	stake	
	take	
	wake	
m	blame	(aim)
	came	(claim)
	dame	
	fame	
	flame	
	frame	
	game	
	lame	
	name	
	same	
	shame	
	tame	
p	ape	
	cape	
	drape	
	gape	
	grape	
	nape	
	scrape	
	shape	
	tape	
← r	bare—(bear)	
	blare	(air)
	care	(chair)
	dare	
	fare—(fair)	
	flare	
	glare	
	hare—(hair)	
	mare	(lair)
	pare—(pair, pear)	
	rare	
	snare	
	spare	
	stare—(stair)	
	ware—(wear)	

	ā_e	
s	↧	
st	baste	
	chaste	
	haste	
	paste	
	taste	
	waste—(waist)	
the (th)	bathe	(faith)
	lathe	
	scathe	
v	↧	
z	↧	

Exception

*their	skate
*there	*they're
heir	suede

*break
steak
great
*where

bear
tear
pear
swear
wear

straight
braille

'ey'=/ā/ (Entire List)

convey	prey
grey	survey
hey	*they
obey	whey

④ **ay=/ā/** ↧

bay
bray
clay
day
fay
fray
flay
gray—(grey)
hay—(hey)
jay
lay
may
nay—(neigh)
pay
play
pray—(prey)
ray
say
slay—(sleigh)
spay
splay
spray
stay
stray
sway
tray
way—(weigh)
Exception: quay

ei=/ā/ (Entire List)

beige
neigh—(nay)
sleigh—(slay)
weigh—(way)
eight—(ate)
freight
weight—(wait)
veil—(vale)
deign
feign—(fain)
reign—(rain)
rein—(rain)
skein
vein—(vain, vane)
feint—(faint)
aweigh—(away)
neighbor
Exception: foreign

☑ Computer checked. *'Everyday Bloopers': Must be memorized. ↧ 'Cliffs(z)' See Unit 4. ← 'R' See Unit 3.

Chart 11

Unit 3 Vowels

Chart 12

Multi-Syllable Words with Long 'a'. The extended list of words with a long 'a' sound in the final syllable reveals that most 'ai' words are with 'l' and 'n'. There are a few with 'd' (most have prefixes added). The 'ai' words with 'm' all have the root '-claim'.

At ends of words there are a lot of '-ay' words. In addition, the French have given us three interesting spellings for the final long 'a' sound—'-et', '-é' and '-ée'. The entire list of these are included. ☛ See page 198 for a poem with the '-é' words.

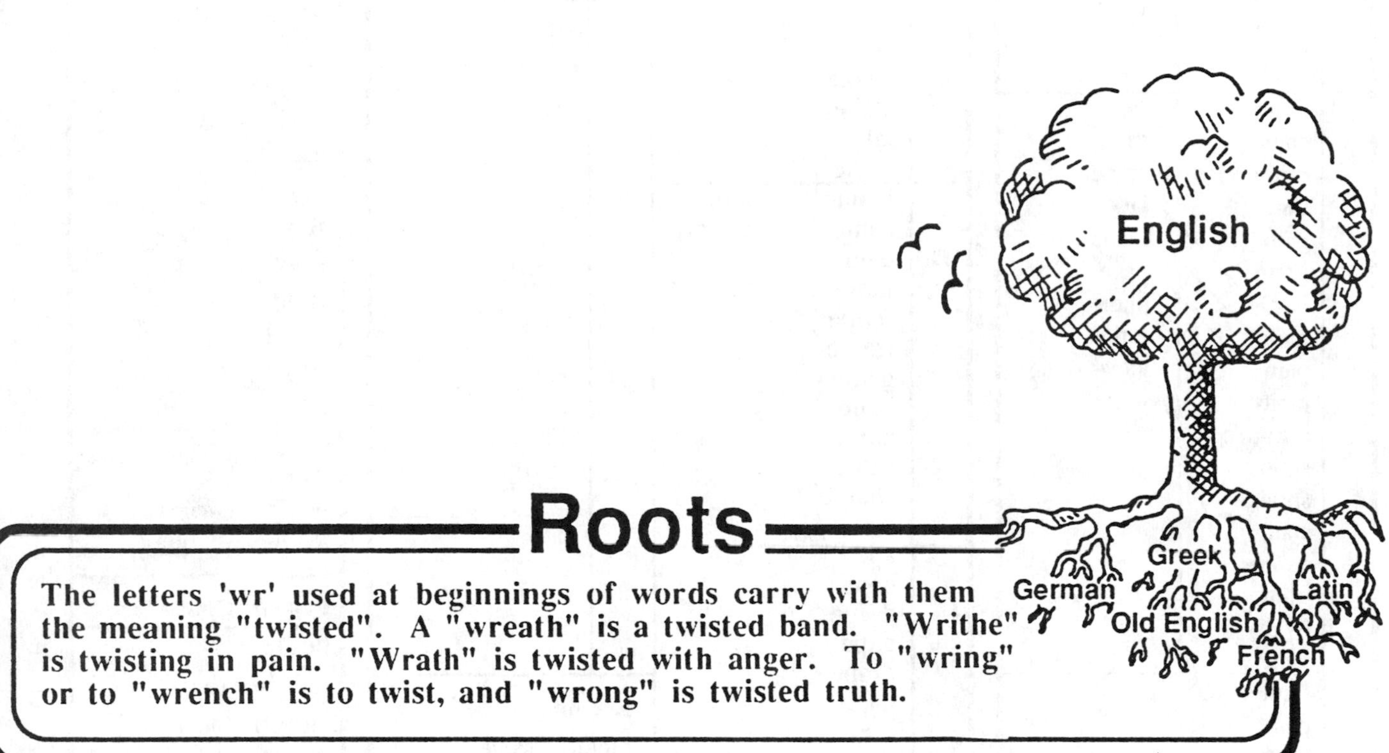
English
Greek
German
Latin
Old English
French

Roots

The letters 'wr' used at beginnings of words carry with them the meaning "twisted". A "wreath" is a twisted band. "Writhe" is twisting in pain. "Wrath" is twisted with anger. To "wring" or to "wrench" is to twist, and "wrong" is twisted truth.

Select List of Long 'a' of Multi-Syllable Words (Final Syllable)

☑	āi		ā_e	
☆ l	assail avail curtail detail	monorail prevail retail travail	exhale female inhale	nightingale resale
☆ n	abstain ascertain attain complain constrain contain detain disdain domain entertain explain acquaint complaint	ingrain maintain obtain ordain pertain refrain regain remain restrain retain sustain constraint restraint	biplane butane cellophane deplane humane hurricane hydroplane inane inhumane membrane methane mundane	octane profane propane urbane
d	afraid inlaid medicaid mislaid prepaid mermaid upbraid		arcade barricade blockade brigade brocade centigrade cascade charade crusade decade degrade dissuade everglade escapade	evade forbade grenade invade lemonade marmalade parade persuade pervade promenade renegade serenade stockade tirade
t	await		abate abbreviate abdicate accelerate calculate captivate communicate contemplate coordinate create cultivate dedicate discriminate	donate duplicate educate estate formulate frustrate hibernate incubate intimidate investigate rebate regulate separate
m	acclaim declaim disclaim	exclaim proclaim reclaim	became inflame	misname surname
p			escape	misshape
st			distaste	foretaste
v			autoclave behave concave deprave enclave	engrave enslave forgave microwave misbehave

/ā/

Compound Words

ai= /ā/

airmail
blackmail
cattail
cottontail
dovetail
fingernail
guardrail
ponytail
thumbnail
bridesmaid
chambermaid
dairymaid
overpaid
overlaid
postpaid
underlaid
waylaid
underpaid
shirtwaist

a_e

airplane
windowpane
tattletale
telltale
wholesale
nickname
overcame
landscape
moonscape
shipshape
videotape
aftertaste
toothpaste
sunbathe
airwave
shortwave

eigh=/ā/

outweigh
counterweight
deadweight
heavyweight
lightweight
paperweight
underweight

ay=/ā/

Sunday
Monday
Tuesday
Wednesday
Thursday
Friday
Saturday

ay= /ā/

array
astray
assay
away
betray
decay
delay
disarray
dismay
display
essay
hurray
okay
moray
parlay
relay
repay
today

Compound Words

anyway
birthday
castaway
cutaway
doorway
everyday
freeway
gateway
hallway
headway
hearsay
highway
holiday
layaway
mainstay
mayday
midday
midway
noonday
overlay
overspray
overstay
partway
pathway
payday
raceway
railway
runaway
someday
someway
speedway
spillway
stingray
stowaway
subway
throwaway
underway
waterway
weekday
workday
yesterday

Other

et=/ā/

(Entire List)

beret
cabaret
bouquet
croquet

é/ée=/ā/

(Entire List)

appliqué
blasé
café
communiqué
consommé
entrée
exposé
fiancé (man)
fiancée (woman)
matinée
melée
negligée
passé
protegé (boy)
protegée (girl)
purée
repartée
resumé
risqué
soufflé
touché

Exception

chow mein
champagne
cocaine
vertebrae

☑ Computer checked.

What makes a long 'e'?

What makes a long 'e'?	Example	
① We use 'ea' or 'y' or double 'e',	bead/baby/deep	ēa 'y ēe
② For silent 'e' rarely helps an 'e'.		e_e
③ And 'i' before 'e' before 'ld', 'f' or 've',	field/brief/grieve	iē> ld f ve
④ Which changes to 'ei' if it's after 'c'	ceiling	(c)ēi

bēad bā´by dēep

① **It takes two vowels to make a long 'e'.** The most common spellings are 'ee' and 'ea'. There is no distinctive pattern to determine which will be used. They must be memorized. The 'ee' pages will help give visual clues for the words that contain 'ee' by giving a mental picture of the word. At the end of words, the most common spelling of a vowel sound is with a 'y' or 'w'. However, in one-syllable words for the long 'e' sound, 'ee' or 'ea' is used. This is because in accented syllables, 'y' says /ī/, "shy". In longer words, in unaccented final syllables, a 'y' is used for the long 'e' sound. For 'ee' words: ☛ See page 202, 203, 204.

② **Silent 'e' rarely helps an 'e' in one-syllable words.** The only single syllable words with 'e'-consonant-silent 'e' that are commonly used are "these" and "here". "There", "where" and "were" have an 'e-consonant-silent e' pattern but do not have a long 'e' sound.

③ Most of the words using 'ie' are followed by 'ld', 'f', or 've'. This is the entire list of 'ie'=/ē/ root words.

cēil ing

④ Words in which the long 'e' sound directly follows a 'c' are usually spelled with 'ei'. This is the entire list of 'ei'=/ē/ independent words.

⑤ The short 'e' sound can be spelled with 'ea'. This is the entire list of 'ea' independent words saying /ĕ/, "head". Several of these words are variations of words that have a long 'e' sound for the 'ea'. ("deal"/"dealt", "heal"/"health") The words in parenthesis show the contrasting long 'e' sound.

Memorize

✏ 'Everyday Words'					*'Everyday Bloopers'		
see	week	between	/ĕ/		*be	*these	/ĕ/
three	real	keep	**head**	**ahead**	*he	*here	*been
tree	seem	eat	**lead**	**instead**	*me	*either	*said
read	green	meet	**read**	**heavy**	*she	*neither	*says
need	seen		**ready**		*we	*people	*friend
cliffs(z) each		reach	teach	ease	please	*these	

/ē/ with 'Cliffs(z)' (Silent 'e' is for the consonant and may or may not affect the vowel)

'ce'=/s/	'se'=/s/	'se'=/z/	'ze'=/z/	'ge'=/j/	've'=/v/	'ch'=/ch/
peace fleece **Exception** niece piece	cease crease grease (n.) lease geese	cheese please ease tease **Exception** *these	breeze squeeze freeze wheeze sneeze **Exception** seize	liege siege	thieve grieve sleeve peeve cleave leave	beach reach bleach teach breach breech each leech peach speech preach

ea=/ĕ/
(Entire List)

Complete List of Long 'e' One-Syllable Words

⑤ ĕa

- ahead
- bread (breed)
- dead (deed)
- dread
- head (heed)
- instead
- lead (lead)
- read (read)
- spread
- stead (steed)
- tread
- thread
- treadle
- ready
- steady
- meadow

- deaf

- breakfast

- jealous
- zealous (zeal)
- realm (real)
- dealt (deal)
- health (heal)
- stealth (steal)
- wealth

- cleanser (clean)
- meant (mean)

- weapon
- leapt (leap)

- peasant
- pleasant (please)
- pheasant
- breast
- abreast
- measure
- pleasure (please)
- treasure

- sweat
- threat
- sweater

- breath (breathe)
- death
- feather
- heather
- leather
- weather

- heaven
- leaven
- endeavor
- heavy (heave)

Exception
- *been
- *friend
- heifer
- conscience
- leopard
- jeopardy
- *said *says

① (Computer checked) ēa / ēe

	ēa	ēe
	flea, pea, plea, sea, tea	bee, fee, flee, free, glee, knee, lee, see, spree, tee, three, tree, wee
c	↧	
ch	↧	
d	bead, knead, lead (lĕad), mead, plead, read (rĕad)	bleed, breed (brĕad), creed, deed (dĕad), feed, freed, greed, heed (hĕad), meed, need, reed, seed, speed, steed (stĕad), tweed, weed
¹f	↧	
k	beak, bleak, creak, freak, leak, peak, sneak, speak, squeak, streak, teak, tweak, weak	cheek, creek, leek, meek, peek, reek, seek, sleek, week
l	deal, heal, meal, peal, real, seal, squeal, steal, teal, veal, weal, zeal	eel, feel (felt), heel, keel, kneel, peel, reel, steel, wheel
m	beam, cream, dream, gleam, ream, scream, seam, steam, stream, team	deem, seem, teem
n	bean (bĕen), clean, dean, glean, jeans, lean, mean, wean	green, keen, preen, queen, screen, seen, sheen, spleen, teen
p	cheap, heap, leap, reap	beep, cheep, creep (crept), deep (depth), jeep, keep (kept), peep, seep, sheep, sleep (slept), steep, sweep (swept), weep (wept)
← r	clear, dear, drear, ear, fear, gear, hear, near, rear, sear, shear, smear, spear, tear(n.), year, beard	beer, cheer, deer, jeer, peer, sheer, sneer, steer, veer
s	↧	
st	beast, east, feast, least, yeast	
sh	leash	
t	beat, bleat, cheat, cleat, eat, feat, heat, meat, neat, peat, seat, treat, wheat	beet, feet, fleet, greet, meet (met), sheet, skeet, sleet, street, sweet, tweet
th	heath, neath, sheath, wreath	seethe, teethe, teeth
¹v	↧	
z	↧	

② ē_e

It takes two vowels to make a long 'e'

For Silent 'e' rarely helps an 'e'.

Exception

e_e (1-syl.)
- gene (jeans)
- scene (seen)
- *these
- *here (hear)
- mere
- sphere
- scheme
- theme
- eve

e
- *be
- *me
- *he
- *she
- *we
- key
- quay

③ ie (Entire List)

ld	field, shield, wield, yield
¹f ↧	brief, chief, grief, thief, belief, relief
¹v ↧	achieve, believe, grieve, relieve, reprieve, retrieve, thieve
↧	niece, piece, fierce, pierce, liege, siege, shriek, frieze
other	fiend, priest, pier, tier, cashier, frontier

④ (c)ei

(Entire List)
- ceiling
- conceit
- conceive
- deceit
- deceive
- perceive
- receipt
- receive

Exceptions
- caffeine
- codeine
- *either
- leisure
- *neither
- protein
- sheik
- seize
- weird

- handkerchief
- hygiene
- mischief
- sieve
- *people

Computer checked. *'Everyday Bloopers': Must be memorized. ↧ 'Cliffs(z)' See Unit 4. ← 'R' See Unit 3.

[1] Before 'f' and 've', the most likely spelling is 'ie'.

Chart 13

Long 'e' in Final Syllable[1]

☑	ēa̸	ēe̸
ch		beseech
d		agreed decreed indeed proceed succeed
l	appeal conceal congeal ideal repeal reveal surreal	genteel
m	abeam agleam inseam	esteem redeem
n	demean **Exception** chlorine gasoline magazine marine sardine submarine	between canteen careen eighteen fifteen fourteen nineteen sixteen thirteen seventeen sateen tureen velveteen
p		asleep
r	endear appear disappear reappear	auctioneer balladeer career charioteer domineer electioneer pioneer reindeer volunteer racketeer veneer
s	decrease displease increase release	
t	defeat entreat maltreat repeat retreat	discreet parakeet semisweet
th	bequeath beneath underneath	
v	bereave	
z		antifreeze

Compound

browbeat
cornmeal
daydream
downstream
drumbeat
flyleaf
forebear
headgear
jellybean
mainstream
oatmeal
offbeat
overeat
overheat
piecemeal
proofread
soybean
southeast
birdseed
bumblebee
cogwheel
crossbreed
evergreen
eyeteeth
foreseen
nosebleed
oversee
oversleep
pinwheel
spreadsheet
tenderfeet
tumbleweed
wintergreen
workweek

'e/consonant/e' Words

☑	ē_e̸ (Entire List)		
d	accede cede centipede concede impede intercede millipede precede recede secede stampede supersede	t	*athlete *compete *complete concrete delete deplete discrete excrete incomplete obsolete replete secrete spirochete
k	eke	r	adhere ampere austere cashmere cohere here interfere mere persevere revere severe sincere sphere *atmosphere bathysphere biosphere hemisphere ionosphere lithosphere troposphere stratosphere **Exception** (don't say /ē/) *there *were *where
m	blaspheme *extreme morpheme phoneme scheme *supreme *theme		
n	contravene convene gangrene gene intervene obscene *scene serene acetylene benzene ethylene kerosene methylene toluene		
s = /z/	Burmese Cantonese Chinese Japanese Lebanese Maltese Melanese Pekinese Portuguese Siamese Sudanese Taiwanese Viennese Vietnamese manganese *these trapeze		
/s/	obese		

☑ Computer checked. *'Everyday Bloopers': Must be memorized.

[1]Complete list for multi-syllable words, not final sound

Chart 14

Multi-Syllable Words with Long 'e' in Final Syllable and Complete List of Common 'e-con-e' Words. The spelling patterns (as well as pronunciation patterns) vary between single and multi-syllable words. In one-syllable words, it usually takes two vowels to make a long 'e' ("bead"). In multi-syllable words however, there are many words that have a silent 'e' helping an 'e' in the final syllable. In the medial position, 'i' says /ē / when it precedes the suffix '-an' ("Indian", see Chart 50) or '-que' ("unique", see Charts 38, 69). However, the rule that it takes two vowels to make a long 'e' still holds true for all other positions. (See Charts 32, 36, 43, 44.)

Chart 15

Multi-Syllable Words ending with /ē /. The **majority** of words ending with an /ē / sound are written with a 'y'. These are included in the section of suffixes, **Chart 43**. Chart 15 deals with the words that do not fall in that pattern. Notice that the words with an 'i' saying /ē / at ends of words have to do with Italian food ("spaghetti"). The '-ie' at the end of words adds the meaning of 'cute' or 'small'. Many children's names have '-ie' (Tammie, Jamie, and so forth.) A large portion of the words with 'ee' at the end describe people who do what the base word means. ("employ" > "employee")The suffix 'ly' is common and changes a base word into an adjective or adverb. ("dear" >"dearly") The 'ey' saying /ē / at ends of words is rare, and these words must be memorized. Other: A final 'e' is normally silent but says /ē / in these exceptions.

Multi-Syllable Words Ending with /ē/

	-i =/ē/ (Entire List)		-ie = /ē/ (Entire List)	-ee = /ē/ (Complete)	ee (people)
Food	broccoli		auntie	agree	absentee
	chili		birdie	chickadee	addressee
	kiwi		brownie	chimpanzee	amputee
	macaroni		calorie	coffee	appointee
	manicotti		collie	committee	assignee
	pastrami		camaraderie	decree	conferee
	ravioli		cookie	degree	devotee
	salami		coolie	disagree	divorcee
	scampi		doggie	dungaree	emcee
	spaghetti		eerie	filigree	escapee
	spumoni		freebie	foresee	employee
	vermicelli		girlie	frisbee	evacuee
	zucchini		hippie	goatee	lessee
Other	confetti	safari	laddie	guarantee	mortgagee
	bikini	sari	lassie	jamboree	nominee
	hibachi	ski	menagerie	jubilee	parolee
	khaki	taxi	movie	levee	pharisee
	potpourri	timpani	pixie	manatee	pledgee
	Israeli		pinkie	pedigree	referee
	Iraqi		prairie	tepee	refugee
	Pakistani		reverie	toffee	sadducee
	Saudi		rookie	warrantee	trainee
			wienie	whoopee	trustee
				yippee	Yankee

-ey = /ē/ (Entire List)			-ly (Samples)			Other
alley	chimney	donkey	blankly	dearly	expertly	**Exception**
barley	honey	hockey	frankly	merely	overtly	abalone
galley	kidney	jockey	trembly	nearly	ghastly	aborigine
medley	money	lackey	assembly	yearly	vastly	acme
motley	journey	monkey	cheaply	severely	mostly	acne
paisley	cagey	turkey	deeply	curly	drizzly	anemone
parley	gooey	whiskey	soundly	early	grizzly	apostrophe
parsley	mosey		barely	surly	entry	bourgeoisie
pulley	mousey		fairly	parsley	gentry	debris
trolley	odyssey		rarely	sparsely	sentry	facsimile
valley	osprey		squarely	partly	corny	hyperbole
volley	phooey		clearly	smartly	thorny	recipe
attorney	surrey			curtly		sesame
baloney						

What makes a long 'i'?

What makes a long 'i'?	Example	
① To make a long 'i', use 'i' with silent 'e',	mine	ī_ė ý īgh
② But at ends of words a 'y' will usually be.	sky	
③ And then 'i' is long with 'igh' or 'ind',	high/find	īnd īgn īld
And again with 'ign', or 'ild'.	sign/child	

mīnė

① The majority of single-syllable words with a long 'i' sound in the middle of the word are spelled with an 'i-consonant-silent e'.

② At the end of words, a 'y' or 'w' usually help in the spelling of a vowel sound. For the /ī/ sound at the end of a word, use 'y'. There are only seven common independent words ending with the 'ie' spelling for the long 'i' sound. However, when a word ending in a 'y' has a suffix added like '-ed', '-er', '-est', or '-es', the 'y' changes to an 'i'. Whether the 'i' and 'e' in these words are actually a "vowel combination" is questionable. Words ending with 'y' retain the 'y' when '-ing' or '-ly' are added.

   hīgh

③ There are several consonant combinations that cause the 'i' to be long—'ld, 'nd', 'gn', and 'gh'. The 'gh' words can be learned with a poem. ☛ See page 205.

✏ 'Everyday Words'

child	ride	time	live
find	side	fine	size
mind	wide	mine	by
night	life	nine	my
right	like	quite	why
light	mile	white	try
hide	while	five	sky

*'Everyday Bloopers'

*hi	*buy	*write
*I	*eye	
*die		
*lie		

cliffs(z)				
nice	twice	rise	wise	
prize	size	drive	five	live

/ī/ with 'Cliffs(z)' **(Silent 'e' is for the consonant and may or may not affect the vowel)**

'ce'=/s/	'se'=/s/	'se'=/z/	'ze'=/z/	'ge'=/j/	've'=/v/	'ch'=/ch/
dice rice ice slice lice spice mice splice nice twice price vice		guise rise wise	prize size		chive strive dive thrive drive knives five wives hive live	

Complete List of Long 'i' in One-Syllable Words

③ ld/nd/gn/gh

☆ ld	child, mild, wild
☆ nd	bind, blind, find, grind, hind, kind, mind, rind, wind (v.)
gn	sign
gh	high— (hi), nigh, sigh, thigh
	night—(knight), right—(rite, write), sight—(site), tight, blight, bright, fight, flight, fright, light, might—(mite), plight, slight

Exception
height
knight
heist
stein

① ī_e

b	bribe, scribe, tribe
c	↧
d	bride, chide, glide, guide, hide, pride, ride, side, slide, snide, stride, tide, wide
f ↧	fife, life (lives), strife (strives), wife (wives)
k	bike, hike, like, mike, pike, spike, strike
l	bile, file, [1]guile, mile, pile, rile, smile, tile, vile, while, wile
m	chime, crime, dime, grime, lime, mime, prime, slime, time
n	brine, dine, fine, line, mine, nine, pine, shine, shrine, spine, swine, thine, twine, vine, whine, wine
p	gripe, pipe, ripe, snipe, stripe, swipe, wipe
← r	fire, ire, mire, sire, tire, wire
s	↧
t	bite, cite (sight), kite, mite (might), quite, rite (right, write), site (sight), smite, spite, trite, white, tithe
v	↧
z	↧

Exception
knife
climb
choir
pint
aisle
isle
pi
*write

② ↧ y=/ī/

y=/ī/	Sample Changes
by	
my	mine
shy	shier/shyly
thy	thine
why	
sky	skies
fly	flies/flying
ply	plies/plying
sly	slier/slyly
spy	spies/spying
cry	cried/crying
dry	driest/drying
fry	fries/frying
pry	pried/prying
try	tries/trying
wry	wryly
spry	spriest/spryly
sty	sties

Exception
*hi *I
*buy guy

aye—(eye, I)
bye—(by, buy)
dye—(die)
*eye—(aye, I)
lye (lie)
rye

dyke
tyke
rhyme
thyme—(time)
type
style

(Entire list of 'ie'=/ī/ root words)

*die—(dye)
fie
hie
*lie—(lye)
pie—(pi)
tie
vie
belie
magpie

Unit 3
Vowels

☑ Computer checked.
*'Everyday Bloopers': Must be memorized.
↧ 'Cliffs(z)' See Unit 4.
← 'R' See Unit 3.

Chart 16

Chart 17

Multi-Syllable Words with Long 'i'. The same rules for long 'i' apply to multi-syllable words as to one-syllable words. There are no new independent words for '-ind' or '-igh'.

There are several Latin-based words ending with '-us' which become plural by changing the '-us' to '-i'. However, the '-us' form for the words are more familiar than the '-i' form. ("nucleus" >"nuclei", "radius" > "radii")

The 'y' at ends of words can say /ī/ or /ē/. When the last syllable is accented, the 'y' says /ī/.

English
Greek
German
Latin
Old English
French

Roots

'Sal' means "salt". From this came "salami" (highly salted meat), "Salzburg" (an Austrian town where the "Sound of Music" was filmed—named after the nearby salt mines), and "salary" (the Roman soldiers were given a 'salary', that is 'money to buy salt rations').

Select List of Multi-Syllable Words with Long 'i' (Final Syllable)

-ind

(no more independent words)

behind
remind
rewind
unkind

-ign (Entire List)

align
assign
benign
consign
design
malign
sign
resign

-igh

(no more independent words)

delight

Compound words

housewife
jackknife
afterlife
downright
forthright
goodnight
headlight
midnight
moonlight
starlight
sunlight
twilight
upright
copyright
watertight
lifetime
sometime
overtime
summertime
spellbind
humankind
mankind
womankind
mastermind
airline
bagpipe
sideswipe
overripe
beehive

-i_e = /ī/

b: ascribe, describe, inscribe, prescribe, transcribe

d: abide, astride, beside, collide, confide, decide, divide, inside, misguide, outside, provide, reside, coincide, homicide, insecticide, suicide

k: alike, dislike, see also '-que'

l: awhile, beguile, compile, defile, exile, senile, crocodile, juvenile

m: sublime, pantomime

n: canine, combine, confine, decline, define, divine, feline, incline, recline, refine, disincline, intertwine, iodine, undermine, valentine

r: ←

s: ↧

t: contrite, despite, excite, ignite, incite, invite, polite, recite, unite, appetite, parasite, satellite, stalactite, stalagmite, meteorite

v: alive, arrive, contrive, deprive, derive, revive, survive

-y´= /ī/

ally
amplify
apply
awry
beautify
butterfly
certify
classify
comply
crucify
decry
defy
deny
fortify
glorify
horrify
imply
rely
justify
lullaby
occupy
magnify
multiply
mystify
reply
standby
supply

-i=/ī/ [plural (singular)] Entire List

abaci (abacus)
alumni (alumnus)
bacilli (bacillus)
cacti (cactus)
foci (focus)
fungi (fungus)
hippopotami (hippopotamus)
loci (locus)
nuclei (nucleus)
octopi (octopus)
operandi (operandus)
radii (radius)
rhombi (rhombus)
stimuli (stimulus)
stratocumuli (stratocumulus)
streptococci (streptococcus)
syllabi (syllabus)
termini (terminus)

alibi
alkali
bonsai
hi
pi
quasi
rabbi

☑ Computer checked. ↧ 'Cliffs(z)' See Unit 4. ← 'R' See Unit 3.

What makes a long 'o'?

What makes a long 'o'?	Example	
① Use 'o', silent 'e', or 'oa' to make long 'o',	bone/boat	ō_ e̸ ōa̸ ō<l r
② And 'o' is long when followed by 'l' or 'r'.	roll/cord	
③ A word may end in 'ow' or 'o',	mow/go	ōw o̸ l r > ōw
But following 'l' or 'r', it's 'ow'.	follow/arrow	

bōne coāt

① The two most common ways to make a long 'o' is with 'o-consonant-silent e' or with the vowel combination 'oa'. Since there is no clear pattern to know where each is used, the 'oa' words must be memorized. (☛ See page 206) [There is a slight pattern—'oa' is used when followed by two consonants and an 'x' which has the sound of two consonants (/ks/, "coax")].

tōll cōal mōre

② 'O' is long when followed by 'l' or 'r'. Most words with an /ōl/, "toll", sound are 'oll'. However, there are also a few 'ole' and 'oal' words. These must be memorized. /ōr/ is spelled 'or' in the middle of a word and 'ore' at the end of a word. The 'or' at the end of a word generally says /ŭr/, "tractor", making the words "or", "nor", and "for" 'Everyday Bloopers'.

slōw

③ At ends of one-syllable words, 'ow' is most commonly used. There are only six common root words with 'oe' at the end. In multi-syllable words, we use 'ow' following an 'l', "follow", or 'r', "arrow". Elsewhere we use an 'o', "potato". See Chart 20. One more thing to note is that verbs ending in 'ow' need only an 'n' added to make them past tense.

✏ 'Everyday Words'

roll	short	home	go
cold	more	hope	no
hold	show	close	so
old	slow	note	
sold	throw	quote	
told	rode	spoke	road
cliffs(z)close		chose	nose	those

***'Everyday Bloopers'**

*for	*most	*know
*four	*don't	*known
*fourth	*won't	*whole
*or	*own	*both
*toe		

/ō/ with 'Cliffs(z)' (Silent 'e' is for the consonant and may or may not affect the vowel)

'ce'=/s/	'se'=/s/	'se'=/z/		'ze'=/z/	'ge'=/j/	've'=/v/		'ch'=/ch/
	close (adj.)	chose	pose	doze		cove	grove	broach
	dose	close (v.)	prose	froze		clove	stove	coach
		hose	rose			dove	strove	poach
		nose	those			drove	wove	roach

Complete List of Long 'o' One-Syllable Words[1]

	ōl(Consonant)	ō_e	ōa
① ☆ l	droll poll roll scroll toll troll stroll bold cold fold gold hold mold old scold sold told bolt colt jolt molt	dole hole(whole) mole pole role sole(soul) stole	coal foal goal

	① ō_e	ōa	③ ōw(ōwn)↧	ō ↧
☆ n	bone cone lone prone scone shone stone throne tone zone	groan loan moan roan	blow (blown) bow crow flow (flown) glow grow (grown) low mow (mown) row show (shown) slow snow sow (sown) stow throw(thrown) tow (toe)	fro no go so lo **Exception** (Entire List of 'oe)' doe toe foe woe hoe oboe folk yolk *don't *won't soul bowl knoll *whole host post *most ghost owe *own *know *known phone sew (sewn) bull pull full *both comb gross whoa

	② ōr(Consonant)	ōre
← r	porch scorch torch cork fork stork form norm storm born (borne) corn horn morn (mourn) scorn shorn sworn thorn torn fort port short snort sport forth (fourth) north	bore (boar) chore core fore (for, four) lore more (moor) pore (poor,pour) score shore snore sore store swore tore **Exception** *for nor *or *four *fourth mourn pour door floor poor boar oar roar soar

①	ō_e	ōa
b	globe lobe probe robe	
c	↧	
ch	↧	
d	bode code mode ode rode strode	load road toad
f		loaf oaf
k	broke choke coke joke poke smoke spoke stroke woke yoke	cloak croak oak soak
m	chrome dome home	foam loam roam
p	cope dope grope hope lope mope nope pope rope scope slope	soap
s	↧	
st		boast coast roast toast
t	dote mote note quote smote tote vote	boat oat bloat throat coat float goat gloat moat
th	clothe	oath loathe
v	↧	
x		coax hoax
z	↧	

☑ Computer checked.

*'Everyday Bloopers': Must be memorized. [1]'eau' see Chart 20; 'ough' see Chart 58; '(w)/ōr/' see Chart 26.

Chart 18

Select List of Multi-Syllable Words with Long 'o'*

☑	/ō/__	o_e=/ō/
☆ l	control idol patrol petrol pistol enroll unroll behold marigold unfold untold revolt	cajole condole console oriole parole rigmarole
☆ n	disown unknown	alone condone ozone chaperone saxophone telephone
	Compound Words	***Compound Words***
	bankroll *payroll* *thunderbolt* *billfold* *blindfold* *foothold* *foretold* *freehold* *household* *manifold* *marigold* *outsold* *scaffold* *stronghold* *tenfold* *threshold* *toehold* *withhold* *downtown* *foreknown* *ingrown* *outgrown* *overgrown* *overthrown* *windblown*	*backbone* *armhole* *buttonhole* *foxhole* *keyhole* *knothole* *loophole* *peephole* *pigeonhole* *pinhole* *porthole* *pothole* *wormhole* *flagpole* *maypole* *tadpole* *milestone*

	/ō/__	o_e=/ō/
b		disrobe
ch	approach cockroach reproach	
d	unload *railroad*	abode erode explode forebode episode
k		awoke evoke provoke
m	*honeycomb*	monochrome
p		elope antelope cantaloupe envelope microscope telescope
s	innermost uppermost uttermost	arose compose disclose expose
st	*fencepost* *signpost*	enclose oppose propose suppose predispose
t	afloat	demote denote devote misquote antidote
v		alcove interwove

☑ Computer checked. *Final syllable, but not final sound. For final 'o' sound, see Chart 20.

Complete List of Long 'o' at Ends of Words

'ow'> 'l' or 'r'

-low
afterglow
aglow
bellow
below
billow
bungalow
callow
deathblow
fallow
fellow
follow
hallow
hollow
inflow
mellow
marshmallow
outflow
overflow
pillow
sallow
schoolfellow
shallow
swallow
tallow
wallow
willow
yellow

-row
arrow
borrow
burrow
escrow
furrow
harrow
marrow
morrow
narrow
outgrow
overthrow
scarecrow
sorrow
sparrow
tomorrow
wheelbarrow

Exception for l & r

halo
polo
silo
kilo
cello
hello
jello
pueblo
armadillo
buffalo
hero
zero
burro

Exception for 'ow'

elbow
rainbow
crossbow
shadow
meadow
widow
window
undertow
minnow

oboe
mistletoe
cocoa
depot

-o

ego
ago
pro (professional)
expo (exposition)
hypo (hypodermic)
memo (memorandum)
also
auto (automobile)
echo
hippo (hippopotamus)
info (information)
judo
logo
veto

bravo
bingo
dingo
cargo
banjo
cameo
combo (combination)
disco (discotheque)
gumbo
limbo
metro (metropolitan)
photo (photograph)
pinto
ratio
video (videotape)
ditto
gizmo
gusto
motto
piano
polio (poliomyelitis)
rhino (rhinoceros)
tango
torso
lasso
mumbo
radio
rodeo
tempo

-o

bronco
embryo
gazebo
ghetto
albino
dynamo
poncho
studio
tuxedo
stereo
weirdo
stucco
tomato
flamingo
avocado
potato
tobacco
volcano

peso
taco
mango
mosquito
patio

eau=/ō/ **(Entire List)**

bandeau
bateau
beau
bureau
chapeau
chateau
flambeau
plateau
tableau
trousseau

Chart 19 and 20: Multi-Syllable Words with Long 'o' (final syllable and final sound): In multi-syllable words, 'l' is usually not doubled unless it is in a compound word or a word that is formed by adding an affix. There are no new independent '-ost' words and just a few new '-oa' words. When the /ō/ sound occurs at ends of words following 'l' or 'r', it is spelled with 'ow' ("follow", "tomorrow"). There are a few '-eau', "bureau", words. Elsewhere, use an 'o'.

Computer checked.

What makes a long 'u'?

What makes a long 'u'?	Example	
① Use 'u', silent 'e', when the sound is /ū/ or /ü/,	cute/duke	ū_ e ü_e
② But in accented syllables, 'oo' for /ü/ is often true,	moon	
③ At ends of words, we usually use 'ew',	few	o͞o ew
But we find 'ue' or 'oo' sometimes too.	blue/zoo	

cūte dūke

① In single-syllable words, there are relatively few words with a 'u' in them. The words using a 'u'-silent -'e' are in a poem. ☛ See page 208. In addition there are two sounds for the long 'u'. The /ū/ sound is like the name of the letter 'u', "cute". The /ü/ (or /o͞o/) is more frequently used for the long 'u' sound, "tune", "moon".

mo͞on

② There are more 'oo' words than 'u-silent-e' words in single-syllable words and in accented syllables of longer words, "moon", "balloon". There are several variations of the common spellings for the /ū/, /ü/ sounds that are put into a poem. ☛ See page 198.

few blüe zo͞o

③ At ends of words, the vowel sounds are most often spelled with a 'y' or 'w'. For the /ū/, /ü/ sounds, 'ew' is often used. Other spellings at ends of words include 'ue', "blue", and 'oo', "zoo".

④ When 'oo' is followed by a 'd' or 'k', it says /o͝o/, "good book".

Memorize:

✏ 'Everyday Words'		
/o͝o/	/ü/, /ū/	
good	food	grew
stood	room	few
book	soon	new
look	rule	blue
took	cute	
cliffs(z)	use	

*'Everyday Bloopers'			
/o͝o/	/ü/, /ū/		
*[1]could	*knew	*do	*two
*[1]should	*school	*to	*you
*[1]would	*group	*shoe	
*put	*youth	*truth	
*push	*through		
*foot			
*lose	*whose	*move	

[1]"I would if I could for I know I should"
Spell these three words with 'o'-'u'-'l'-'d'.

/ū/ with 'Cliffs(z)'(Silent 'e' is for the consonant and may or may not affect the vowel)

'ce'=/s/	'se'=/s/	'se'=/z/	'ze'=/z/	'ge'=/j/	've'=/v/	'ch'=/ch/
spruce truce **Exception** juice sluice	use (n.) goose loose moose noose	fuse muse use (v.) **Exception** bruise cruise *lose *whose	ooze snooze	huge stooge	groove **Exception** *move prove	pooch smooch

Complete List of One-Syllable Long 'u' and 'oo' Sounds

☑	④ oo=/ŏŏ/
d	good hood stood wood (would)
k	book brook cook crook hook look nook rook shook took **Exception** *could *should *would *put push bush foot soot

☑	② oo=/ü/		① u_e / ū_e	
b			cube	tube
c	↧			
d	brood food	mood	crude dude **Exception** feud	prude rude lewd
f	goof proof	roof spoof		
g	↧			
k	spook		duke	fluke
l	cool drool fool pool **Exception:** school	spool stool tool wool	mule rule **Exception** cruel	yule fuel
m	bloom boom broom doom gloom	groom loom room zoom	fume plume **Exception** tomb *whom	 womb
n	boon coon croon goon loon	moon noon soon spoon swoon	prune tune **Exception** hewn	
p	coop droop hoop loop poop scoop	sloop snoop stoop swoop troop whoop	dupe **Exception** croup group	 soup troupe
← r			cure lure	pure sure
s	↧			
t	boot coot hoot loot root	shoot toot scoot	brute cute flute **Exception** route youth	jute lute mute truth
	booth tooth smooth soothe		**ui =/ü/ (Entire List)**	
			bruise cruise fruit juice nuisance pursuit	sluice suit suitor
v	↧			
z	↧			

③ **ew=/ü/,/ū/ ↧**

blew (blue)
brew
chew
crew
dew (do, due)
drew
few
flew (flue)
grew
hew (hue)
mew
new (knew)
pew
screw
shrew
slew (slough)
skew
spew
stew
strew
threw (through)
whew
yew (you, ewe)
Exception
ewe (you)
view
*knew

ue=/ü/, /ū/ ↧

blue (blew)
clue
cue
due (dew, do)
flue (flew)
glue
hue (hew)
rue
sue
true

oo=/ü/ ↧

boo
coo
goo
moo
too (to, two)
woo
zoo

Exception
*do
*to
*two
*who
*you
gnu
*shoe
*through

☑ Computer checked. *'Everyday Bloopers': Must be memorized. ↧ 'Cliffs(z)' See Unit 4. ← 'R' See Unit 3.

Chart 21

Unit 3 Vowels

Chart 22

Multi-Syllable Words with 'u' and 'oo'. The multi-syllable words with /ü/ in the final syllable are almost equally divided between 'oo', "balloon", and 'u_e', "costume". The 'u_e' words end in '-ude', '-ute' and '-ume'. At ends of words, the /ü/ sound can be divided between '-ew', '-ue' and '-oo'.

Many of the multi-syllable words with /ŏŏ/ contain the suffix '-hood', meaning "a member of a group" ("childhood").

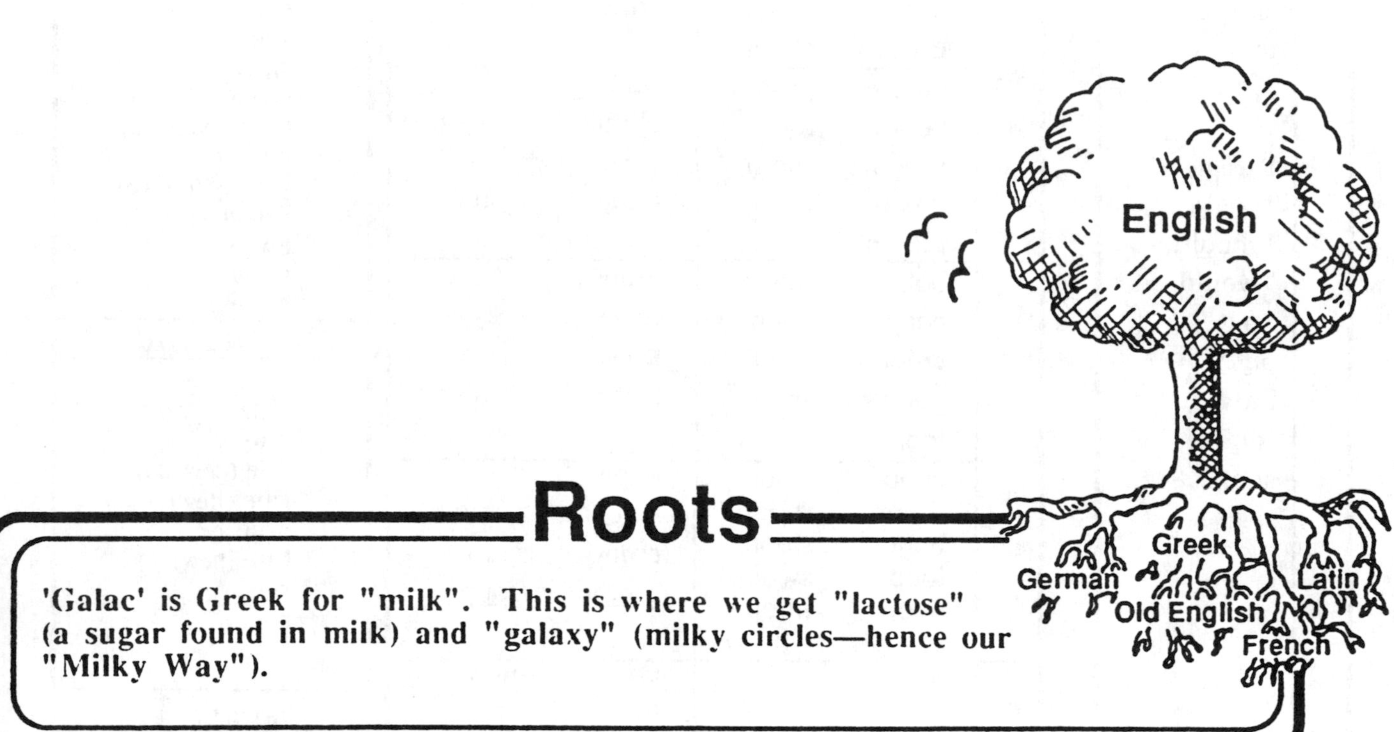
English
Roots
Greek
German
Latin
Old English
French
'Galac' is Greek for "milk". This is where we get "lactose" (a sugar found in milk) and "galaxy" (milky circles—hence our "Milky Way").

Select Multi-Syllable Words with /ü/ and /ū/ *

	oo = /ŏŏ/
d	brotherhood childhood falsehood likelihood livelihood misunderstood motherhood neighborhood parenthood priesthood understood withstood
t	betook chinook forsook mistook partook
	Compound Words *cookbook* *driftwood* *firewood* *outlook* *overlook* *pocketbook* *sketchbook* *workbook* *yearbook*

	oo = /ü/	ü_e, ū_e	
c		deduce produce	introduce reproduce
d		altitude aptitude certitude collude conclude delude elude exclude extrude fortitude include	interlude intrude latitude longitude magnitude occlude preclude prelude protrude seclude solitude
f	aloof disproof behoof		
g		centrifuge subterfuge	vermifuge
k	gobbledygook	rebuke	
l		ampule molecule	ridicule vestibule
m	heirloom mushroom	consume costume exhume legume perfume	presume resume
n	balloon macaroon bassoon maroon buffoon pantaloon cartoon platoon cocoon pontoon dragoon quadroon festoon raccoon harpoon tycoon lagoon typhoon	attune commune immune opportune	
p	nincompoop paratroop		
s	caboose papoose mongoose vamoose	accuse confuse enthuse	excuse refuse transfuse
t	cahoot uproot forsooth	absolute acute astute attribute commute constitute destitute	execute institute persecute pollute resolute repute substitute
v	behoove		
Compound	*afternoon* *courtroom* *elbowroom* *fireproof* *foolproof* *schoolroom* *soundproof* *whirlpool*	*suitcase*	

-ue = /ü/, /ū/ ↧
accrue argue avenue barbecue construe continue curlicue ensue fondue imbue issue overdue pursue rescue residue revenue statue subdue tissue value virtue
-ew = /ü/ ↧
anew askew cashew corkscrew curfew eschew mildew nephew renew sinew **Exception** interview preview review
-oo = /ü/ ↧
bamboo buckaroo cockatoo cuckoo hullabaloo igloo kangaroo kazoo shampoo taboo tattoo yahoo **Exception:** rendezvous canoe

Unit 3

Vowels

Computer checked.

*Final syllable and final sound. For '-ure', see Chart 66.

What about /ŭ/?

What about /ŭ/?	Example	
① In unaccented syllables, most often 'a' stands in for 'u',	about	a- (u) -a (u↓)
② Unless the prefix is 'up' or 'un'.	upon/uneven	up- un-
③ The /ŭ/ sound is always an 'a' at the end.	banana	
④ And 'o' can take 'u's place with 'v', 'th,' and 'n'.	love mother/son	o (u) ⟨ v th (n)☆

① The vowel 'u' is the least used vowel. A short 'u' spelled with a 'u' is very rare in unaccented syllables. What many dictionaries refer to as the schwa can be any vowel in an unaccented syllable. However, most often 'a' is used for the /ŭ/ sound at the beginning of a word and almost always at the end of a word.

above (u u) ŭpŏn ŭnēvĕn

② If the beginning syllable of a word is not accented and begins with an /ŭ/ sound, it will be an 'a', with the exceptions of the prefixes 'up-' and 'un-'.

③ If an /ŭ/ sound is heard at the end of a word, it will be spelled almost exclusively with an 'a'.

love (u) mother (u x u) son (u)

④ The vowel 'o' takes 'u's place for all the sounds of 'u' only when followed by 'v' and 'th'. There are no 'uv' words and only two 'uth' words ("truth" and "ruthless"). Many 'on' words say /ŭn/, "onion". The complete break-down of what happens is on Chart 24.

✏ 'Everyday Words'

about	along	America
above	aloud	extra
across	amount	grandma
afraid	apart	grandpa
ago	around	idea
agree	awake	
alike	aware	
alone	away	

***'Everyday Bloopers'**

*again

Select Words Where 'a' Stands in for /ŭ/.

Initial		Medial	Final	
aback	agenda	banana	alpaca	hysteria
abandon	aglow	balance	America	koala
abide	ago	career	area	idea
ablaze	agree	contradict	aroma	lava
abloom	aground	excavate	bacteria	larva
abode	alas	extravagant	camera	mama
abolish	alike	gelatin	candelabra	nausea
about	alone	hesitant	cobra	okra
above	along	madam	cola	orchestra
abroad	aloud	malaria	coma	panda
abrupt	allow	pajama	comma	pizza
abuse	amaze	parade	data	quota
academy	among	propaganda	drama	saga
accompany	amount	payable	dilemma	saliva
acquit	amuse	singable	diploma	soda
across	apart	sacrament	encyclopedia	stanza
acute	around	salad	extra	stamina
adapt	awake	salute	formula	tuna
adore	award	sesame	gorilla	umbrella
adrift	aware	tentacle	grandma	vanilla
adult	awash	tentative	grandpa	zebra
afraid	away		**Exception**	
again	awoke		ah blah	hurrah shah

Select Words with 'un-' and 'up-'

up- (up)	**un-** (not)	
upbeat	unarmed	unheard-of
upbringing	unbecoming	unhook
update	unbolt	unpopular
upend	unclean	unqualified
upheld	uncommon	unreal
uphill	uncork	unreasonable
uphold	uncover	unruly
uplift	undone	unseemly
upright	unearthed	unsuitable
uproot	uneasy	untangle
upset	unemployed	untie
upside-down	uneven	unused
upstage	unfair	unwise
upstairs	unfriendly	unwritten
upstream	unlace	
upsurge	unless	**Exception**
upsweep	unloved	umbilical
upturn	unload	umbrella
upward	unmade	umpire

Chart 24
When 'o' Stands in for 'u'. This chart clearly shows the unique ability of 'o' to stand in for 'u'. There are certain consonants that 'u' will never be next to. In these words, the 'o' takes on the sounds of 'u' (long or short). Most words with any 'u' sound before a 'v', 'th', 'm', or 'n' and before or following a 'w' or 'qu' will be spelled with an 'o'. There are less than a handful of exceptions with the combinations of 'uv', 'wu', 'uth', 'quu', and a very limited number of words with '-un' or '-um' (excluding the affixes 'un-' or 'um-'). This is helpful to know for spelling purposes, but presents some difficulty in reading these words. The Family Tree poem would be helpful in learning several of these words which have to do with family members. ☛ See page 207.

English
Greek
German
Latin
Old English
French

Roots

'Quar' means "four". From it we get words like "quart" (1/4 part of a gallon), "quarter" (1/4 part of a dollar), "quartet" (musical group of four), and "quarantine". "Quarantine" means four, ten times (= 40) which is the number of days people or goods were held in ports if they were suspected of carrying contagious diseases.

When 'o' Stands in for 'u'

'o' is used exclusively with 'v', 'w', 'qu', 'wh' and 'th.

ov=/ŭv/	ove/oove =/üv/	ov=/ŏv/	ov=/ōv/
above	*move	novice	cove
dove	prove	novel	clove
glove	movie	poverty	clover
love	hooves	grovel	dove
shove	groove		drove
hovel	approve		grove
shovel	behoove		stove
oven	disapprove		strove
cover	disprove		wove
hover	improve		over
govern	remove		rover
covenant	reprove		covert
discover	**(No 'uv' words)**		overt
turtledove			nova
(No 'uv' words)			mangrove
Exception			interwove
*of			

wo=/wo͝o/	wo=/wü/	who=/hwü/	wo=/wō/
wolf	womb	*who	woe
wolverine	swoon	whom	woke
woman	swoop	whoop	won't
wood (would)		*whose	wore
wool			wove
(would)			swollen

oth=/ŭth/	ooth=/üth/	oth=/ŏth/	oth=/ōth/
*another	booth	broth	*both
*brother	tooth	cloth	
*mother	smooth	froth	**Exception**
*other		moth	growth
smother	**Exception**	sloth	
nothing	**(Entire List of 'uth' words)**		
(no 'uth' words)	ruthless		
	truth		
	youth		
	uncouth		

quo=/kwu/	quo=/kwō/
(No /u/ or /ü/ words with 'qu'. /kü/ is spelled 'cu', "cute".)	quota
	quote
	quotient

a=/ŭ/	oo=/ü/
see Chart 23	see Chart 22

Where 'o' and 'u' overlap.[1]

on=/ŭn/	on=/ŏn/ (samples)
son	on
ton	con
won	bond
apron	fond
lemon	pond
lion	ponder
melon	mongrel
Monday	bonnet
ribbon	sonnet
almond	monster
wonder	nonsense
wonderful	sponsor
honey	
money	
*among	
sponge	
tongue	(Accented initial 'con-' such as: con´cert con´crete con´tact con´tract)
monk	
monkey	
*front	
frontier	
*month	
(Unaccented initial 'con-' such as: con duct´, con fide´, con ti nue´)	**ood=/ŭd/**
Exception	blood
*one *once	flood
*done *none	

ou=/ŭ/	om=/ŭm/
*double	comfort
*trouble	company
*touch	compass
*young	complain
couple	compress
cousin	from
country	blossom
southern	kingdom
	wisdom
(Numerous words with suffix '-ous', such as: pious porous momentous)	*become
	*come
	*some
Exception	
dozen	

Computer checked. *'Everyday Bloopers': Must be memorized. [1]Note: /u/, see Chart 23.

Chart 24

What else about 'o'?

What else about 'o'?	Example	
① 'Oi' says /oi/ and is spelled 'oy' at the end,	coin/boy	oi/oy
② 'Ou' says /ou/ and is spelled 'ow' at the end.	loud/now	
③ And use 'ow' before 'l' or 'n',	owl/town	ou/ow<n, l
Whenever they are not in a blend.	found	

coin boy

① The /oi/, "coin", sound is quite predictable. It is a unique sound called a diphthong. We mark it as a unique sound by putting an 'x' under it. It is spelled 'oi' in the middle of a syllable, "coin", and 'oy' at the end of syllables or words, "boy".

out cow

② Another diphthong is /ou/, "out". It is also a unique sound and is marked with an 'x' under it. Its sound is like the sound of pain a child makes when hurt, "Ow!" At the beginning or middle of a syllable, the /ou/ sound is spelled 'ou', "couch". At the end of a syllable or word, it is 'ow', "cow".

down owl found count

③ There are two consonants, 'l' and 'n', that affect vowel spelling and sounds more than any others. When the /ou/ sound is followed by a single 'l' or 'n', it is spelled 'ow', "owl", "crown". However, if 'n' is in a blend (as 'nd' or 'nt'), the /ou/ sound is spelled 'ou', "found", "count".

✏ 'Everyday Words'

loud	count	about	brown
found	hour	around	town
ground	our	how	
round	out	now	
sound	shout		
coin	join	point	
boy	toy	joy	
cliffs(z)choice		house	noise

***'Everyday Bloopers'**

*noun *doubt

/oi/ and /ou/ with 'Cliffs(z)' (Silent 'e' is for consonant and may/may not affect vowel)

'ce'=/s/	'se'=/s/	'se'=/z/	'ze'=/z/	'ge'=/j/	've'=/v/	'ch'=/ch/
choice voice		noise poise				
bounce flounce ounce pounce	blouse douse grouse house louse mouse spouse	rouse **Exception** browse		gouge lounge scrounge **Exception** rouge		couch crouch grouch ouch pouch slouch vouch

ou/ow (Entire List)

	ou
c	↧
ch	couch, crouch, grouch, ouch, pouch, slouch, vouch
d	cloud, loud, proud
g	↧
n_	bound, found, ground, hound, mound, pound, round, sound, wound, count, mount
r	dour, hour, flour (flower), our, scour, sour
s	↧
t	bout, clout, grout, out, pout, scout, shout, snout, spout, sprout, stout, trout, mouth, south
	aloud, about, abound, around, account, amount, founder, flounder, fountain, mountain, devour, trouser, outer

	ow (↧ / l / n)	
↧	bow, brow, chow, cow, how, now, plow, pow, prow, row (n.), scow, sow (n.), vow, wow	allow, avow, disallow, endow, meow, chowder, powder, dowdy, howdy, bower, cower, flower, glower, power, shower, tower, renown, dowry
☆ l	cowl, fowl, growl, howl, jowl, owl, prowl, scowl, yowl, bowel, towel, vowel	**Exception** sauerkraut
☆ n	brown, clown, crown, down, drown, frown, gown, town	***Compound Words*** *anyhow, eyebrow, highbrow, powwow, snowplow, somehow, breakdown, countdown, crackdown, rubdown, rundown, showdown, sundown, hometown, cauliflower, mayflower, sunflower, wallflower, empower, horsepower, manpower, waterpower, willpower, thundershower, watchtower*
	Exception foul, noun, crowd, doubt	

oi/oy (Entire List)

	oi	oy ↧
☆ l	boil, broil, coil, foil, oil, soil, spoil, toil	boy, coy, joy, ploy, soy, toy
☆ n	coin, groin, join, loin, joint, point	**Exception** buoy
c	↧	
d	void	
s	↧	
st	hoist, moist	
	anoint, appoint, asteroid, avoid, cloister, disappoint, disjoin, exploit, loiter, moisture, ointment, recoil, sirloin, tabloid, tenderloin, trapezoid, turmoil	alloy, annoy, corduroy, decoy, deploy, destroy, employ, enjoy, envoy, viceroy
	Exception boycott, buoyant, flamboyant, loyal, oyster, voyage	***Compound Words*** *busboy, cowboy, killjoy, newsboy, overjoy, schoolboy, tomboy*

Unit 3

Vowels

Computer checked.

*'Everyday Bloopers': Must be memorized.

Chart 25

More about 'o' and 'a'.

More about 'o' and 'a'.	Example	
① Before and after 'w' and 'u',	won't/want quota/squat row/raw fraud	w ō/wå quō/quå ōw/åw åu
And when in front of 'l' and 'r',	toll/tall form/farm	ōl/ål ōr/år
'o' says, /ō/, and 'a' says /å/,		
② But with 'w', 'or' is /wŭr/ and 'ar' is /wōr/.	worm/warm	wor=/wŭr/ war=/wōr/

① Before and after 'w' and 'u', ('wo', 'ow', 'quo'), and in front of 'l' and 'r', ('ol', 'oll', 'oll'), the 'o' will say /ō/. On occasion, the 'ow' may sometimes say /ou/, "cow". The 'ou' almost always says /ou/, "pout". Also, when we see an 'a' before and after 'w' and 'u', ('wa', 'aw', 'qua', 'au'), and in front of 'l' and 'r', ('ar', and 'al'), the 'a' will say /å/, "tall". The /å/ sound is very close to the /ŏ/, "cot", sound. Certain regions make a greater distinction between the two sounds than do other areas. The fact that 'o' will never say an /ŏ/ in any of these positions shows that they are mutually exclusive and therefore for all practical purposes /ŏ/, "off", and /å/, "awful", are the same sound. The 'awk', 'awl', 'alk', and 'awn' words must be memorized since these sounds do not clearly indicate their spelling. For a complete list of words with 'au', see Chart 27.

② Although a 'w' or an 'r' by itself will make the 'a' say /å/, "saw", and the 'o' say /ō/, "for", when they are both together, there is an interesting switch in the sounds. In these cases, 'wor' says /wŭr/, "worm" and 'war' says /wōr/, "warm".

✏ 'Everyday Words'

roll	call	throw	work
cold	fall	caught	world
fold	small	taught	worse
hold	tall	bought	worth
old	draw	brought	for
sold	saw	thought	large
told	grow	talk	torn
own	know	warm	short
all	low	word	sport

***'Everyday Bloopers'**

*aunt	*father
*for	*mama
*four	*papa
*nor	*gone
*or	*on
*doll	
*shall	

/å/ (& 'or') with **'Cliffs(z)'** **(Silent 'e' is for consonant and may/may not affect the vowel)**

'ce'=/s/	'se'=/s/	'se'=/z/	'ze'=/z/	'ge'=/j/	've'=/v/	'ch'=/ch/
farce sauce	parse sparse	cause clause pause	gauze	barge charge large	carve starve	
force	horse			forge gorge		

Comparison of 'a' and 'o'

Mutually Exclusive

☑

☆ l

oll=/ōl/	all=/ål/	awl=/ål/
'ole'	all	bawl
droll	ball	brawl
knoll	call	crawl
poll	fall	drawl
roll	gall	scrawl
scroll	hall (haul)	shawl
stroll	mall (maul)	sprawl
toll	stall	
troll	small	
bold	squall	
cold	tall	
fold	wall	
gold	bald	
hold	scald	
mold	false	
old	halt	
sold	malt	
scold	salt	
told	exalt	
bolt	(Silent 'l')	
colt	balm	
jolt	calm	
molt	palm	
(Silent 'l')	psalm	
folk	qualm	
yolk	**Exception**	
	doll	
	loll	
	shall	
	fault	
	vault	
	haul	
	maul	

↧

aw=/å/	ow=/ō/
caw	blow
claw	crow
craw	flow
draw	glow
flaw	grow
gnaw	know
jaw	low
law	mow
paw	row
raw	show
saw	snow
slaw	sow
squaw	stow
straw	throw
thaw	tow
bylaw	
handsaw	
jigsaw	
rickshaw	
seesaw	
southpaw	
withdraw	

☆ n

own=/ōn/	awn=/ån/	aun=/ån/	on=/ōn/
blown	brawn	aunt[1]	don't
flown	dawn	daunt	won't
grown	drawn	gaunt	
known	fawn	haunt	
mown	lawn	jaunt	
own	pawn	taunt	
shown	spawn	launch	
sown	yawn	staunch	
thrown			
	Exception	**Exception**	
	con	font	
	*gone	[1]aunt (can be /ănt/ or /ânt/)	
	*on		

ar=/år/	or=/ōr/
bar	porch
car	scorch
char	torch
far	cork
jar	fork
mar	stork
star	form
tar	norm
barb	storm
garb	born (borne)
arch	corn
march	horn
starch	morn(mourn)
card	scorn
hard	shorn
lard	thorn
yard	torn
ark	fort
bark	port
dark	short
hark	snort
lark	sort
mark	sport
park	forth (fourth)
shark	north
spark	
stark	
snarl	
arm	
charm	
farm	
harm	
alarm	
barn	
darn	
yarn	
carp	
harp	
sharp	
art	
cart	**Exception**
chart	*father
hart (heart)	*mama
part	*papa
smart	schwa
start	*for
tart	*four
	*nor
	*or

wa=/wå/	wo=/wō/
wad	won't
wall	
wand	
wash	
wasp	
watch	
swab	
swamp	
swat	
squad	
squall	
squash	
squat	
war=/wor/	**wor=/wŭr/**
war	word
ward	work
warm	world
warn	worm
warp	worse
wart	worst
swarm	worth
dwarf	**Exception**
thwart	sword
quart	sworn
quartz	

Overlapping

augh/ough	ot=/ŏt/
aught	cot
caught	dot
naught	got
taught	hot
bought	jot
brought	lot
fought	not
thought	rot
wrought	tot
cough	
trough	
awk=/åk/	**ock=/ŏk/**
hawk	block
gawk	clock
squawk	cock
balk	crock
chalk	dock
stalk	flock
	hock
	lock
	mock
	rock
	shock
	smock
	sock
	stock
	tock
auce/ause	**oss=/ŏs/**
sauce	boss
cause	floss
clause	gloss
pause	loss
gauze	moss
	toss

☑ Computer checked. *'Everyday Bloopers': Must be memorized. [1]See Chart 19 and 20.

Chart 26

Complete List of 'au'/'aw' Words

au = /å/

b	bauble bedaub daub
c	Caucasian caucus faucet raucous sauce saucer
d	applaud audible audience audio audit auditorium fraud gaudy laud vaudeville
g[2]	auger augment August inaugural
gh	aught caught daughter fraught haughty naughty onslaught slaughter taught
l	assault cauliflower fault hydraulic somersault vault **Exception** haul maul
m	trauma
n[3]	aunt[1] daunt flaunt gaunt haunt haunch jaundice jaunt launch laundry leprechaun paunch saunter staunch taunt vaunt **Exception** faun fauna sauna
p	pauper
s	austere auspicious Australia applause cause caustic clause exhaust holocaust nausea pause sausage
t[4]	authentic author autocrat autograph automatic automobile autonomous autonomy autopsy autumn aquanaut astronaut caution nautical nautilus sauté taut
x	auxiliary
z	gauze
	Exception aunt[1] beauty because chauffeur gauge laugh mauve taupe **au = /ōr/** aura aural aurora brontosaur dinosaur laurel thesaurus

aw = /å/

	awl
☆ l	bawl brawl crawl drawl scrawl shawl sprawl **Exception:** squall
☆ n	brawn dawn drawn fawn lawn pawn spawn yawn tawny
k	gawk hawk squawk
↧	caw, claw, craw, draw, flaw, gnaw, haw law, paw, raw, saw, squaw, straw, thaw awful awkward bawdy dawdle lawyer ***Compound Words*** *awesome* *awestruck* *drawback* *strawberry* *withdraw*

☑ Computer checked. [1]Note: 'Aunt' may be pronounced either /ånt/ or /ănt/. [2]Note: No words begin with 'og' = /ŏg/

[3]Note: 'font' is only 'ont' word. [4]Note: 'otter' is the only word beginning with 'ot'.

Chart 27
Complete List of 'au'/'aw' Words. This is the majority of words with 'au' and 'aw'. Many of these words begin with 'au'. The prefix 'auto-' means 'self'. Again, as with 'ow', we use 'aw' before 'l' and 'n' if they are not in a blend and if it is at ends of words. For '-augh' words: ☛ See page 213.

Chart 28
One-Syllable Words with /ūr/ sounds.

her
u

The /ŭr/ sound can be spelled many ways. There is no way of knowing if it is 'ur', 'ir', 'or', 'er', or 'ear'. The only /ŭr/ spelling that is certain is when the /ŭr/ sound follows a 'w', it is always spelled 'wor'. To learn the different /ŭr/ words, for 'ur': ☛ See page 209, and for the 'ir' words: ☛ See page 210.

✏ 'Everyday Words'

turn	search	bird	word
hurt	heard	third	work
her	early	girl	world
serve	earn	first	worse
	learn		worth

***'Everyday Bloopers'**

*were
*sure

Chart 29
One-Syllable Words with 'r'. The 'r' greatly affects the sounds of the vowels. In this chart, the long vowels with 'r' are presented. Notice that it often takes two vowels to make a long vowel sound with 'r'. They may be next to each other, "fair", or may be arranged with a vowel, the 'r', silent 'e'.

In front of 'r' (if no other vowel is present) an 'a' says /å/, "car", and an 'o' says /ō/, "born" . The sound that 'a' says when followed by an 'r' is very close to a short 'o' sound. Certain regions make more of a distinction between the two sounds than other areas do. However, the fact that the 'o' will never say the /ŏ/ sound when followed by an 'r', shows that they are mutually exclusive and therefore for all practical purposes, the /å/ and the /ŏ/ are the same sound. The other places where the 'o' is long and the 'a' says /å/ are found on Chart 26.

✏ 'Everyday Words'

car	arm	scare	clear	short
far	farm	share	dear	sport
star	barn	square	ear	north
march	sharp	stare	fear	chore
yard	part	air	near	more
bark	smart	fair	year	store
mark	start	pair	deer	door
park	rare	stair	born	floor
war	warm	warn	quart	

***'Everyday Bloopers'**

*your	*you're	*here
*our	*are	*there
*where	*for	*their
*four	*or	
*pour		

'r' words with 'Cliffs(z)' (Silent 'e' is for consonant and may/may not affect the vowel)

'ce'=/s/	'se'=/s/	'se'=/z/	'ze'=/z/	'ge'=/j/	've'=/v/	'ch'=/ch/
farce force source	parse sparse coarse course horse			barge charge large forge gorge	carve starve	

Unit 3
Vowels

Complete List of One-Syllable Words with /ŭr/ Sound

☑	① ur=/ŭr/	② er=/ŭr/	③ ear=/ŭr/ (Entire List)	④ ir=/ŭr/	⑤ (w)or=(w)/ŭr/
r	blur slur cur spur fur–(fir) **Exception** burr purr lure sure	her per–(purr)		fir–(fur) sir stir whir	**Exception** were
b	blurb curb	herb verb			
ch	lurch church	perch	search (research)	birch smirch	
d	curd	herd–(heard)	heard–(herd)	bird gird third	word
f	surf turf				
k	lurk murk	perk		kirk shirk quirk smirk	work
l	burl hurl curl purl churl furl		earl pearl early	girl swirl twirl whirl	world
m		germ term		firm squirm	worm
n	burn urn burnt churn spurn turn	fern tern	earn learn yearn		
p	burp slurp			chirp	
st	burst			first thirst	worst
t	blurt curt hurt spurt	pert		dirt squirt flirt shirt skirt	
th		berth–(birth)	earth (earthen) dearth	birth–(berth) mirth girth	worth

Cliffs(z)

ge ↧	purge surge scourge urge splurge	merge serge verge		dirge	
se ↧	curse purse nurse	verse terse	hearse (rehearse)		worse
ve ↧	curve	nerve serve			**Exception** swerve

☑ Computer checked. *'Everyday Bloopers': Must be memorized.

Complete List of One-Syllable 'r' Words (Excluding /ŭr/ words)

① /år/

bar
car
far
jar
mar
scar
star
tar
barb
garb
arch
march
parch
starch
bard
card
hard
lard
yard
scarf
ark
bark
dark
hark
lark
mark
park
shark
spark
stark
snarl
arm
charm
farm
harm
barn
darn
yarn
harp
sharp
art
cart
chart
dart
part
mart
smart
start
tart

Cliffs ↧
farce sparse
carve starve
barge charge
large

Exception
*are heart
*our hearth
guard hearty
barre

② /ār/

are
bare (bear)
blare
care
dare
fare (fair)
flare (flair)
glare
hare (hair)
mare
pare (pair, pear)
rare
scare
share
snare
spare
square
stare (stair)
ware (wear)

air
air (heir)
chair
fair (fare)
flair
hair (hare)
lair
pair (pare, pear)
stair (stare)

Exception
ear
bear (bare)
tear (tare)
pear (pair, pare)
swear
wear (ware)

*where
*there--their
ere
heir (air)

③ /ēr/

ear
clear
dear (deer)
drear
ear
fear
gear
hear (here)
near
rear
shear
smear
spear
tear (n.)
year
beard

eer
beer
cheer
deer
jeer
leer
peer (pier)
queer
seer
sheer (shear)
sneer
steer
veer

Exception
ere
'e' rarely helps an 'e' see Ch. 13
*here
mere
sphere

pier
tier

Cliffs ↧
fierce
pierce

④ /ōr/

or
porch
scorch
torch
cord
ford
lord
cork
fork
pork
stork
dorm
form
norm
storm
born (borne)
corn
horn
morn (mourn)
scorn
shorn
sworn
thorn
torn
fort
port
short
snort
sort
sport
forth (fourth)
north

Cliffs ↧
corpse
force
horse (hoarse)
forge
gorge

Exception
horde (hoard)

our
gourd
mourn
four (fore, fore)
pour (poor,pore)
court
fourth (forth)

Cliffs ↧
course (coarse)
source

Exception
borne

⑤ /ōr/

ore
bore(boar, boor)
chore
core
fore (for, four)
gore
lore
more (moor)
pore(poor, pour)
score
shore
snore
sore
spore
store
swore
tore

Exception
*for nor
*or

oar
boar (boor,bore)
hoard (horde)
oar (or, ore)
roar
soar

Cliffs ↧
coarse (course)
hoarse (horse)

oor
door
floor
boor (boar, bore)
poor (pore pour)
moor (more)

(w)ar
war (wore)
ward
warp
thwart
wart
warn (worn)
swarm
warm
(quart)

Exception
wore
*worn

⑥ /īr/

dire
fire
hire
ire
mire
shire
sire
spire
squire
tire
wire

Exception
choir

⑦ /ūr/

cure
pure

Exception
tour
you're
your

⑧ /our/

our
flour (flower)
hour
our
sour
scour

ower
bower
flower
power
shower
tower

☑ Computer checked. *'Everyday Bloopers': Must be memorized. ↧ 'Cliffs(z)' See Unit 4.

UNIT 4

FOCUS ON:
ENDS OF WORDS AND SILENT 'E' HELPING CONSONANTS
['CLIFFS(Z)']

Unit Four is about ends of words. At ends of words, there are consonants that often double or have a silent 'e' with them: when following short vowels ('ck', 'll', 'ff', 'ss', 'zz', 'tch', 'dge', 've'), when not following short vowels, ('ce', 'se', 'ze', 'ge', 'ch', 've') and in multi-syllable words ('le', 'que', 'gue', and so forth). The following poem/song (from Alphabet Island Phonics) summarizes what happens.

At Ends of Words

Ends of Words:	Examples:
At ends of words when by a short vowel	
Use 'ck', double 'l', 'f', 's', 'z'.	—băck, fĭll, clĭff, frĭzz
Use 't' with 'ch', 'd' with 'ge',	—bătch, fŭdge
But always have 'e' with 'v'.	—hăve
At ends of words when not by a short vowel	
'c', 's', and 'z' always need an 'e'.	—rejoice, mouse, frēeze
No 't' with 'ch', no 'd' with 'ge',	—ēach, cāge
But always have 'e' with 'v'.	—sāve

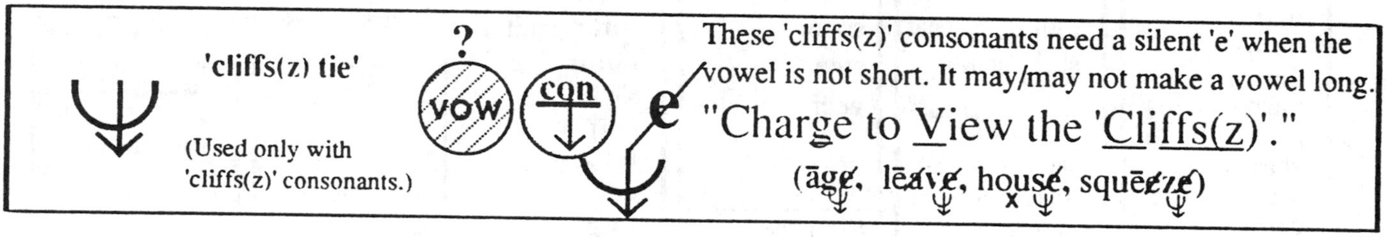

'cliffs(z) tie'

(Used only with 'cliffs(z)' consonants.)

?

VOW con e

These 'cliffs(z)' consonants need a silent 'e' when the vowel is not short. It may/may not make a vowel long.

"Charge to View the 'Cliffs(z)'."

(āge, lēave, house, squēeze)

More about 'cliffs(z)'.

The concept of 'cliffs(z) in an exciting new concept that brings together many seemingly unrelated rules under one theme. There are certain letters that predictably change their spellings at ends of words. These same letters are the ones that double or have another consonant with them following a short vowel. And these same letters need a silent 'e' when following anything other than a short vowel.

We will first deal with the words that have a short vowel followed by two consonants that make a single consonant sound, v̆cc/. Following a short vowel, the consonants that double at ends of words to make a single consonant sound are found in the word "cliffs(z)". The 'cliffs(z)' symbol indicates that the extra consonant is not heard but is needed at ends of words for the consonant. The following analogy may be helpful in understanding and remembering this concept.

Cliffs(z) Story

When letters get together to form words, the last letter is by a 'cliff'. And as with people, some are afraid to be there and others are not. Although many letters do not mind being at the end of a word, some letters will never be there and others will be there only if another letter is with them. All the vowels are afraid of the 'cliffs' and usually have a 'y' or 'w' to help them. The key phrase, "Charge to view the 'cliffs(z)'" contains the consonants that are afraid of ends of words.

c /k/>ck "back"

l /l/>ll "fell"*

i (All vowels change their spelling at ends of words.)

ff /f/>ff "off"

s /s/>ss "pass"

z /z/>zz "fizz"

*['all' says /ål/, "ball", and 'oll' says /ōl/ "poll", and is studied in detail on Charts 64 and 65.]

The complete list of consonants that change their spelling at ends of words are underlined in the phrase, "Charge to view the cliffs(z)." It is important to note that these consonants usually have a silent 'e' with them when not directly following a short vowel (house, hinge, apple, snooze, sleeve, and so on.) In these words, the silent 'e' is there for the consonant and may or may not help the vowel.

In this unit, we will be looking at the rest of the 'cliffs(z)' letters and will also see what happens with each of these letters in multi-syllable words.

Chart 30

One-Syllable 'Cliffs(z)' with Short Vowels. This chart is a review of the beginning study of 'cliffs(z)' in Unit 2. It deals with one-syllable, short-vowel words ending with consonants that change their spellings at ends of words.

Chart 31

Multi-Syllable Words ending in 'l', 'f', or 's'. This chart is a sample of multi-syllable words ending with /l/, /f/, and /s/ following a short vowel. There are a few words that double the 'l' and 'f', many of which are compound words. The suffix '-ful' does not double the 'l'.

There are numerous independent words that end with a double 's'. There are hundreds of words with the suffixes '-ess', '-ness', and '-less'. The suffix '-ous' is pronounced /ŭs/ and the 'o' is an unexpected part of its spelling. Many of the independent words that end in a single 's' are related to math or science. They come from Latin and Greek.

Complete List of One-Syllable 'Cliffs(z)' with Short Vowels

	ck ↧	ll ↧	ff ↧	ss ↧	zz ↧
ă	back hack jack lack pack rack sack tack black clack crack flack quack shack slack smack snack stack track whack	'all'=/ål/	chaff	bass lass mass pass sass brass class crass glass grass	jazz razz
ĕ	deck peck neck check fleck speck	bell cell dell fell hell jell sell tell well yell dwell smell quell spell swell		less mess bless chess dress press tress stress	
ĭ	hick kick lick tick nick pick sick tick wick brick click crick flick prick quick trick slick stick thick	bill dill fill gill[1] hill ill kill mill pill sill till will drill frill grill quill trill skill spill still twill chill shrill thrill	cliff sniff stiff whiff	hiss kiss miss bliss	fizz frizz
ŏ	cock dock hock lock mock rock sock block clock crock flock frock shock smock stock	'oll'=/ōl/	off scoff	boss loss moss toss floss gloss cross dross	
ŭ	buck duck luck muck puck suck tuck cluck chuck pluck truck shuck snuck stuck struck	cull dull gull hull lull mull	buff cuff huff puff muff bluff fluff gruff scuff scruff snuff stuff	cuss fuss muss truss	buzz fuzz
	Exception knock trek wrack wreck yak	**Exception** *full *pull nil	**Exception** calf half graph rough tough *if *of	**Exception** gas alas *yes bus pus *plus *us *[1]guess *this *thus	**Exception** *does *has *his *is *says *was quiz whiz

Computer checked. *'Everyday Bloopers': Must be memorized. [1]'gu'=/g/ before 'e', 'i', or 'y'.

Select Multi-Syllable Words Ending in 'l', 'f' or 's' (Following short vowels)

l

(Complete List)

appall
chlorophyll
distill
enroll
enthrall
forestall
idyll
indwell
install
instill
marshall
misspell
recall
refill
unroll
whippoorwill

-ful

armful
bashful
beautiful
careful
cheerful
colorful
cupful
doubtful
dreadful
forceful
forgetful
grateful
harmful
hopeful
houseful
joyful
lawful
meaningful
mindful
mouthful
needful
painful
peaceful
playful
pocketful
regretful
resentful
roomful
sackful
scornful
skillful
successful
tearful
thankful
truthful

f

(Complete List)

bailiff
dandruff
mastiff
middriff
plaintiff
pontiff
rebuff
riffraff
sheriff
stroganoff
tariff

Exception

giraffe

Compound Words

blastoff
flagstaff
handcuff
layoff
liftoff
runoff
showoff
shutoff
standoff
anthill
baseball
basketball
birdcall
bombshell
carryall
catchall
doorbell
downfall
eggshell
eyeball
farewell
football
foothill
fulfill
goodwill
handbill
landfill
meatball
nightfall
nutshell
oddball
overall
pitfall
rainfall
seashell
snowfall
softball
stairwell
standstill
treadmill
uphill
waterfall
windmill
windowsill

s

amass
amiss
assess
business
buttress
canvass
carcass
caress
compass
compress
confess
congress
cypress
depress
digress
discuss
dismiss
distress
duress
embarrass
emboss
encompass
engross
excess
express
fortress
harass
harness
impress
mattress
obsess
oppress
possess
profess
prowess
progress
recess
regress
repossess
repress
reprocess
remiss
success
suppress
surpass
trespass
witness

US (math/science)

apparatus
cactus
crocus
esophagus
focus
fungus
hibiscus
locus
minus
mucus
virus

'-ess' (Female)

countess
duchess
empress
heiress
goddess
highness
hostess
laundress
governess
mistress
lioness
princess
prioress
shepherdess
sculptress
tigress
waitress

-ous (full of)

anonymous
cantankerous
continuous
curious
dangerous
delicious
delirious
dubious
enormous
fabulous
famous
frivolous
furious
generous
glamorous
humorous
incredulous
jealous
lustrous
marvelous
perilous
ravenous
ridiculous
venomous

advantageous
igneous

luxurious
mysterious
notorious
obvious
precious
previous
scrumptious
serious
suspicious
tenacious

'-ness'=state or condition of being

alertness
apprehensiveness
attractiveness
awesomeness
bashfulness
blackness
blindness
business
cheerfulness
cleanliness
closeness
dampness
deceptiveness
drowsiness
effectiveness
fairness
faithfulness
foolishness
forgiveness
gladness
grumpiness
haughtiness
hideousness
hilliness
holiness
homesickness
immenseness
impulsiveness
kindness
loudness
mischievousness
mysteriousness
neglectfulness
nervousness
openness
productiveness
purposefulness
quietness
respectfulness
shyness
sincereness
spaciousness
squeakiness
suspiciousness
sweatiness
thickness
tightness
uniqueness
uneasiness
unhappiness
weakness
weariness
weightlessness
wilderness
wishfulness
witness
youthfulness

'less'=without

ageless
aimless
blameless
breathless
careless
ceaseless
changeless
cheerless
childless
cloudless
colorless
countless
defenseless
doubtless
effortless
emotionless
endless
fatherless
fathomless
faultless
fearless
flavorless
friendless
fruitless
godless
groundless
hairless
harmless
heartless
helpless
homeless
hopeless
jobless
lawless
lifeless
matchless
meaningless
motionless
nameless
nevertheless
noiseless
painless
penniless
pointless
powerless
priceless
regardless
restless
ruthless
senseless
speechless
spotless
sugarless
thankless
timeless
unless
useless
worthless

Computer checked.

Chart 32
A Study of Silent 'e' with 'c', 's' and 'z' (One-Syllable). When they are not following short vowels, 'c', 's', and 'z' always need an 'e' unless the word has the suffix '-s' or '-es' added to make the word plural or to change a verb tense.

There is an overlap between the 'ce' and the 'se' and between the 'se' and the 'ze'. The only clear prediction that can be made regarding the spellings of these words occurs following 'i'. In these words, the 's' says /z/ and the 'c' is used for the /s/ sound. Note that the 'i's are bold to emphasis this pattern.

Chart 33
A Study of Silent 'e' with 'c', 's' and 'z' (Multi-Syllable). The study of 'ce', 'se', and 'ze' is expanded in this chart to include multi-syllable words. There are only a few words ending in '-ze' that are not formed with the suffix '-ize'. Learn the list of '-ise' words that say /īz/. The rest of the /īz/ words will be spelled '-ize'. There is an overlapping in all the other areas.

Chart 34
A Study of Silent 'e' with '-nce'. This chart is a sampling of words ending in '-ance', '-ence' and '-ense'. Many of the words on this page can be modified by changing the '-ance' to '-ant', the '-ence' to '-ent', and the '-ense' to '-end'. In many of these words, the vowel sound is difficult to distinguish. For spelling purposes, practice by exaggerating the vowel sound when learning it. (Instead of saying "entrŭnce, say "entrănce".) By working on a few at a time, they can be mastered.

-ance changes to:	**-ence** changes to:	**-ense** changes to:	**-nce/-nse** (other) changes :
-ant	-ent	-end	-nd (other)
abundance >abundant	innocence > innocent	defense > defend	response > respond

A Study of Silent 'e' in One-Syllable Words with 'c', 's', and 'z'

☑	ce=/s/	se=/s/	se=/z/	ze=/z/
ā	ace, face, lace, mace, pace, race, brace, grace, place, space, trace	base, case, chase, vase	braise, praise, raise, phase, phrase	daze, faze, gaze, haze, laze, maze, raze, blaze, braze, craze, glaze, graze
ē	fleece, peace **Exception** niece, piece	cease, crease, geese, vise, grease(n.), lease	cheese, ease, grease(v.), please, tease **Exception:** these	breeze, freeze, sneeze, squeeze, tweeze, wheeze **Exception:** seize
ī[1]	dice, ice, lice, mice, nice, price, rice, slice, spice, splice, thrice, twice, trice, vice		guise, rise, arise, wise	prize, size (Numerous words with '-ize' suffix--see Ch. 33)
ō		close(adj.), dose **Exception** gross	chose, close(v.), hose, nose, pose, prose, rose, those	doze, froze
oi	choice, voice		noise, poise	
ou		blouse, douse, grouse, house, louse, mouse, spouse	rouse **Exception** browse, drowse	
ü/ū	spruce, truce **Exception** juice, sluice, deuce	use (n.) goose, loose, moose, noose	fuse, muse, use (v.), ruse, choose, bruise, cruise **Exception** *whose, lose	booze, snooze, ooze
å	sauce		cause, clause, pause	gauze
n	chance, dance, glance, lance, prance, stance, trance, fence, hence, pence, thence, whence, mince, prince, quince, since, bounce, flounce, jounce, ounce, pounce, trounce, dunce **Exception:** once	manse, dense, sense, tense, rinse	cleanse	bronze
l		false, else, pulse		
p		corpse, glimpse, lapse, traipse		
r	farce, scarce, fierce, pierce, force, source	parse, sparse, terse, verse, horse, worse, curse, nurse, purse **Exception** hearse, coarse, hoarse		

☑ Computer checked. *'Everyday Bloopers': Must be memorized. [1]Note: ice=/īs/; ise=/īz/; notice bold ice and ise in above words.

Unit 4

Ends of Words

A Study of Silent 'e' in Multi-Syllable Words with 'c', 's', and 'z'

	ce=/s/	se=/s/
ā	disgrace efface embrace retrace unlace marketplace	amylase encase erase
ē	**Exception** police *mantelpiece*	decease decrease increase release
ī	advice device entice sacrifice suffice	concise merchandise precise paradise
ĭ	apprentice armistice artifice auspice avarice bodice chalice cowardice crevice edifice jaundice justice lattice malice notice novice office prejudice orifice poultice practice precipice prejudice pumice service solstice **Exception** furnace menace populace palace preface solace surface terrace	anise premise promise treatise **Exception** lettuce porpoise purchase purpose tortoise also see-iss
ō		adipose cellulose comatose diagnose fructose glucose grandiose lactose overdose sucrose varicose verbose
oi	invoice rejoice	turquoise
ou	birdhouse jailhouse poorhouse warehouse	espouse
ū / oo	deduce produce reduce introduce reproduce	abuse (n) excuse (n) profuse refuse (n) recluse caboose papoose vamoose
[1]Blends	coerce commerce divorce enforce resource convalesce effervesce fluoresce incandesce	convulse impulse repulse collapse eclipse elapse ellipse prolapse relapse synapse adverse averse concourse converse enforce disburse disperse diverse endorse immerse perverse recourse rehearse reimburse remorse reverse submerse transverse traverse

	se=/z/	ze=/z/
ā	appraise malaise mayonnaise paraphrase	ablaze amaze
ē	appease disease displease Japanese	antifreeze
ī	advise (v) advertise apprise arise chastise comprise compromise demise despise devise disguise enterprise excise exercise franchise incise improvise otherwise reprise revise supervise sunrise surmise surprise televise unwise	apologize authorize baptize capitalize capsize civilize criticize demoralize dramatize emphasize equalize familiarize fertilize formalize fossilize galvanize harmonize idolize improvise legalize legitimize localize maximize mechanize memorize minimize mobilize modernize neutralize normalize organize penalize personalize pluralize popularize rationalize realize recognize specialize stabilize standardize sterilize summarize sympathize tranquilize utilize vaporize verbalize (and many more)
ō	arose compose decompose disclose dispose enclose expose foreclose impose indispose oppose predispose propose repose suppose transpose	
ū	abuse accuse bemuse confuse enthuse excuse (v) refuse (v) transfuse	
ou	arouse	

[1]For -nce, -nse see Chart 34.

Chart 33

A Study of Silent 'e' in '-nce', '-nse

-ance

abundance
acceptance
accordance
acquaintance
admittance
advance
allegiance
alliance
allowance
ambulance
annoyance
appearance
appliance
arrogance
askance
assistance
assurance
attendance
avoidance
balance
brilliance
chance
circumstance
clearance
compliance
concordance
conformance
continuance
contrivance
conveyance
countenance
dalliance
defiance
deliverance
disappearance
discordance
dissonance
distance
disturbance
dominance
elegance
encumbrance
endurance
enhance
entrance
exorbitance
expectance
extravagance
exuberance
finance
flagrance
flamboyance
forbearance
fragrance
furtherance
grievance
guidance
happenstance
hesitance
hindrance
ignorance
imbalance
importance
inheritance
insignificance
instance
insurance
intolerance
maintenance
nonchalance
nuisance
observance
ordinance
participance
perchance
perseverance
performance
preponderance
pursuance
purveyance
radiance
recognizance
reconnaissance
relevance
reliance
reluctance
remembrance
remittance
repentance
resemblance
resonance
riddance
romance
semblance
severance
significance
substance
surveillance
sustenance
temperance
tolerance
utterance
vengeance
vigilance

-ence

abhorrence
absence
abstinence
acquiescence
adherence
adolescence
affluence
ambivalence
ascendence
astringence
audience
belligerence
beneficence
benevolence
cadence
circumference
coexistence
coherence
commence
competence
concurrence
condescendence
condolence
conference
confidence
consequence
consistence
convenience
convergence
correspondence
credence
decadence
difference
diligence
disobedience
dissidence
divergence
effervescence
eloquence
eminence
equivalence
essence
evidence
excellence
existence
expedience
experience
fraudulence
impatience
impertinence
inadvertence
incidence
inconsistence
inconvenience
independence
indifference
indigence
indolence
inference
influence
innocence
insistence
insurgence
intelligence
interference
intermittence
magnificence
negligence
obedience
obsolescence
occurrence
omnipotence
opulence
patience
penitence
permanence
persistence
pertinence
pestilence
precedence
preeminence
preference
presence
prominence
providence
prudence
pungence
quintessence
recurrence
residence
resilience
resplendence
resurgence
reverence
science
sentence
sequence
silence
subsistence
subsequence
stridence
transference
transparence
turbulence
vehemence
violence
virulence

-ense

condense
defense
dispense
expense
frankincense
immense
incense
intense
license
nonsense
offense
pretense
recompense
suspense

-nce/nse

expanse
announce
pronounce
renounce
response

Chart 35 and 36

Multi-syllable Words Ending with /l/. At the end of a single syllable word following a short vowel, we use 'll', 'ff', and 'ck'. However following a long vowel or consonant, unlike 'c', 's', and 'z' which need an 'e', these letters do not have a silent 'e' unless it is needed to make the vowel long. For instance, the words "pail", "peel", and "bank" do not have a final silent 'e'.

ăpple māple

In multi-syllable words, the 'l' needs an 'e' if it is at the end of a word in a syllable without a vowel in it. The 'le' is a unit that makes a 'long-vowel-tie' to the letter next to it. Therefore if the vowel is to be short, the consonant must be doubled.

In these charts we deal with the endings '-al', '-el', and '-le'. The ending '-al' is a suffix that indicates a connection to the base word (bride > bridal). The other two endings, however, are an integral part of their words. Many of the '-el' words follow a 'v'. A large portion of the words with a medial 'v' have an 'e' following it. The exceptions "devil" and "evil" seem appropriately related.

Chart 37

A Study of Silent 'e' with 'g' and 'v' (One-Syllable).

bădge cāge

Neither 'v' and 'j' will ever be found alone at ends of words. The 'j' is replaced with 'dge' following a short vowel and 'ge' elsewhere. The 'd' is needed only to make the vowel short.

The 'v' always needs a silent 'e' regardless of the vowel sound. The vowel may be long or short followed by a 've'. Also, we never find a 'uv'. Any 'u' sound (/ŭ/, /ü/) will be made by an 'o' ("love", "prove"). And the rule, "It takes two vowels to make a long 'e'" holds true here (leave, sleeve).

Chart 38

A Study of Silent 'e' with /g/, /j/, /k/ and /v/ (Multi-Syllable). In multi-syllable words, the patterns seem to change drastically for the /g/ sound. At ends of one-syllable words, not following a short vowel, a '-gue' is needed. The 'u' is there to keep the 'g' saying /g/—without it, 'ge' says /j/. The suffix '-age' sounds like /ĭj/, "bandage". There are several '-ge' words that say /zh/, "garage". Learn to recognize these.

The /k/ sound also goes through many changes. At the beginning or in the middle of words, it can be 'k' before 'i', 'e', and 'y', and can be 'c' elsewhere. At ends of words, following a short vowel in a one-syllable word, it is 'ck'. Elsewhere in a one-syllable word it will usually end with 'k' or 'ke'. In multi-syllable words (not including compound words), the final /k/ is likely to be spelled '-que' with the exception of the suffix '-ic'. It is interesting to note that words ending in a single 'c' will add a 'k' before adding a suffix beginning with a vowel (picnic > picnicking).

For '-ve', again whether the vowel is long or short, always have an 'e' with 'v'.

A Study of '-al' and '-el'

	-al		-el
d	bridal	b	label
	pedal		rebel
	medal	c	nickel
	modal		parcel
	sandal	d	strudel
	scandal		yodel
	tidal	g	angel
t	accidental	m	camel
	acquittal		enamel
	brutal	n	channel
	coastal		funnel
	committal		kennel
	fatal		panel
	frontal		tunnel
	governmental	p	chapel
	mental	r	barrel
	mortal		quarrel
	ornamental		squirrel
	petal	s	chisel
	postal		weasel
	sentimental	st	hostel
	total	v	gravel
	vital		marvel
c	fiscal		navel
	local		shovel
	rascal		travel
	vocal		level
/s/	dorsal		grovel
/z/	appraisal		hovel
	nasal		novel
/sh/	facial	w	bowel
	glacial		jewel
	palatial		towel
	martial		vowel
	partial		**-il**
	marshal		council
m	animal		devil
	mammal		evil
	minimal		fossil
n	criminal		pupil
	final		**-ile**
	penal		agile
u	manual		fragile
v	naval		futile
	upheaval		hostile
y	loyal		**-ol**
	royal		idol
			patrol
			pistol
			symbol

A Study of Silent 'e' in Multi-Syllable Words with 'l'

	ă	ā	ĕ	ē	ĭ	ī	ŏ	ō	ŭ	ū
b	babble dabble scrabble	able cable fable table stable	pebble	feeble	dribble nibble quibble scribble	Bible	cobble hobble gobble wabble[1]	ogle	bubble rubble stubble Exc:double Exc:trouble	
ck	crackle shackle		heckle		pickle tickle	Exc:cycle			buckle chuckle knuckle	
d	paddle saddle straddle	cradle ladle	meddle	needle	fiddle middle riddle twiddle	bridle	coddle [1]swaddle [1]waddle		cuddle puddle	doodle noodle poodle
f	baffle					rifle stifle trifle			muffle shuffle	
g	straggle			eagle beagle	giggle jiggle		boggle goggle		smuggle struggle	bugle
p	apple ample	maple staple		steeple Exc:people	cripple ripple Exc:triple		topple		supple	scruple
t	battle cattle rattle		kettle nettle settle	beetle	brittle little	title	bottle throttle [1]wattle		shuttle subtle	
z	dazzle			**Exception** measles	drizzle fizzle		nozzle		nuzzle puzzle	
Blends	ample sample trample example		tremble assemble temple		nimble thimble dimple simple				bumble crumble grumble humble stumble tumble crumple rumple	
Blends	candle handle angle dangle strangle triangle ankle mantle		gentle		dwindle spindle swindle jingle shingle single tingle crinkle sprinkle wrinkle				uncle bundle bungle jungle	
r					girdle		marble startle	[1]warble	curdle hurdle hurtle turtle	
st	castle **Exception** hassle		nestle wrestle		bristle gristle thistle whistle Exc:missile		jostle apostle		bustle hustle rustle **Exception** muscle	

[1]'wa' = /wå/ and 'war'

Unit 4

Ends of Words

Chart 36

A Study of Silent 'e' with 'g' and 'v'

(v̆)g= /g/
bag
brag
drag
flag
gag
hag
lag
nag
rag
sag
shag
snag
beg
keg
leg
peg
big
dig
fig
gig
jig
pig
sprig
swig
twig
wig
bog
clog
cog
dog
flog
fog
frog
hog
jog
log
bug
chug
dug
drug
hug
jug
lug
mug
plug
pug
rug
shrug
slug
smug
snug
thug
tug
Exception
egg

(v̆)ge=/j/	(v̆)nge=/nj/	(v̆)dge=/j/	(v)rge=/rj/
age	binge	badge (bag)	large
cage	cringe	edge (egg)	merge
page	fringe	dredge	serge
rage (rag)	hinge	fledge	verge
sage (sag)	singe (sing)	hedge	forge
stage (stag)	(sting)	ledge (leg)	gorge
wage (wag)	tinge	pledge	purge
huge (hug)	twinge	sledge	surge
stooge	lunge (lung)	wedge	splurge
gouge	plunge	bridge (brig)	
	Exception	midge	
Exception	sponge	ridge (rig)	
gauge (gag)	orange	dodge (dog)	
liege		lodge (log)	
siege	**ānge**	budge (bug)	
	change	drudge (drug)	
	mange	fudge	
	range (rang)	grudge	
	strange	judge (jug)	
		nudge	
		sludge (slug)	
		smudge (smug)	
		trudge	
		Exception	
		bulge	

ove=/ŭv/	ove=/üv/	ove=/ōv/	lve
above	move	cove	valve
dove	prove	clove	twelve
glove	groove	dove	solve
love		drove	(Silent 'l')
shove	**(v̄)ve**	grove	calves (calf)
Exception	brave	stove	halves (half)
*of	cave	strove	salve
	crave	wove	
	knave		
	save		
(v̆)ve	slave	**/ē/ve**	**rve**
have	wave	cleave	carve
live	chive	grieve	scarves (scarf)
sieve	dive	heave	starve
	drive	leaves (leaf)	nerve
	five	leave	serve
	hive	peeve	swerve
	live	sleeve	curve
	lives (life)		
	knives (knife)		
	strive		
	thrive		
	wives (wife)		

A Study of Silent 'e' in Multi-Syllable Words with 'g', 'k', and 'v'

g

gue=/g/
(final position)
catalogue
colleague
demagogue
dialogue
epilogue
fatigue
intrigue
league (liege)
monologue
plague
prologue
rogue
synagogue
travelogue
vague
vogue

/ng/
harangue
meringue
tongue

g=/zh/
Complete List
arbitrage
barrage
bourgeois
beige
camouflage
collage
entourage
fuselage
garage
gavage
lavage
lingerie
massage
menagerie
mirage
negligee
prestige
regime
rouge
sabotage

ge = /j/
acreage
adage
advantage
average
baggage
bandage
bondage
carriage
cartilage
cottage
courage
damage
disadvantage
drainage
engage
enrage
exaggerate
exchange
foliage
garbage
language
manage
marriage
message
mileage
orphanage
outrage
package
plumage
postage
rummage
sausage
usage

arrange
challenge
orange
barge
bulge

Exception
allege
besiege
college
privilege
sacrilege

dg = /j/
abridge
cartridge
dislodge
judgment
knowledge
partridge
porridge

vowels and 'r'

/ā/
behave
engrave

/ē/
achieve
aggrieve
believe
bereave
conceive
deceive
disbelieve
interweave
perceive
receive
relieve
reprieve
retrieve

/ī/
alive
arrive
connive
contrive
deprive
derive
revive
survive

/oov/
approve
behoove
disapprove
disprove
improve
remove
reprove

/r/
conserve
deserve
observe
preserve
reserve
unnerve

/ĭ/
active
adaptive
adhesive
adjective
aggressive
assertive
attentive
collective
conclusive
conductive
connective
conservative
constructive
creative
decorative
descriptive
digestive
distinctive
exclusive
expensive
extensive
informative
imaginative
instinctive
intensive
locomotive
motive
offensive
preventive
reactive
respective
sensitive
suggestive

Exception
octave

c/k

ic = /ik/
academic
arithmetic
artistic
athletic
atomic
attic
autographic
automatic
barbaric
biographic
caloric
classic
cleric
colic
comic
cosmetic
critic
drastic
egotistic
elastic
electric
erratic
frantic
frolic
gigantic
graphic
gymnastic
garlic
hectic
humanistic
individualistic
lunatic
magic
mechanic
metallic
mimic
mosaic
music
nomadic
panic
pathetic
phonetic
photographic
picnic
plastic
romantic
sarcastic
scenic
scientific
skeptic
specific
static
statistic
traffic
tragic

ac = /ăk/
cardiac
maniac
shellac

ck
attack
peacock
ransack
unlock
wedlock

k = /k/
awoke
dislike
handiwork
keepsake
mistake
provoke
rebuke
tiddlywink

-que = /k/
(Entire List)
antique
baroque
boutique
brusque
cheque
clique
critique
discotheque
grotesque
masque
mosque
mystique
oblique
opaque
picturesque
pique
physique
plaque
statuesque
technique
torque
unique

Compound Words
candlestick
deadlock
fiddlestick
haystack
henpeck
hunchback
potluck
yardstick
cornflake
daybreak
earthquake
landmark
outbreak
overlook
pocketbook
snowbank
turnpike

A Further Study of Digraphs at Ends of Words

tch = /ch/	ch = /ch/			ch = /k/	the = /th/	ph = /f/
batch	blanch	breech	***Compound Words***	matriarch	bathe (bath)	graph
catch	branch	preach	*backstretch*	monarch	blithe	autograph
hatch	ranch	speech	*homestretch*	patriarch	breathe (breath)	epitaph
latch	bench	broach	*inasmuch*	oligarch	clothe (cloth)	phonograph
match	clench	coach	*nonesuch*	Pentateuch	lathe	telegraph
patch	drench	poach	*overreach*	ache	lithe	**gh = /f/**
watch	quench	roach	*crosshatch*	epoch	loathe	enough
fetch	stench	pooch	*outreach*	stomach	scathe	rough
etch	trench	smooch	*overmatch*		scythe	tough
retch	cinch	couch	*stagecoach*		seethe	slough
wretch	clinch	crouch	*blowtorch*		sheathe (sheath)	cough
ditch	finch	grouch	*cornstarch*		soothe (sooth)	trough
hitch	flinch	ouch	*goldfinch*		spathe	laugh
itch	inch	pouch	*hopscotch*		sunbathe (sunbath)	
pitch	pinch	slouch	*keypunch*		swathe	
witch	winch	vouch	*outstretch*		teethe (teath)	
notch	conch	cockroach	*topnotch*		tithe	
hutch	bunch	approach	*workbench*		wreathe (wreath)	
bewitch	brunch	avouch	*stopwatch*		writhe	
dispatch	crunch	encroach				
mismatch	hunch	reproach				
unhitch	lunch	retouch				
Exception	munch	impeach				
niche	punch	unclench				
rich	scrunch	besmirch				
spinach	beach	research				
touch	bleach					
much	breach					
such						

Chart 39

A Further Study of Digraphs at Ends of Words. This chart concludes our extended study of 'cliffs(z)'. It focuses on 'ph', 'gh', 'th', 'ch' and 'tch' at ends of words.

The main digraph that changes its spelling at ends of words is 'ch'. Following a short vowel, it is '-tch'. Elsehwere it is 'ch'. The 't' is needed to make the vowel short.

The digraph 'th' says /th/, "bath", at ends of words, unless silent 'e' is with it. Then it is voiced, **/th/**, "ba**the**".

The root, "graph", catches almost all of the multi-syllable words ending with '-ph' = /f/. The '-gh' says /f/ in only these few words, which can be memorized.

UNIT 5

FOCUS ON:
SUFFIXES AND ENDINGS

Unit Five is about syllables and adding suffixes. It will show how and when to double a consonant or drop a silent 'e'. There is also further discussion about the spellings for long 'e' in multi-syllable words.

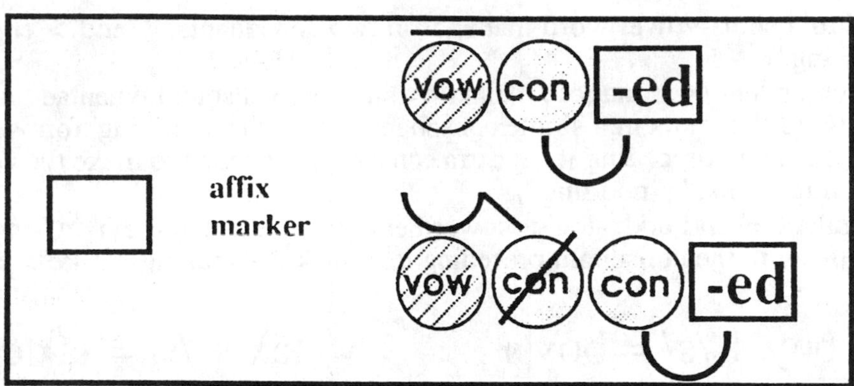
affix
marker
vow
con
-ed
vow
con
con
-ed

Unit 5
Suffixes

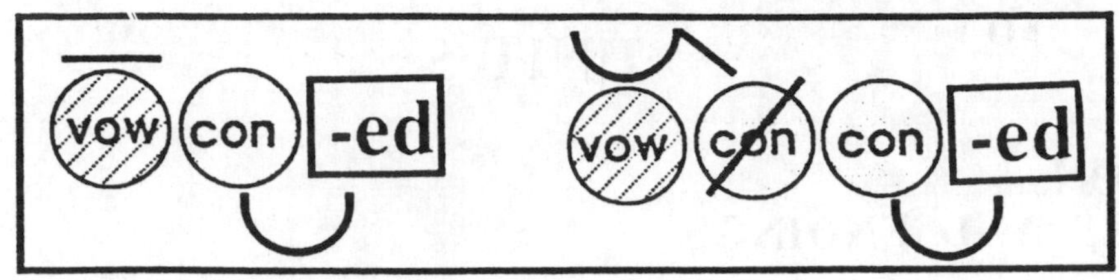

vow
con
-ed
vow
con
con
-ed

bĕd + /ĭng/ = bĕdd ing   ĕnd + /ĭng/ = ĕnd ing

Chart 40: Adding '-ing'

① Add '-ing' to a short-vowel word that ends in two consonants. ("end">"ending", "back">"backing")
② Add a second silent consonant to maintain a short-vowel sound when adding '-ing' to a short-vowel word that ends in a single consonant. Since the 'i' in '-ing' forms a 'long-vowel-tie' with the consonant preceding it, an extra consonant is needed to make the vowel short. ("bed">"bedding", "nod">"nodding")
③ Drop the silent 'e' and add '-ing' to a word ending in 'e' since the 'i' in '-ing' forms a 'long-vowel-tie' with the consonant preceding it. ("make">"making", "like">"liking")

boy + /s/ = boy s   tăx + /s/ = tăx es

Chart 41: Adding '-s' or '-es'. (These guidelines apply whether pluralizing or changing a verb tense.)

① Add '-es' following all letters whose sounds are somehow related to 's'. ['s', 'sh', 'ch', 'x' ('x'=/ks/), and 'z'] ("bus">"buses", "tax">"taxes")
② Add '-s' to every other word. ("sleep">"sleeps") The 'e' is retained with words ending in 'e'. ("fade">"fades")
③ Change 'y' to 'i' and add '-es' when the 'y' is preceded by a consonant. ("try">"tries", "baby">"babies") The 'y' is retained as 'y' when in a vowel team. ("monkey">"monkeys", "boy">"boys")
④ Add '-s' to words ending in 'ff'. ("puff">"puffs") If the word ends in a single 'f' or 'fe', it often changes to 'ves'. ("half">"halves", "leaf">"leaves", "wife">"wives")

păd + /ĕd/ = pădd ed   fāde + /ĕd/ = fād ed

Chart 42: Adding '-ed'

① The '-ed' ending has three distinctive and predictable sounds: /ĕd/, /t/, and /d/:

'-ed' = /t/	with words that end in 'c', 's', 'ch', 'sh', 'f', 'p', and 'x'
'-ed'= /ĕd/	with words that end in 't' or 'd'
'-ed'= /d/	with words ending in any other letter

② Add '-ed' to a short-vowel word that ends in two consonants. ("end">"ended", "back">"backed")
③ Add a second silent consonant to maintain a short-vowel sound when adding '-ed' to a short-vowel word that ends in a single consonant. Since the 'e' in '-ed' forms a 'long-vowel-tie' with the consonant preceding it, an extra consonant is needed to make the vowel short. ("pad">"padded", "nod">"nodded")
④ Drop the silent 'e' and add '-ed' to a word ending in 'e' since the 'e' in '-ed' forms a 'long-vowel-tie' with the consonant preceding it. ("bake">"baked", "like">"liked")
⑤ Change 'y' to 'i' before adding '-ed' when 'y' is preceded by a consonant ("try" >"tried", "baby" > "babied") The 'y' is retained when in a vowel team ("play" > "played").

To Double or not to Double—Adding '-ing'

short vowels

Blends/Digraphs

Blends	landing	acting
	sanding	rafting
	ending	lifting
	mending	sifting
	bonding	crafting
	funding	drafting
	handing	grafting
	branding	drifting
	welding	shifting
	banging	hunting
	longing	punting
	wronging	jilting
	camping	quilting
	limping	tilting
	romping	wilting
	bumping	chatting
	dumping	tempting
	jumping	prompting
	gasping	planting
	helping	squinting
	gulping	fasting
	slumping	lasting
	thumping	besting
	clasping	nesting
	grasping	resting
	cashing	testing
	mashing	cresting
	dishing	twisting
	fishing	listing
	wishing	frosting
	hushing	busting
	rushing	dusting
	crashing	rusting
	flashing	trusting
	smashing	thrusting
	splashing	matching
	thrashing	patching
	blushing	pitching
	brushing	bunching
	crushing	branching
		clenching
		blotching
		snatching
		scratching

'Cliffs(z)'

s	passing	stressing	bossing
	blessing	hissing	flossing
	messing	kissing	tossing
	pressing	missing	fussing
k	backing	sucking	banking
	packing	tucking	linking
	sacking	blocking	conking
	decking	clicking	honking
	pecking	flicking	asking
	kicking	plucking	masking
	licking	pricking	milking
	picking	tricking	sulking
	cocking	slicking	blanking
	docking	smacking	cranking
	locking	smocking	spanking
	rocking	snacking	thanking
f	staffing	bluffing	puffing
	sniffing	buffing	scuffing
	scoffing	huffing	stuffing
l	shelling	drilling	tilling
	smelling	filling	trilling
	spelling	grilling	willing
	swelling	killing	hulling
	telling	spilling	mulling
	yelling	stilling	
	chilling	thrilling	
z	razzing	frizzing	quizzing
	fizzing	buzzing	
x[1]	taxing	flexing	mixing
	waxing	fixing	boxing

Double Consonant

b	blabbing	scabbing	mobbing
	grabbing	stabbing	sobbing
	jabbing	fibbing	scrubbing
	nabbing	ribbing	rubbing
d	padding	kidding	prodding
	bedding	skidding	budding
	shredding	nodding	thudding
g	bragging	tagging	bugging
	dragging	wagging	hugging
	flagging	pegging	mugging
	lagging	bogging	plugging
	nagging	flogging	
	sagging	hogging	
	snagging	jogging	
m	clamming	dimming	drumming
	cramming	slimming	humming
	slamming	trimming	
n	fanning	tanning	skinning
	planning	penning	stunning
	scanning	grinning	shunning
	spanning	sinning	
p	clapping	gripping	dropping
	napping	skipping	flopping
	snapping	slipping	hopping
	trapping	ripping	mopping
	stepping	zipping	popping
	clipping	cropping	stopping
t	patting	pitting	jotting
	fretting	blotting	slotting
	petting	clotting	spotting
	fitting	dotting	rotting

long vowels with silent 'e'.

d	fading	hiding
	shading	priding
	chiding	siding
	gliding	coding
t	hating	
	quoting	
	noting	
	toting	
	voting	

k	baking	hiking	yoking
	faking	biking	smoking
	raking	joking	
	liking	poking	
f			
p	draping	piping	coping
	scraping	striping	groping
	shaping	swiping	hoping
	taping	wiping	moping
	griping		sloping

b	cubing	probing	
m	blaming	shaming	priming
	laming	taming	timing
	naming	chiming	fuming
n	dining	stoning	tuning
	mining	throning	
	whining	pruning	
v	braving	raving	slaving
	caving	saving	waving
	craving	shaving	thriving

[1] 'X'= /ks/=2 consonant sounds, and is never doubled.

Chart 40

To Double or not to Double—Adding '-s' or '-es'.

short vowels

-s

d	pads	lands
	beds	sands
	shreds	ends
	kids	mends
	skids	bonds
	nods	funds
	prods	hands
	buds	brands
	thuds	welds
t	pats	quilts
	frets	tilts
	pets	wilts
	fits	chats
	pits	tempts
	dots	prompts
	jots	plants
	rots	squints
	blots	fasts
	clots	lasts
	slots	bests
	spots	nests
	acts	rests
	rafts	tests
	gifts	crests
	lifts	twists
	crafts	lists
	drafts	frosts
	grafts	busts
	drifts	dusts
	shifts	rusts
	hunts	trusts
	punts	thrusts
	jilts	

-es

s	passes	flosses	rushes
	bosses	presses	crashes
	tosses	stresses	flashes
	hisses	cashes	smashes
	kisses	mashes	splashes
	misses	dishes	thrashes
	messes	fishes	blushes
	fusses	wishes	brushes
	blesses	hushes	crushes
ch	branches	scratches	pitches
	matches	snatches	blotches
	patches	clenches	bunches
x[1]	taxes	flexes	mixes
	waxes	fixes	boxes
z	razzes	frizzes	quizzes
	fizzes	buzzes	

k	backs	pricks	banks
	packs	slicks	links
	sacks	tricks	conks
	smacks	blocks	honks
	snacks	cocks	asks
	decks	docks	masks
	pecks	locks	milks
	clicks	rocks	sulks
	flicks	smocks	blanks
	kicks	plucks	cranks
	licks	sucks	spanks
	picks	tucks	thanks
f	staffs	bluffs	scuffs
	sniffs	huffs	stuffs
	scoffs	puffs	
p	naps	drops	bumps
	rips	grips	dumps
	zips	traps	jumps
	hops	skips	gasps
	mops	slips	helps
	pops	snaps	gulps
	cups	steps	slumps
	claps	stops	thumps
	clips	camps	clasps
	flops	limps	grasps
	crops	romps	shops

-s

b	blabs	scabs	mobs
	grabs	stabs	sobs
	jabs	fibs	rubs
	nabs	ribs	scrubs
g	brags	tags	bugs
	drags	wags	hugs
	flags	pegs	mugs
	lags	bogs	plugs
	nags	flogs	bangs
	sags	hogs	longs
	snags	jogs	wrongs
l	stalls	drills	tills
	shells	fills	trills
	smells	grills	thrills
	spells	kills	wills
	swells	skills	hulls
	yells	spills	mulls
	chills	stills	
m	clams	dims	drums
	crams	slims	hums
	slams	trims	
n	fans	tans	skins
	plans	pens	stuns
	scans	grins	shuns
	spans	sins	

long vowels with silent 'e'.

d	fades	hides
	shades	prides
	chides	sides
	glides	codes
t	hates	
	quotes	
	notes	
	totes	
	votes	

k	bakes	hikes	smokes
	fakes	likes	yokes
	rakes	jokes	
	bikes	pokes	
f			
p	drapes	pipes	gropes
	scrapes	swipes	hopes
	shapes	stripes	mopes
	tapes	wipes	slopes
	gripes	copes	

b	cubes	probes	
m	blames	shames	primes
	lames	tames	times
	names	chimes	fumes
n	dines	whines	tunes
	mines	stones	
	shines	prunes	
v	braves	raves	slaves
	caves	saves	waves
	craves	shaves	thrives

[1] 'X'= /ks/=2 consonant sounds, and is never doubled.

Chart 41

To Double or not to Double—Adding '-ed'

short vowels

-ed=/ĕd/		
d	padded	landed
	bedded	sanded
	shredded	ended
	kidded	mended
	skidded	bonded
	nodded	funded
	prodded	handed
	budded	branded
	thudded	welded
t	patted	quilted
	fretted	tilted
	petted	wilted
	fitted	chatted
	pitted	tempted
	blotted	prompted
	clotted	planted
	dotted	squinted
	jotted	fasted
	rotted	lasted
	slotted	bested
	spotted	nested
	acted	rested
	rafted	tested
	gifted	crested
	lifted	twisted
	crafted	listed
	drafted	frosted
	grafted	busted
	drifted	dusted
	shifted	rusted
	hunted	trusted
	punted	thrusted
	jilted	

-ed=/t/			
s	passed	flossed	thrashed
	blessed	tossed	dished
	messed	fussed	fished
	pressed	cashed	wished
	stressed	crashed	blushed
	hissed	flashed	brushed
	kissed	mashed	crushed
	missed	smashed	hushed
	bossed	splashed	rushed
ch	branched	scratched	pitched
	matched	snatched	blotched
	patched	clenched	bunched
x[1]	taxed	flexed	mixed
	waxed	fixed	boxed
k	backed	sucked	banked
	packed	tucked	linked
	sacked	blocked	conked
	decked	clicked	honked
	pecked	flicked	asked
	kicked	plucked	masked
	licked	pricked	milked
	picked	tricked	sulked
	cocked	slicked	blanked
	docked	smacked	cranked
	locked	smocked	spanked
	rocked	snacked	thanked
f	staffed	bluffed	scuffed
	sniffed	huffed	stuffed
	scoffed	puffed	
p	napped	dropped	bumped
	ripped	gripped	dumped
	zipped	trapped	jumped
	hopped	skipped	gasped
	mopped	slipped	helped
	popped	snapped	gulped
	cupped	stepped	slumped
	clapped	stopped	thumped
	clipped	camped	clasped
	flopped	limped	grasped
	cropped	romped	shopped

-ed=/d/			
b	blabbed	scabbed	mobbed
	grabbed	stabbed	sobbed
	jabbed	fibbed	rubbed
	nabbed	ribbed	scrubbed
g	bragged	tagged	plugged
	dragged	wagged	bugged
	flagged	pegged	hugged
	lagged	bogged	mugged
	nagged	flogged	banged
	sagged	hogged	longed
	snagged	jogged	wronged
l	shelled	filled	tilled
	smelled	grilled	trilled
	spelled	killed	willed
	swelled	skilled	hulled
	yelled	spilled	mulled
	chilled	stilled	
	drilled	thrilled	
m	crammed	dimmed	drummed
	clammed	slimmed	hummed
	slammed	trimmed	
n	fanned	tanned	skinned
	planned	penned	shunned
	scanned	grinned	stunned
	spanned	sinned	
z	razzed	frizzed	quizzed
	fizzed	buzzed	

long vowels with silent 'e'.

-ed=/ĕd/		
d	faded	prided
	shaded	sided
	chided	coded
	glided	
t	hated	
	noted	
	quoted	
	toted	
	voted	

-ed=/t/			
k	baked	hiked	smoked
	faked	liked	yoked
	raked	joked	
	biked	poked	
f			
p	draped	piped	moped
	scraped	wiped	sloped
	shaped	coped	swiped
	taped	groped	striped
	griped	hoped	

-ed=/d/			
b	cubed	probed	
m	blamed	tamed	primed
	lamed	shamed	timed
	named	chimed	fumed
n	dined	whined	tuned
	mined	stoned	
	shined	pruned	
v	braved	raved	slaved
	caved	saved	waved
	craved	shaved	thrived

[1] 'X'= /ks/=2 consonant sounds, and is never doubled.

Chart 42

Chart 43, 44, 45
Studies with '-y' and '-er'. When adding a '-y' or '-er' to a word, we follow the basic pattern of when to double and when not to. There are several other things to note. The rule, "It takes two vowels to make a long 'e'" shows up clearly in this study. All single syllable words with a long 'e' that end in 'y' have two vowels to make the /ē/, "greedy". They must be memorized, but many are independent words that have been covered in previous charts. There are a few 'ea' words with the short 'e' sound, "ready".

The 'ai', /ā/, "rainy" occurs as expected before 'l' and 'n'.

The 'oa' words, /ō/, "loader", come from independent one-syllable words that have been previously studied.

Chart 46
Multi-Syllable Words with /ŭr/ ('-ar' and '-ure). This chart deals with '-ar' and '-ure' at the ends of words saying the /ŭr/ sound. Almost all the '-ture' words say /chŭr/, "venture", and the '-sure' words say /shŭr/, "insure" or /zhŭr/, "exposure". The '-ar' words must be memorized.

Chart 47
Multi-Syllable Words with /ŭr/ ('or'). This is a complete list of final '-or' words saying /ŭr/, "doctor". The largest percentage of these words refer to people. Of these, most end with '-tor'. Numerous other '-or' words also end in '-tor'. However, hearing /tŭr/ at the end of a word does not insure that it will be spelled '-tor'. There are many words that end in '-ter'. Only samples of these were included on Chart 45. So, the '-or' words must still be memorized.

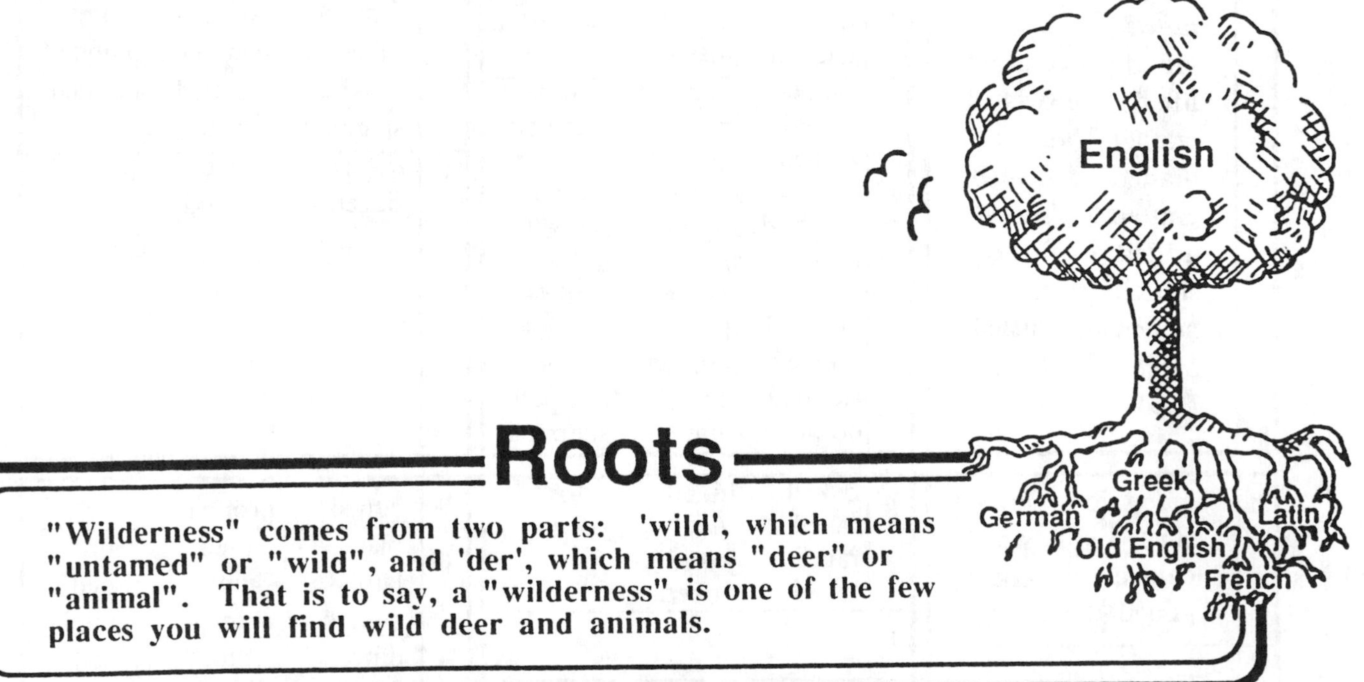
English
Roots
Greek
German
Latin
Old English
French
"Wilderness" comes from two parts: 'wild', which means "untamed" or "wild", and 'der', which means "deer" or "animal". That is to say, a "wilderness" is one of the few places you will find wild deer and animals.

To Double or not to Double—Adding 'y'[1]

	ă	ā	ĕ	ē[2]	ĭ	ī	ŏ	ō	ŭ	ū
b	crabby flabby shabby	baby					hobby lobby snobby		chubby grubby stubby	ruby
k	tacky wacky	flaky		freaky streaky	sticky tricky		cocky rocky stocky	poky smoky	lucky mucky yucky	
d	caddy daddy paddy	lady shady	ready steady already	greedy needy speedy weedy		tidy	shoddy **Exc.** *body		muddy **Exc.** *study	broody moody
f	daffy taffy			beefy leafy					fluffy huffy puffy	
g	baggy craggy shaggy		leggy		piggy		doggy groggy soggy		buggy muggy	
l	rally	daily **Exc.** scaly	belly jelly smelly		hilly silly **Exc:**lily				bully /o͝o/ dully /o͝o/ fully /o͝o/	
m	clammy	gamy			shimmy	grimy slimy	mommy		dummy tummy yummy	gloomy roomy
n	granny nanny	brainy grainy rainy	penny **Exc.** *many		skinny tinny	shiny spiny tiny		bony phony pony stony	bunny funny sunny	
p	happy sappy scrappy snappy			creepy sleepy weepy	drippy snippy zippy		floppy poppy sloppy **Exc:**copy		puppy	**Exc.** beauty fruity soupy
s/z	brassy classy glassy grassy	crazy hazy lazy **Exc:**daisy	dressy messy	cheesy greasy	dizzy frizzy tizzy **Exc:**busy		bossy mossy glossy **Exc:**saucy	posy rosy cozy	fussy fuzzy	
t		**Exc.** eighty	petty sweaty	meaty treaty	ditty **Exc:**city **Exc:**pretty			throaty	nutty putty	duty
v		gravy navy wavy	heavy			ivy				
blends	scratchy crafty drafty scanty chancy fancy candy dandy handy sandy pantry flashy splashy trashy		sketchy stretchy lefty plenty twenty testy	peachy	fifty nifty shifty thrifty minty dinky inky fishy wishy flimsy scrimpy skimpy crispy misty		blotchy splotchy lofty softy		chunky spunky gushy mushy dusty rusty **Exc.** country	

[1]Use 'ai' before 'l' and 'n', unless it is a homonym. [2]It takes two vowels to make a long 'e'.

Chart 43

To Double or not to Double—Adding 'er'

	① ă	ā	② ĕ	(Takes 2 vowels) ē	③ ĭ	ī	④ ŏ/å	ō	⑤ ŭ	ū
b	grabber nabber				fibber	briber fiber	clobber robber sobber slobber [1]swabber	prober sober	blubber rubber scrubber	
ck k	sacker snacker stacker	baker maker raker taker	checker wrecker	beaker weaker sneaker meeker seeker	bicker flicker quicker sicker	biker hiker	knocker locker mocker rocker shocker	broker choker joker poker stroker	pucker sucker tucker trucker	
d	bladder gladder ladder madder sadder	grader trader raider	redder	leader pleader reader feeder speeder	bidder kidder	cider glider hider rider spider wider	nodder plodder	loader	rudder shudder	cruder ruder
f	staffer	safer wafer			sniffer	lifer **Exception** cipher	offer scoffer	loafer **Exception** gopher	bluffer puffer suffer	roofer woofer
g	bagger bragger	pager wager		eager meager	bigger chigger trigger	geiger tiger	hogger jogger logger		bugger hugger plugger	
m	hammer slammer stammer	namer		creamer dreamer steamer streamer redeemer	dimmer glimmer shimmer swimmer trimmer	timer primer **Exception** climber		roamer homer	drummer hummer summer **Exception** plumber	boomer
n	banner planner scanner tanner	drainer strainer trainer		greener cleaner gleaner meaner	dinner inner sinner	diner finer liner miner shiner		loner toner groaner loaner moaner	gunner runner	pruner sooner schooner tuner
p	flapper trapper wrapper	caper paper scraper taper		cheaper creeper deeper reaper sleeper steeper sweeper	clipper dipper gripper ripper slipper stripper zipper	griper riper striper wiper viper **Exception** diaper	chopper copper hopper shopper topper **Exception** proper	moper roper	upper supper	grouper super trooper
/s/	passer	chaser pacer racer	dresser guesser lesser			dicer nicer pricer slicer	crosser tosser	closer		juicer looser (adj.)
t	batter chatter flatter hatter matter scatter shatter splatter	crater later hater skater waiter	better letter setter wetter **Exception** sweater	beater cheater eater heater greeter sweeter	bitter glitter jitter litter twitter splinter	brighter fighter lighter tighter writer	blotter hotter otter potter [1]squatter [1]swatter **Exception** [1]water		butter cutter gutter sputter	cuter looter

[1]'wa' and 'ua' = /wå/.

Chart 44

Continuing with '-er' (Following a blend, digraph, or vowel)

	a	e	i	o—/å/	u
f_	after drafter rafter		drifter lifter shifter sifter		
m_	amber camper hamper scamper	ember member remember tempter	limper simper whimper		bumper jumper stumper number slumber cucumber encumber
n_	cancer dancer prancer sander commander grander hanger banker tanker planter danger manger ranger stranger **Exception** anger	blender fender lender sender slender spender tender defender pretender center enter renter	blinker sinker stinker thinker finger singer stinger winter binder finder kinder reminder **Exception** cinder	blonder fonder squander wander longer stronger bounder founder rounder sounder encounter	blunder thunder under wonder bunker hunger drunker hunter punter
s_	blaster faster master plaster disaster		minister spinster whisker		luster bluster
th	gather rather lather	feather heather leather weather whether together		father	brother mother other smother smoother
r_	charmer farmer sharper barter carter charter starter		drier flier fryer shyer spryer	order border recorder forger former warmer scorner	murder herder curer purer curler twirler burner earner learner hurter server observer
Vowel	layer prayer	freer seer		blower lower slower flower power tower	fewer newer sewer bluer truer

More About /ŭr/

ar = /ŭr/

cellar
caterpillar
pillar
similar
collar
dollar
molar
polar
solar
circular
globular
modular
regular
singular
calendar
beggar
sugar
vinegar
briar
liar
peculiar
grammar
lunar

'-ar'=/år/

cigar
guitar
registrar
seminar

Exception

bazaar
bizarre
jaguar

Exception

Group 1
ignore
either
proper
answer
water

Group 2
choir
dinosaur
engineer
glamour
martyr
femur
lemur

ture = /chŭr/

adventure
agriculture
armature
capture
caricature
creature
culture
curvature
denture
departure
feature
fixture
forfeiture
fracture
furniture
future
gesture
horticulture
immature
indenture
juncture
lecture
legislature
literature
manufacture
mature
miniature
mixture
moisture
nature
nurture
overture
pasture
picture
posture
puncture
rapture
rupture
sculpture
signature
stature
stricture
structure
temperature
texture
tincture
torture
venture
vulture

Exception

amateur

'-cher' = /chŭr/

catcher
matcher
scratcher
snatcher
dispatcher
etcher
stretcher
bleacher
preacher
teacher
scorcher
snitcher
richer
clincher
watcher

ur = /ŭr/

your
you're
allure
endure
manure
demure
impure
voyageur
obscure
procure
secure
manicure
occur
concur
incur

sure=/zhŭr/

closure
composure
disclosure
displeasure
enclosure
exposure
foreclosure
leisure
measure
pleasure
treasure

Exception

seizure

sure=/shŭr/

assure
censure
ensure
erasure
fissure
insure
pressure

Exception

brochure

Chart 46

Complete List of Final '-or' = /ŭr/ Words

"People":

abductor
actor
administrator
advocator
ancestor
animator
auditor
aviator
benefactor
captivator
captor
chiropractor
collector
commentator
communicator
competitor
conservator
conspirator
contaminator
contractor
contradictor
contributor
coordinator
creator
creditor
cultivator
debtor
decorator
defector
demonstrator
depositor
designator
detector
dictator
director
discriminator
dissipator
distributor
doctor
editor
educator
elector
eliminator
emancipator
eradicator
exaggerator

'-tor'

excavator
executor
exhibitor
exterminator
fabricator
fumigator
hibernator
illustrator
impersonator
impostor
infiltrator
inheritor
inquisitor
inspector
instructor
inventor
investigator
janitor
mediator
mentor
monitor
narrator
navigator
objector
operator
orator
pastor
predator
proprietor
prosecutor
prospector
protector
realtor
regulator
sculptor
selector
senator
solicitor
spectator
tenor
tormentor
traitor
tutor
vendor
victor
visitor

'-or'

advisor
aggressor
ambassador
author
bachelor
censor
chancellor
confessor
conqueror
conquistador
counselor
donor
emperor
governor
intercessor
juror
major
mayor
minor
neighbor
oppressor
predecessor
professor
sailor
sponsor
successor
supervisor
survivor
tailor
transgressor

Other '-or' Words

-tor

accelerator
alligator
alternator
calibrator
calculator
carburetor
constrictor
deflector
detector
detonator
duplicator
elevator
erector
escalator
evaporator
factor
incubator
percolator
perforator
projector
radiator
reflector
refrigerator
respirator
sector
tractor
vector

Other

anchor
arbor
ardor
armor
camphor
candor
castor
clamor
color
corridor
cursor
demeanor
enamor
endeavor
equator
error
favor
fervor
flavor
flexor
furor
glamor
harbor
honor
horror
humor
incisor
labor
liquor
manor
metaphor
meteor
mirror
odor
parlor
phosphor
razor
rigor
rumor
savor
scissors
splendor
stupor
terror
tremor
tumor
valor
vapor
vigor
visor

-ior=/yŭr/

anterior
behavior
exterior
inferior
interior
junior
posterior
prior
savior
senior
superior
warrior

Charts 48 and 49: Words with /shŭn/ and /zhŭn/. The words included in the charts on this page and the next are often a source of confusion. These words are spelled with '-tion', '-sion', '-ssion', and '-cian', all of which can say the /shŭn/ sound. This check list will help to determine which spelling to use.

① 1. Use '-**cian**' for a person or profession. (A musi**cian**, physi**cian**, or beauti**cian** can say, "See, I'm human." [**C I**'m hum**AN**])

② 2. If it says /zhŭn/, always use '-**sion**'. (There's no revi**sion** if your deci**sion** is '-**sion**'.

⑧ ⑥ 3. Use '-**sion**' following 'l' and sometimes 'n'. (ten**sion**, compul**sion**)

③ ④ 4. Use '-**ssion**' following a short 'e' or a short 'u', and always with the base word '**mission**'. (You have pers**mission** to use double 's' with '-**mission**'.

⑥ ⑦ ⑧ 5. Use '-**tion**' everywhere else. (There is a nation of words with '-**tion**'.)

If a further question remains, try adding the suffix '-ive' to the base word. The '-si' or '-ti' becomes clearly distinguishable by doing this. (/nā · shŭn/ >native>nation, /pĕn · shŭn/ >pensive>pension) For a summary, see the 'Eagle's Wings /shŭn/ Check List' (☛ page 217).

Exceptions to learn:
fashion, cushion, luncheon, ocean, suspicion, equation, coercion, complexion, crucifixion.

Multi-Syllable Words with '-cian' and '-sion'

① '-cian'=/shŭn/
(human) Entire List
academician
arithmetician
beautician
cosmetician
clinician
electrician
geometrician
logician
magician
mathematician
physician
metaphysician
mortician
musician
obstetrician
optician
patrician
pediatrician
phonetician
politician
physician
rhetorician
statistician
tactician
theoretician

② Entire List of '-sion'=/zhŭn/	
abrasion (abrasive)	incision (incisive)
adhesion (adhesive)	inclusion (inclusive)
allusion (allusive)	indecision (indecisive)
aspersion	infusion
aversion	interspersion
cohesion (cohesive)	introversion (introversive)
collision	intrusion (intrusive)
conclusion (conclusive)	invasion (invasive)
confusion	inversion (inversive)
contusion	lesion
conversion	obtrusion (obtrusive)
corrosion (corrosive)	occasion
decision (decisive)	occlusion (occlusive)
delusion	persuasion (persuasive)
derision (derisive)	pervasion (pervasive)
diffusion	perversion (perversive)
disillusion	precision
dissuasion (dissuasive)	preclusion (preclusive)
diversion	pretension
division (divisive)	profusion
effusion (effusive)	protrusion (protrusive)
elusion (elusive)	provision
envision	reclusion (reclusive)
erosion (erosive)	reversion
evasion (evasive)	revision
excision	seclusion (seclusive)
exclusion (exclusive)	subdivision
excursion	submersion
explosion (explosive)	subversion (subversive)
extroversion (extroversive)	supervision
extrusion (extrusive)	television
fusion	transfusion
illusion (illusive)	version
immersion	vision
implosion (implosive)	**Exception:** Caucasian, equation, coercion, Asian

 Computer checked.

Chart 50: Words with /-'n/

There are many words ending with /n/ in which the vowel before it may be difficult to hear. The '-ian' and words are people. The words with '-en', which is often a suffix, are verbs and adjectives. The endings '-in '-on' are mostly nouns. The /yŭn/, "union", sound is spelled '-ion'. The limited number of '-ain' and '-un' w are all shown here.

Select List of Words with /shŭn/ and '-ive' Endings

⑦ -tion/-tive Following a Long Vowel

admiration
appreciation (appreciative)
carnation
combination
complication
congratulation
conservation (conservative)
conversation
cooperation (cooperative)
decoration
demonstration (demonstrative)
dictation
donation
duplication
education (educative)
elevation
estimation
evaporation (evaporative)
examination
exploration (explorative)
fascination
frustration
generation
graduation
hibernation
humiliation
identification
information (informative)
inspiration
investigation (investigative)
medication
multiplication
nation (native)
navigation
observation
population
plantation
publication
recreation (recreative)
refrigeration
relaxation
reservation
sensation
simulation
station
stimulation
temptation
transformation
transportation
ventilation
completion
depletion
secretion
lotion
motion (motive)
notion
potion
commotion
devotion
emotion (emotive)
promotion
locomotion (locomotive)

⑧ Following Consonants -tion/-tive (Except 'l'☆ or 'n'☆)

action (active)
attraction (attractive)
collection (collective)
connection (connective)
construction (constructive)
deduction (deductive)
conviction
correction (corrective)
destruction (destructive)
direction (directive)
election (elective)
introduction

adoption (adoptive)
caption
contraption

assertion (assertive)
exertion

digestion (digestive)
suggestion (suggestive)

③ -tion/-tive Following a Short 'i' (except for -mission)

addition (additive)
ambition
condition
disposition
edition
ignition
nutrition
tradition
transition
competition (competitive)
composition
definition (definitive)
demolition
exhibition
opposition
preposition
recognition
repetition (repetitive)
superstition

(Entire List)
mission
admission (admissive)
commission
emission
intermission
omission
permission (permissive
remission
submission (submissive)
transmission
missionary

Exception
fission

⑤ Following 'l' ☆ -sion/-sive (Entire List)

compulsion (compulsive)
convulsion (convulsive)
emulsion
expulsion
impulsion (impulsive)
propulsion
repulsion (repulsive)
revulsion

④ (Entire List) -ssion/-ssive (short 'e', 'u')

accession
aggression (aggressive)
cession
compassion
compression
concession
concussion
confession
depression
digression
discussion
expression (expressive)
impression
intercession
obsession (obsessive)
oppression (oppressive)
percussion (percussive)
possession (possessive)
procession
recession (recessive)
regression (regressive)
repercussion
repression (repressive)
retrogression
succession (successive)
suppression (suppressive
transgression

Exception
passion

⑥ Overlap of /shŭn/ Following 'n'☆

-tion/-tive (Entire List)	-sion/-sive (Entire List)
abstention	mansion
attention (attentive)	expansion (expansive)
circumvention (circumventive)	apprehension (apprehensive)
contention	ascension
convention	comprehension (comprehensive
detention	condescension
intention	dimension
intervention	dissension
invention (inventive)	distension
mention	extension (extensive)
prevention (preventive)	pension
retention (retentive)	pretension
	reprehension
	suspension
	tension

Exception: cushion; fashion; complexion; crucifixion; freshen; luncheon; ocean; crustacean; fission; suspicion, dalmatian; Russian

Chart 49

Select Multi-Syllable Words with /-'n/

'-an' (= human)[1]

businessman
cameraman
clergyman
countryman
fireman
fisherman
foreman
horseman
middleman
newsman
nobleman
repairman
salesman
watchman
weatherman
woman
workingman
yardman

orphan
pagan
veteran
civilian
custodian
guardian
humanitarian
arithmetician
beautician
clinician
electrician
magician
mathematician
physician
mortician
musician
obstetrician
optician
pediatrician
politician
physician

African
American
Australian
Bohemian
Bolivian
Brazilian
Californian
Chilean
Egyptian
Episcopalian
Indonesian
Indian
Italian
Mexican
Puritan
Republican
Texan

'-en'

beaten
bitten
broken
cheapen
chosen
darken
deafen
deepen
driven
enlighten
frighten
forgiven
given
gladden
loosen
moisten
ridden
shaken
stolen
taken
tighten

flaxen
golden
oaken

abdomen
brethren
children
even
happen
heaven
hyphen
kitchen
kitten
leaven
linen
listen
mitten
open
oven
raven
regimen
seven
siren
specimen
token

allergen
antigen
estrogen
hallucinogen
halogen
hydrogen
nitrogen
oxygen
pathogen

'-in'

assassin
basin
begin
bobbin
bulletin
cabin
cumin
mandolin
mannequin
margin
moccasin
muffin
napkin
origin
paraffin
penguin
raisin
robin
satin
sequin
terrapin
urchin
vermin
violin
virgin
within

Medical words

adrenalin
albumin
aspirin
heroin
insulin
lanolin
lecithin
myelin
niacin
nitroglycerin
penicillin
rennin
toxin
vitamin

ain = /ĭn/

(Entire List)

bargain
captain
certain
chaplain
chieftain
curtain
fountain
mountain
porcelain
villain

'-on'

abandon
accordion
bacon
beacon
beckon
bison
button
caldron
carbon
carton
cinnamon
dragon
environ
falcon
felon
gallon
glutton
heron
horizon
lemon
lesson
matron
melon
mutton
pardon
parson
patron
person
piston
prison
reason
reckon
region
ribbon
season
sermon
simpleton
skeleton
summon
surgeon
tendon
treason
unison
venison
wanton
wagon
watermelon
weapon

'-ion' = /yun/

battalion
billion
bullion
bunion
communion
companion
dominion
galleon
medallion
million
mullion
oblivion
onion
opinion
pavilion
pillion
pinion
quadrillion
quintillion
rebellion
scullion
stallion
trillion
union
vermilion
zillion

-un = /ŭn/

(Entire List)

begun
bun
Cajun
dun
fun
gun
nun
pun
run
shun
spun
stun
sun

Compound Words

blowgun
handgun
homespun
outrun
overrun
popgun
shotgun
Shogun

[1]**Exception:** amphibian; reptilian; obsidian; cardigan; median; organ; slogan; turban.

Chart 50

UNIT 6

FOCUS ON:
LETTER STUDIES

Unit Six takes a look at many letters to see how they function in all positions within a word. This helps bring a better understanding of why words are spelled the way they are.

Eagle's Wings Comprehensive Chart of Consonants

Consonant Sounds: Consistent Spelling ① Chart 1, 51

Sound/Spelling	
/b/	boy
/d/	dad
/h/	hop
/m/[1]	mat
/n/[1]	not
/p/	pat
/r/[1]	ran
/t/	top
/w/[2]	wet
/y/[2]	yes Chart 70

'Cliffs(z) Consonants': "Charge to View the Cliffs(z)!"

Varied spellings:

②	Chart	At beginnings	Chart	↧ At ends of words [Cliffs(z)] ③ Following a short vowel.		Chart	Not following a short vowel	
/k/[3]	51/59	cat; kit; chord	30/38	-ck/-c	back; picnic	38	-k/-que	bank; opaque
/l/	51	lot	30/31	-ll[5]	tell; awful	36	-l/-le	sail; apple
/f/[1]	51 58	fan; photo	30/31 39	-ff/-ph (-ffs)[6]	cliff; graph (cliffs)	7/31 39	-f/-gh (-ves)[4]	leaf; tough (leaves)
/s/[1;3]	51	sat; city	30/31	-ss[7]	pass	32-34	-ce/-se[7]	dance; house
/z/	51	zoo; xylophone	30	-zz	fizz	32-34	-se/-ze	cheese; sneeze
/ch/[4]	57	cheese	39	-tch	catch	39	-ch	each
/j/[3]	51/61	jam; gem	37/62	-dge	judge	37/62	-ge	hinge
/g/[3]	61	got; guitar	37/38 62	-g/-gue	bag catalogue	38	-gue	vague
/v/	51.63	vine	37/38 63	-ve[8]	have	37/38 63	-ve[8]	sleeve

[1] See "Silent Consonants", below. [2] 'w' and 'y' act as consonants only at the beginning of syllables.
[3] /k/= c & /s/= s>a,o,u, & consonants; /k/= k & /s/= c & s>e,i,y. Generally: /g/= g & /j/= j>a,o,u, & consonants; /j/=g & /g/=gu>e,i,y.
[4] See "Blends". [5] 'all'=/ăl/,"tall"; 'oll'=/ōl/,"toll". [6] To pluralize words ending in 'ff', add 's'. To pluralize a word ending in a single 'f' or 'fe', change to 'ves'. [7] A single 's' or 'es' is used for plurals, possesives, and tense. [8] 'ove'=/uv/, /ūv/, /ov/, /ov/ ('u' is never next to a 'v'.)

Beginning Blends Chart 4, 52, 53, 54 ④

'-l'	'-r'	'-w'	's-'
bl black	br brag		sc scab
cl clam	cr crab		sk skid;school
	dr drag	dw dwarf	sm smog
fl flag	fr frog		sn snap
gl glad	gr grin		sp span
pl plan	pr prim		st stop
	tr trap	tw twig	spl splash
		/kw/[1] quote	scr scrap
		choir	spr sprig
sl slam		sw swing	str strap
			squ[1] squid

Ending Blends[3] Chart 6, 7, 8 ④

'-t'	'-d'	'-p'	'-k'
-ct act			
-ft gift			
		-mp camp	
-nt bent	-nd bend		-nk[4] bank
-pt wept			
-st mast		-sp gasp	-sk mask
-xt next			
-lt belt	-ld held	-lp help	-lk milk
			/ks/[2] mix;licks[3]

[1] 'qu' = /kw/; 'qua'=/kwŏ/ [2] 'x' = /ks/ [3] Adding 's' to a word will make a consonant blend with the consonant preceding it; cat/cats. [4] 'nk' = /ngk/

Digraphs (unique sounds) ⑤

	Chart	Beginning	Chart	Medial	Chart	Final
/ch/	8/55	cheese;cello	46/57	picture;question	9/57	catch;each
/sh/	8 55 57	shh!;shut chandelier	49 57	caption;mission physician;pension conscious	9 56	fish
/zh/			46/48/58	vision;pleasure	57	garage
/th/	8/55	think			9/56	path
/th/	8/55	that	56	other	9/56	loathe
/hw/	8/55	when				
-/ng/			6/8	bank; anchor	6/8	sing;tongue

Silent Consonants Chart 71 ⑥

lf=/f/ calf	ps=/s/ psychiatrist
sle=/l/ aisle	sc=/s/ scene
chm=/m/ drachm	st=/s/ castle
gm=/m/ phlegm	sw=/s/ sword
lm=/m/ palm	bt=/t/ debt
mb=/m/ comb	rh=/r/ rhythm
gn=/n/ gnat, sign	wr=/r/ wren
kn=/n/ knee	dj=/j/ adjacent
mn=/n/ mnemonic	lk=/k/ walk
pn=/n/ pneumonia	gh=/ / sigh (Chart 58)
	h=/ / exhibit, hour

Unit 6 Letter Studies

Chart 51
Initial Sounds. This study of Initial Sounds of every letter in the alphabet gives ten words for each of the most common sounds for the letters. It is to be used for **auditory** skills. Being able to hear a sound in a word and knowing which sound it is, is a skill that must be developed. Note that 'c' has no unique sound. It says /s/ before 'i', 'e' and 'y' and /k/ elsewhere. Also, 'g' says /j/ before 'i', 'e', and 'y' if they are a single vowel followed by a single consonant. It says /g/ elsewhere.

Chart 52
Beginning Blends with 'r' and 'l'. The study of beginning blends with 'l' and 'r' is to help develop auditory recognition skills of blends with 'l' and 'r'.

Beginning consonant blends are made only with 'l', 'r', and 'w' following a consonant, and 's' preceding a consonant. A blend is two (or three) letters put together which still make their own individual sounds. (We circle these consonants to show that they are a blend.) A blend can be broken apart. When sustaining a blend, we end up saying the last letter of the blend. Try sustaining 'bl'— 'bl • l • l • l'. We end up saying an 'l'.

Chart 53
Beginning Blends with 's'. The study of beginning blends with 's' is to develop auditory recognition of initial blends with 's'. Remember: 'c' says /s/ before 'i', 'e' and 'y' and /k/ elsewhere. So for /sk/ before 'i', 'e', or 'y', use 'sk'. Use 'sc' elsewhere.

Chart 54
Blends and Study of 'w' and 'qu'. This is a study of blends with 'w' and 'qu'.
Remember:

> Before and after 'w' and 'u',
> 'o' says /ō/ and 'a' says /å/.
> But with 'w', 'or' is /wŭr/ and 'ar' is /wōr/.

The lower portion of the page deals with 'w' and 'qu' and their unique effect on 'a' and 'o'.

'wa' = /wå/, "want"	'wo' = /wōr/, "won't" (rare)
'qua' = /kwå/, "qualify"	'quo' = /kwōr/, "quota" (rare)
'war' = /wōr/, "warm"	'wor' = /wŭr/, "worm"
'quar' = /kwōr/, "quart"	

A Study of Initial Sounds

ă	ā	b	c=/k/>a,o,u	c=/s/>e, i, y	d	ĕ	ē	f
antler	able	ball	cabbage	cent	double	exterior	even	fan
active	ache	baboon	cage	cider	desk	echo	eat	faith
address	aviation	bark	case	city	daisy	embroidery	evaporate	film
after	aid	bed	corn	cycle	dance	eggs	ego	finger
answer	acorn	butterfly	cattle	century	dove	envelope	eagle	fire
athlete	acre	bird	camp	cement	deer	excite	easy	feather
at	aim	banana	cave	cinch	duck	edge	evil	fawn
animal	aviator	bat	car	cellar	dive	establish	erase	face
and	agent	bench	calendar	cinnamon	dark	explore	elect	fun
apple	alien	bicycle	camp	center	dime	examine	easel	fill
ax	ail	bell	cut	cypress	day	every	electric	feed
absent	angel	bat	cake	central	damp	end	east	false
atom	amiable	button	came	cinder	dip	enter	eel	fine
astronaut	ate	boat	corner	centipede	deep	empty	emotion	future

g=/g/>a,o,u	g=/j/> i, e, y	h	ĭ	ī	j = /j/> a, o, u	k= /k/> e, i , y	l	m
gone	gem	hard	important	iron	jam	kite	lifeboat	maple
gain	gentle	horse	inchworm	ice	jump	kidnap	lightening	milk
gum	Gypsy	headdress	igloo	ideal	jubilant	key	lantern	market
gallop	giraffe	hammock	inside	ivy	justice	kitchen	lobster	map
goat	gym	hand	insect	idle	joke	keep	lighthouse	mile
guitar	genius	hat	ignore	iris	jar	kindergarten	live	monkey
goose	gelatin	hope	inning	idea	judge	kind	lake	magnet
gun	geography	heat	interior	icecream	jug	kick	laugh	mail
gold	gigantic	history	improve	ivory	jail	king	love	manners
gorilla	generous	hair	itch	icicle	juggle	kid	lend	mad
gang	gyp	humor	in	ironic	job	key	loose	math
gate	ginger	hear	import	identical	jolly	kitten	land	mole
got	general	harvest	imagine	island	junk	kettle	loud	mend
game	gene	hunt	interest	identify	journey	kiss	leave	meet

n	ŏ	ō	p	qu=/kw/	r	s	t	
number	octopus	oak	pepper	quilt	remain	swan	tangle	
no	otter	occasion	pilot	quail	reindeer	sunflower	temperature	
nurse	offer	ocean	palm	queen	raft	saddle	time	
nest	ox	over	pass	quack	rose	sack	toast	
nut	ostrich	open	part	quality	raccoon	sun	table	
nail	odd	odor	peacock	quit	rainbow	salt	tender	
nose	onward	old	palace	quarter	rabbit	sail	toothbrush	
name	off	owe	parakeet	quote	race	sea	tiger	
nibble	often	oat	painter	quick	radio	soil	toucan	
new	odd	omit	possible	quantity	reason	safe	tulip	
noodle	object	obey	polish	quart	relax	sack	touch	
night	office	ozone	people	quite	read	salad	town	
near	on	oath	park	quake	red	seat	telescope	
nothing	opera	oboe	paper	quiet	right	sadden	tangerine	

ŭ	ū	v	w	x (final position)	y	z
uncle	usual	volcano	wake	box	yak	zip
upward	ukulele	violin	wet	flax	yawn	zero
until	unite	vulture	wasp	fix	yodel	zipper
us	unique	valentine	witness	relax	yes	zebra
usher	unify	vest	worship	mix	yield	zany
unzip	unicorn	vacuum	walrus	coax	yard	zeal
under	utility	varnish	wolf	ax	yoke	zigzag
up	use	vent	window	fox	yellow	zinnia
unhappy	universe	vacation	wade	complex	year	zone
umbrella	union	valley	wag	six	yam	zoo
ugly	utensil	van	wall	flex	young	zucchini
unarmed	useless	violet	wait	wax	yank	zealot
utter	university	value	waltz	ox	yell	zoom
umpire	utilize	vacant	wild	tax	yo-yo	zinc

Chart for Initial Sounds

The primary purpose of this chart is to familiarize students with the initial sounds of the alphabet, including long and short vowels, as well as the two sounds of 'c' and 'g'. Students are not expected to be able to spell the words at this level, and meanings of the words may be discussed if desired.

A Study of Beginning Blends with 'r' and 'l'

Blends with 'r'

br: brace, bracket, braid, brain, braise, brake, brave, brawl, brawn, bray, bread, break, breath, breathe, breed, breeze, brew, bribe, bride, bridge, bridle, brief, bright, broad, broke, bronze, brooch, brood, brook, broom, brother, brown, bruise, brute

cr: crane, crave, crawl, craze, cream, crease, create, credit, creed, creek, crime, critic, crook, crow, crowd, crown, crude, cruel, crystal

dr: drain, draw, drawl, dread, dream, drive, drizzle, droll, drool, drove, drowsy, dry

fr: fraction, fragile, frail, frame, fraud, freak, freckle, free, freeze, freight, frenzy, friend, fright, front, frown, fruit, fry

gr: grace, grade, grain, grammar, grape, graph, grate, grave, gravity, gravy, gray, graze, grease, green, grew, grief, grime, gripe, groan

gr: groom, groove, grouch, ground, grove, grow, grumble

pr: practice, prairie, prance, pray, preach, preen, prefer, prepare, present, presume, pretend, pretty, prevent, price, pride, prime, prince, principal, principle, prison, prize, probe, proceed, process, produce, profit, progress, project, property, prose, protect, proud, prove, prowl, prude, prune, pry

tr: trace, traffic, tragedy, trail, train, trait, traitor, transport, transplant, travel, tray, tread, treasure, treat, tree, tremble, triangle, tribe, trio, triple, triumph, troop, tropic, trouble, trousers, true, truth, try

*Blends with 'l'

bl: blade, blame, blanket, blare, blast, blaze, bleach, bleak, bleed, blew, blister, blood, bloom, blossom, blotch, blow, blue, blur

cl: classic, clause, clean, clear, cleave, clerk, cloak, close, clothe, cloud, clove, clown

fl: flake, flame, flannel, flare, flaunt, flow, flea, fleece, fleet, flew, flight, flirt, float, flood, floor, flora, flour, flow, flue, flute, fly

gl: glacier, glade, glance, glare, glaze, gleam, glean, glide, globe, gloom, glory, glove, glow

pl: place, plague, plaid, plain, plane, planet, plaque, plate, play, plead, please, plight, plow, ply

* Note: 'd' and 't' do not blend with 'l'.

Chart 52

A Study of Beginning Blends with 's'

[3]sc	scab	[3]sk	skeleton	sl	slope	sp	space	spr	sprain	str	strand
=	scald	=	skeptic		slot		spaghetti		sprang		strap
/sk/	scale	/sk/	sketch		sloth		span		sprawl		straw
>	scalp	>	skewer		slouch		spank		spray		stress
a	scamp	e	ski		slough		spangle		spree		stretch
o	scan	i	skid		slow		spaniel		sprinkle		strict
u	scandal	y	skill		slumber		spark		sprig		string
	scant		skillet		slump		sparrow		spring		strip
	scapula		skim		slurp		sparse		sprint		stripe
	scarce		skimp		sly		spasm	st	stab		strong
	scare		skin	sm	small		spat		stack		stroll
	scarf		skip		smash		spatter		staff		struck
	scarlet		skipper		smear		spawn		stag		strung
	scary		skirmish		smell		spear		stall		strut
	scat		skirt		smile		specific		stamp	sw	swab
	scavenger		sky		smirk		speck		stand		swaddle
	scoff	sl	slab		smith		spectator		stem		swagger
	scold		slack		smock		sped		step		swallow
	scoop		slander		smog		speed		stick		swam
	scoot		slap		smoke		spell		stiff		swamp
	scope		slash		smooth		spend		still		swan
	scorch		slat		smother		spice		sting		swarm
	score		slate		smudge		spider		stink		swat
	scorn		slaughter		smug		spike		stitch		sway
	scotch		slave	sn	snack		spill		stock		swear
	scout		slay		snag		spin		stoke		sweat
	scowl		sleeve		snail		spine		stole		sweep
	scum		sleazy		snake		spirit		stone		sweet
	scuttle		sleek		snap		spit		stood		swell
scr	scrabble		sleep		snarl		spite		stoop		swept
	scram		sleet		snatch		spoil		stop		swift
	scrap		sleeve		sneak		spoke		stub		swig
	scrape		slender		sneer		sponge		stuck		swim
	scratch		slew		sneeze		spoof		stud		swing
	scrawl		slice		sniff		spook		stuff		swish
	scrawny		slick		snip		spore		stump		switch
	screech		slid		snipe		sport		stun		swum
	screen		slide		snob		spun		stung		
	screw		slight		snoop		spunk		stunk		
	scribble		slim		snooze	spl	splatter		stunt		
	script		slime		snore		splice				
	scrimp		sling		snort		splint				
	scroll		slink		snow						
	scrub		slip		snub						
	scrunch		slit		snuff						
	scruple		sliver		snug						

[1]sc=/s/ >e, i, or y [2]sch=/sk/ [3]/sk/ is normally 'sc' > a, o, or u and 'sk'> e, i, or y.

Chart 53

A Study of Beginning Blends with 'w' and 'qu'

dw	sw		qu=/kw/	squ=/skw/
[2]dwarf	[1]swab	swig	quail	[1]squab
dwelt	[1]swallow	swim	quake	[1]squabble
dwindle	[1]swamp	swindle	[1]quality	[1]squad
tw	[1]swan	swine	[1]qualm	[1]squadron
twain	[1]swap	swing	[2]quart	[1]squall
tweak	[2]swarm	swipe	[2]quarter	[1]squander
tweed	[2]swarthy	swirl	[2]quartet	[1]square
tweet	[1]swat	swish	[2]quartz	[1]squash
tweezers	[1]swath	swiss	queen	[1]squat
twelve	[1]sway	switch	quench	[1]squaw
twenty	swear	swivel	quest	[1]squawk
twice	sweat	swore	quick	squeak
twiddle	sweater	[1]swollen	quiet	squeal
twig	sweep	swoop	quill	squeeze
twilight	sweet	**Exception**	quilt	squid
twin	swell	swag	quintet	squint
twine	swelter	swagger	quip	squirm
twinge	swept	swain	quit	squirrel
twinkle	swerve	swam	quite	squirt
twirl	swift	swang	[1]quota	
twist		swank	[1]quote	
twitch		sword	[1]quotient	
twitter		sworn	**Exception**	
between		swung	quack	
thwart			quiz	
Exception				
two				

A Study of 'w' and 'qu'

[1]wa and ua=/wå/		[1]wo=/wō/	wo=/wŭ/	[2]wor=/wŭr/	[2]war=/wōr/	wa=/wā/
wad	swab	woe	won	word	war	wade
wall	swamp	woke	wonder	work	ward	wafer
waltz	swan	won't	wonderful	world	warble	wage
wand	swap	wore	**Exception**	worm	warm	wail
want	swash	wove	*was	worry	warn	waist
wash	swat	swollen	wobble	worse	warp	wait
wasp	swatch	**[1]quo=/kwō/**	**(wa=/wă/)**	worship	wart	waiter
watch	swaddle	quota	wacky	worst	swarm	waitress
wabble	swallow	quote	wag	worth	quart	wake
wadding	squad	quotient	wagon	**Exception**	quartz	ware
waddle	squall	**wo=/wo͝o/**	wangle	*were	dwarf	wary
waffle	squash	wolf	wax	forward	warrior	waste
wallaby	squat	wolverine	swag		quarantine	wave
wallet	squaw	woman	swam		quarrel	way
wallop	squawk	would	swank		quarter	sway
wallow	squabble	**wo=/wü/**	quack		thwart	quail
walnut	squander	womb	twang		**Exception**	quaint
walrus	squatter	swoon			sword	quake
wander	qualm	**who=/hü/**			sworn	square
water	quadrangle	who whom			worn	
twaddle	quadruplet	whoop				
	qualify	whose				
	quality					

Computer checked. *'Everyday Bloopers': Must be memorized. [1]wa=/wå/ wo=/wō/ qua=/kwå/ quo = /kwō/ [2]war=/wōr/ wor=/wŭr/ quar=/kwōr/

Digraphs Again

The majority of digraphs are with 'h'. A digraph is a sound that can be sustained and will not break down into its parts. The sound of a digraph is unrelated to the individual letters used to create it. In other words, a digraph is a unique sound that must be memorized. We mark an 'x' underneath it to show that it is a unique sound. The following hand symbols may help in remembering these 'h' digraphs.

'sh' says /sh/, "shush": Put finger to mouth and say "Shhh!"

'wh' says /hw/, "what": Put finger up like a candle and blow.

'ch' says /ch/, "cheese": Put a finger on either side of mouth, smile as if posing for a picture and say "Ch-ch-cheese."

'th' says /th/, "thing", and /th/, "that": This is the only sound that is made with the tongue between the teeth. Stick your tongue out slightly and blow /th/, "thing", and then repeat with a buzz or voiced sound, /th/, "that".

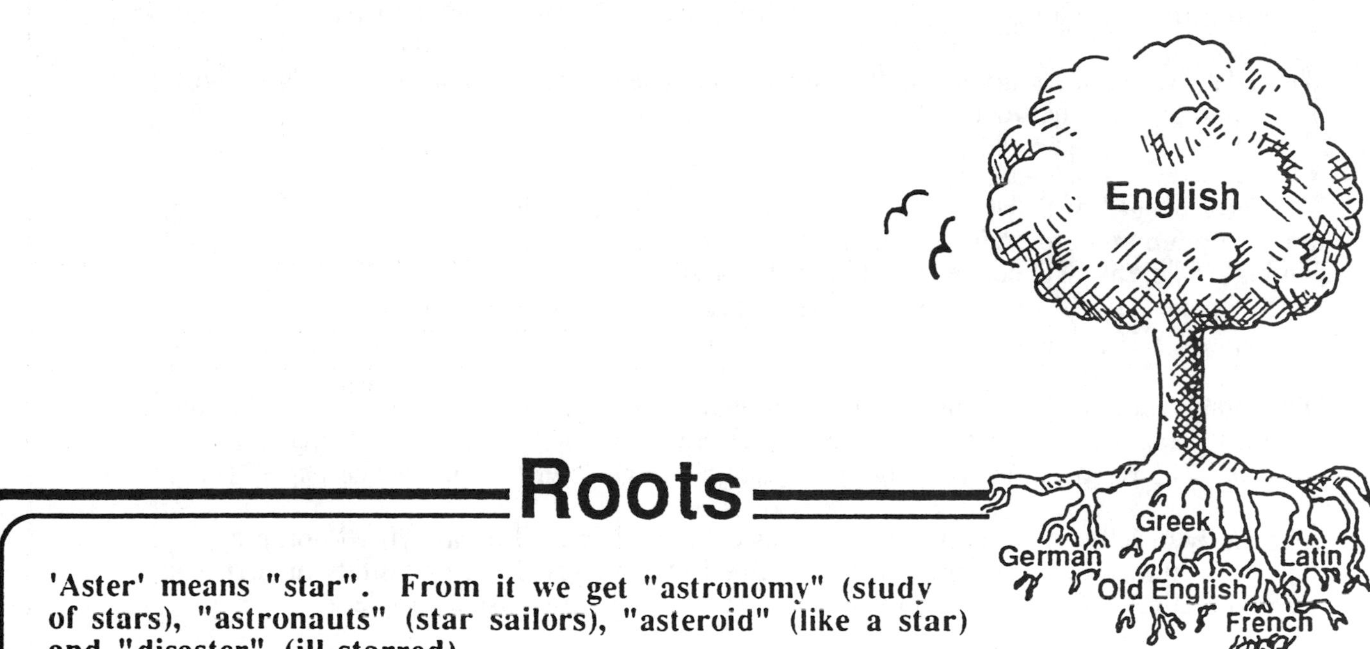
English
Greek
German
Latin
Old English
French

Roots

'Aster' means "star". From it we get "astronomy" (study of stars), "astronauts" (star sailors), "asteroid" (like a star) and "disaster" (ill-starred).

Chart 55
One-Syllable Words with Beginning 'h' Digraphs. This is a study of beginning 'h' digraphs to be used primarily for improving auditory skills and, much later, for spelling skills.

Chart 56
A Study of 'sh' and 'th'. Of particular interest in this study is the fact that, in the final syllable with the suffix '-ish', no consonants are double as they are in almost all other suffixes beginning with a vowel, '-le' or 'y'. There are few independent words with 'sh' in the medial position. This is because the medial /sh/ sound is generally spelled with '-si-', '-ci-', '-ti-', or '-s(u)-' ("compassion", "facial", "circumstantial", "pressure"). See Chart 57.

The digraph, 'th', is voiced when it is between vowels ("mother"). At the ends of words it is unvoiced unless it is spelled '-the' ("breath", "breat**he**").

Chart 57
A Study of /ch/, /sh/, and /zh/ (Multi-Syllable). This chart deals with the various ways to spell the /ch/, /sh/, and /zh/ sounds. At first glance, many are unexpected. For the /ch/, "cheap", 'ch' is used at the beginnings of words. At ends of words directly following a short vowel, use 'tch', "match". For a medial /ch/ sound, '-tu-', "mixture", is often found.

The /sh/, "shape", sound at beginning and ends of words is most often spelled 'sh'. There are several 'ch' words saying /sh/, "chandelier". These are of French origin. In the medial position, the /sh/ can be '-si', '-ssi', '-ci', '-su', or '-ti', "nation". ☛ See page 217.

The /zh/, "casual", sound is usually '-si' or '-su'. The entire list of words with 'ge' saying /zh/, "garage", are included in this chart.

Chart 58
A Study of 'gh' and 'ph'. There are several sets of combinations with 'gh'. There are only 5 common words with 'gh' saying /g/. There are 23 independent words with '-igh' saying /ī/, "high". These are found in the helps section under "The Knight's Plight".
☛ See page 205. There are only 8 independent words with '-eigh' saying /ā/, "neigh".
☛ See page 198.

The '-augh' and '-ough' forms are very confusing. They can say different sounds, but there are only 30 words. It is easier and much more practical to learn the 30 words than the 7 sounds. The poem, "The Taming of the '-augh'/'-ough' " will help. ☛ See page 213.

The study of 'ph' covers all the base words containing 'ph'. 'Ph' says /f/, "Photograph". Many of these words are words we would find in text books. When we study them, think about needing a Ph.D. to learn the 'ph' words. Simple words use a simple 'f'.

A Study of Beginning 'h' Digraphs

sh	wh	ph=/f/	gh[1]	ch	th
shabby	whack	Pharaoh		chain	thank
shack	whale	pharmacy		chair	thatch
shade	what	phase		chalk	thaw
shadow	wheat	pheasant		challenge	theater
shaft	wheel	philosophy		chamber	theft
shake	wheeze	phone		champ	theme
shale	when	phonetic		chance	theology
shall	where	phoney		change	theory
shallow	whether	phonograph		channel	therapy
shame	whew	photograph		chant	thermometer
shank	whey	phrase		chap	thick
shape	which	physical		chapel	thief
share	whiff	physics		chapter	thigh
shark	while			charcoal	thimble
sharp	whim			charge	thing
shatter	whimper			chariot	think
shave	whine			charm	third
shawl	whinny			chart	thirst
she	whip			chase	thirteen
shear	whippoorwill			chat	thirty
shed	whirl			cheap	thistle
sheep	whish			cheat	thong
sheet	whisk			check	thorn
shelf	whisper			cheek	thousand
shell	whistle			cheer	thread
shelter	white			cheese	three
shepherd	whittle			cheetah	threw
shield	whiz			chess	thrill
shift	whop			chest	thrive
shin	why			chew	throat
shine				chide	throb
shingle				chief	throne
ship				child	throw
shirt				chill	thrust
shiver				chime	thumb
shock				chimney	thunder
shot				chimpanzee	**Voiced th**
shoe				chin	than
shook				china	that
shoot				chip	the
shop	**Exception**			chipmunk	their
shore	who			chisel	them
short	whole			chocolate	then
shrank	whose			choice	there
shred				choke	these
shrewd				choose	they
shrill				chop	this
shrimp				chore	those
shrine				chuckle	thy
shrub				church	
Exception					
sugar					
sure					

[1] 'Gh' is at the beginning of "ghost", "ghoul", "ghastly", and "ghetto". In these **gh** = /g/. In all other positions, 'gh' is silent.

A Study of 'sh'

Final 'sh'		Medial 'sh'
One-Syllable	**Multi-Syllable**	**Multi-Syllable**
ash	abash	ashore
bash	abolish	ashamed
dash	ambush	bashful
gash	anguish	bishop
hash	banish	blusher
lash	bulrush	bushel
mash	cherish	cashew
rash	finish	galoshes
sash	foolish	marshal
mesh	furnish	marshmallow
dish	garnish	mushroom
wish	harsh	nourishment
gosh	impish	refreshment
josh	lavish	reshape
bush	leash	sashay
gush	marsh	unshackle
hush	nourish	unshorn
lush	oafish	washer
mush	parish	worship
push	perish	***Compound Words***
rush	polish	*ashtray*
blush	publish	*bookshelf*
brush	punish	*bushwhack*
clash	quash	*dishcloth*
crash	radish	*dishtowel*
flash	ravish	*eggshell*
flesh	refresh	*fishhook*
flush	relish	*flashbulb*
fresh	selfish	*flashlight*
gnash	tarnish	*foreshadow*
plush	vanish	*freshman*
slash	varnish	*freshwater*
slosh		*handshake*
smash		*horseshoe*
splash		*hotshot*
squash		*offshoot*
squish		*lordship*
swish		*makeshift*
stash		*mishmash*
thrash		*overshadow*
thresh		*overshoe*
thrush		*pushcart*
trash		*slingshot*
whoosh		*snapshot*
		snowshoe
		spaceship
		splashdown
		sunshine
		undershirt
		warship
		washbasin
		watershed
		workshop

A Study of 'th'

Final 'th'	Medial 'th'	
One-Syllable	**Multi-Syllable**	
bath/bathe	although	panther
birth	amethyst	parenthesis
berth	anesthesia	pathetic
breath/breathe	anthem	pathology
cloth/clothe	anthology	polytheism
dearth	anthrax	python
death	apathy	Sabbath
depth	arithmetic	seventh
earth	arthritis	stethoscope
eighth	atheist	sympathy
faith	athlete	synthetic
fifth	authentic	telethon
filth	author	together
forth	bother	weather
fourth	brethren	whether
froth	brother	whither
girth	cathedral	zenith
health	diphtheria	zither
hearth	diphthong	
lath/lathe	either	**Exception**
length	empathy	asthma
mirth	enthrall	
month	enthuse	***Compound Words***
moth	ethyl	*bathrobe*
mouth	ether	*bathtub*
myth	ethics	*birthday*
ninth	father	*earthworm*
north	fathom	*everything*
oath	feather	*northwest*
path	further	*outthink*
pith	gather	*southeast*
scythe	hither	*weatherman*
sheath/sheathe	hypothesis	*withdraw*
sixth	kinesthetic	*withhold*
sleuth	lather	*withstand*
sloth	leather	
sooth/soothe	lethal	
south	lethargic	
stealth	lithograph	
swath/swathe	mammoth	
teeth/teethe	marathon	
tenth	mathematic	
tithe	methane	
tooth	method	
truth	mother	
wealth	neither	
worth	nothing	
wrath	orthodontic	
wreath/wreathe	orthodox	
writhe	orthopedic	
youth		

A Study of /ch/, /sh/, and /zh/

/ch/ (Initial)	/ch/ (Final)	/ch/ (Medial)	ch, si, su = /sh/	ci, ti = /sh/	si, su, zu, ge=/zh/
ch	**-tch**	**tu**	**(Initial)**	**(Medial)**	**(Medial)**
chafe	batch	adventure	**ch (French)**	**ci**	**si**
chaff	catch	capture	chagrin	crucial	cohesion
chain	hatch	creature	chaise	facial	confusion
chair	latch	feature	chalet	financial	division
chalk	match	gesture	champagne	glacial	erosion
challenge	patch	lecture	chandelier	judicial	explosion
chamber	fetch	manufacture	chaperon	social	incision
champion	etch	mixture	charade	capricious	invasion
chance	retch	moisture	charlatan	delicious	occasion
chancellor	ditch	nature	chartreuse	malicious	profusion
change	hitch	picture	chateau	precious	television
channel	itch	puncture	chauffeur	spacious	**su /zu**
chant	pitch	temperature	chauvinist	suspicious	casual
chapel	witch	venture	chef	vicious	closure
chapter	notch	actuary	chic	ancient	exposure
charcoal	hutch	century	chicanery	efficient	leisure
chariot	**-ch**	factual	chiffon	omniscient	measure
charity	inch	fluctuate	chivalry	appreciate	pleasure
charm	pinch	fortune	chute	beautician	treasure
chart	winch	gargantuan	**(Medial)**	electrician	usual
chase	conch	habitual	**-che-**	musician	visual
chaste	bunch	mortuary	attache	physician	azure
cheap	brunch	natural	crochet	politician	seizure
cheat	crunch	obituary	cliche	**ti**	**ge**
check	hunch	punctual	machine	circumstantial	**(Entire List)**
cheek	lunch	ritual	mustache	differential	arbitrage
cheer	munch	sanctuary	parachute	impartial	barrage
cheese	punch	situate	pistachio	initial	bourgeois
cherish	scrunch	spiritual	echelon	martial	beige
cherry	beach	spatula	ricochet	militia	camouflage
chess	bleach	**Exception**	**-si-/-ssi-**	palatial	collage
chest	breach	anxious	compassion	partial	entourage
chew	breech	conscience	concession	quotient	fuselage
chicken	preach	conscious	confession	scrumptious	garage
chief	speech	achieve	expansion	combination	gavage
child	broach	artichoke	expulsion	decoration	lavage
chill	coach	crotchety	intermission	duplication	lingerie
chime	poach	franchise	revulsion	education	massage
chimney	roach	luncheon	submission	emotion	menagerie
chimpanzee	smooch	nonchalant	**su**	generation	mirage
china	couch	treachery	assure	investigation	negligee
chip	crouch		censure	motion	prestige
chisel	grouch		erasure	population	regime
chocolate	ouch		fissure	sensation	rouge
choice	pouch		insure		sabotage
choke	slouch		issue		
choose	vouch		pressure		
chop	**Exception**		sugar		
chortle	watch		sure		
church	niche		tissue		
Exception	rich				
cello	touch				
concerto	much				
	such				

A Study of 'gh' (Complete List)

-igh=/ī/		*Compound Words*
high	*alight*	*airtight*
nigh	*delight*	*birthright*
thigh	*foresight*	*bullfight*
sigh	*forthright*	*candlelight*
blight	*preflight*	*copyright*
bright	*twilight*	*daylight*
fight		*downright*
flight		*eyesight*
fright		*firelight*
height		*flashlight*
knight		*floodlight*
light		*footlight*
might		*highlight*
night		*lamplight*
plight		*midnight*
right		*moonlight*
sight		*outright*
sleight		*overnight*
slight		*oversight*
tight		*playwright*
		searchlight
		skylight
		spotlight
		starlight
		stoplight
		sunlight
		taillight
		torchlight
		watertight

-eigh=/ā/
neigh
sleigh
weigh
eight
freight
straight
weight
-eign=/ān/
feign
reign
Compound Words
counterweight
deadweight
featherweight
heavyweight
lightweight
middleweight
overweight
paperweight
underweight

-augh/-ough		
/ŏ/	caught	although
	taught	besought
	daughter	distraught
	haughty	forethought
	naughty	onslaught
	slaughter	untaught
	bought	
	brought	
	fought	
	nought	
	ought	***Compound Words***
	sought	*afterthought*
	thought	*breakthrough*
	wrought	*overbought*
/ü/	through	*overwrought*
	slough (n)	
/ou/	bough	
	drought	
/ō/	borough	
	dough	
	furlough	
	thorough	
	though	
/ŭf/	enough	
	rough	
	tough	
	slough (v)	
/ŏf/	cough	
	trough	
/af/	draught	
	laugh	

gh=/g/
ghastly
ghetto
ghost
ghoul
spaghetti

A Study of 'ph' (Entire List)

Animals	Science	Medical	Language/Sound		People	Other
aphid	biosphere	amphetamine	alphabet	megaphone	nephew	asphalt
amphibian	camphor	asphyxiate	autobiography	metaphor	orphan	cellophane
dolphin	chlorophyll	atrophy	autograph	microphone	Pharaoh	ephemeral
elephant	geography	diaphragm	biography	morpheme	Pharisee	peripheral
gopher	geophysics	diphtheria	blasphemy	pamphlet	philanthropist	phenomenal
pheasant	graph	encephalitis	cacophony	paraphrase	photographer	philosophy
	hemisphere	endomorph	cipher	phonograph	prophet	phony
	photon	euphoria	choreography	phrase	sophomore	photo
	photosynthesis	hemophiliac	decipher	prophecy		photogenic
	physics	hydrophobia	diphthong	prophesy		seraphim
	sapphire	lymph	emphasis	saxophone		siphon
	sphere	morphine	epitaph	symphony		sophisticate
	sulphur	pharmacy	euphony	telegraph		triumphant
	typhoon	phobia	euphoric	telephone		trophy
	zephyr	phlebitis	headphones			xerography
		phlegm	hyphen			
		physical	phonetic			

☑ Computer checked.

Chart 59

A Study of /k/. This chart has all the words beginning with 'k'. Note that most are followed by 'i', 'e', or 'y'. The exceptions in the last row show that many of these are recently borrowed words. Therefore the rule is, if you can use a 'c' for a /k/ sound, use it. The rest of the chart deals with multi-syllable words with a 'k' in them. Most of the words fall into patterns: '-kle', '-ket', '-ker', and so forth. There are a few 'qu' word saying /k/.

At the ends of one-syllable words, following a short vowel, 'ck', "back", is used. Elsewhere, 'k', "beak", or 'ke', "bake", is used. (For 'ck' words, see Chart 30.)

Chart 60

A Further Study of /k/ and A Study of 'x'. This is a further study of the /k/ sound. Here are the 'ch' words that say /k/, "character". We also see that 'sc' is used for /sk/ sounds after 'a', 'o', or 'u', "scan", and 'sk' is used for the /sk/ sound after 'i', 'e', or 'y', "skip". If 'sc' is used with 'i', 'e', or 'y', the 'c' is silent, "science". These must be memorized.

Few words begin with an 'x'. Those that do say /z/, "xylophone". Most words with 'x' either end in 'x' or have the prefix 'ex-'. The 'ex-' has two sounds. When followed by a consonant, it is /ks/, "exclaim". When followed by a vowel, it is /gz/, "exact". To keep the 'ks' sound with a vowel, a silent 'c' ("excess") must be added. The silent 'h' in some of these words does not appear to have any particular function.

An 'x' is never doubled. Its sound, /ks/ or /gz/, functions as two consonants. Therefore, when adding a suffix, never double an 'x', (boxes).

Chart 61

A Study of Initial 'g' and 'j'. The study of initial 'g' and 'j' show an interesting interaction. We use 'g' to say /j/, "gem", before 'i', 'e', and 'y' (if they are a single vowel followed by a single consonant), and 'j' to say /j/ elsewhere. The relationship is similar to that between 'c' and 'k'. However, there is a little 'kink' in the pattern. If there are two vowels ('ee', 'ea', 'ei', 'ey') or two consonants following the 'i', 'e', or 'y', the 'g' will say /g/, "gear", "giggle", and the 'j' will be needed for the /j/, "jeer", "jiggle".

There are two more important points to note. The /g/ sound can also be maintained by adding 'u', "guide". And second, Jewish names never use a 'g' for the 'j' sound ("Jerusalem").

Chart 62

A Study of Final 'g' and 'j' (Multi-Syllable). For a study of the /j/ and /g/ sound at the ends of one-syllable words, see Chart 37. In most one-syllable words, we use 'g' for the /g/ sound at the end of the word. For the /j/ sound we use 'dge' following a short vowel and '-ge' elsewhere. The 'd' is only there to make the vowel short ("fudge").

This chart is a continuation of the study of /j/ and /g/ and their spellings in multi-syllable words. In the medial position we see 'g' is used for the /j/ sound before 'i', 'e', and 'y' (if they are a single vowel followed by a single consonant), and 'j' is used for the /j/ sound and 'g' for the /g/ sound elsewhere. There are a few words with 'du' in which the 'd' says the /j/ sound, "educate".

There are several options for spellings and sounds at ends of words. When a word ends in '-ger' it can say /jŭr/, "danger", or /gŭr/, "hunger".

At ends of words, we have the suffix '-age' that says /ĭj/, "advantage", and many multi-syllable words with '-gue' saying /g/, "fatigue". There are several words in which the 'ge' says /z/, "garage". The entire list of these is included.

Chart 63

A study of 'v'. This is basically a study of 'v' and 'e'. Other than in the beginning position, most words with a 'v' are followed directly by an 'e'. The rule, therefore, is 've'. The fewer other options need to be memorized.

A Study of /k/

Beginning	Medial		End		Exceptions
k> i, e, y	**-kl/-ckl**	**-k_n/-ck_n**	**ic**	**ck**	**k> a, o, u, consonants**
(Complete)	ankle	beckon	academic	attack	kale
keel	anklet	bumpkin	arithmetic	peacock	kaleidoscope
keen	booklet	chicken	artistic	ransack	karat (carrot)
keep	cackle	manikin	athletic	unlock	katydid
keg	chuckle	napkin	atomic	wedlock	krypton
kelp	cockle	plankton	attic	**k = /k/**	acknowledge
kennel	crackle	reckon	autographic	awoke	alkali
kept	crinkle	stricken	automatic	dislike	askance
keratin	freckle	frankincense	barbaric	handiwork	awkward
kerchief	fickle	**-ker/-cker**	biographic	keepsake	bazooka
kernel	grackle	bakery	botanic	mistake	blockage
kerosene	heckle	bunker	caloric	provoke	gecko
ketchup	knuckle	canker	classic	rebuke	package
kettle	prickle	checker	cleric	tiddlywink	stockade
key	rankle	checkers	colic	**-que = /k/**	ukulele
kick	shackle	flicker	comic	**(Entire List)**	yokel
kid	sparkle	marker	cosmetic	antique	nickel
kidnap	sparkler	slicker	critic	baroque	snorkel
kidney	speckle	sticker	drastic	boutique	jackal
kill	sprinkler	sucker	egotistic	brusque	**Recently borrowed**
kiln	stickler	tanker	elastic	cheque	Africa
kilo	suckle	tucker	electric	clique	kaftan
kilt	tackle	whisker	erratic	critique	khaki
kin	tickle	wicker	frantic	discotheque	okra
kind	tickle	**/ki/**	frolic	grotesque	Alaska
kindergarten	trickle	cocky	gigantic	masque	kayak
kindle	twinkle	cookie	graphic	mosque	parka
kindred	wrinkle	jockey	gymnastic	mystique	Australia
kinetic	**-ket/-cket**	lanky	garlic	oblique	buckaroo
king	basket	monkey	hectic	opaque	cockatoo
kink	blanket	turkey	humanistic	picturesque	kangaroo
kinsfolk	bracket	wacky	individualistic	pique	koala
kipper	casket	hockey	lunatic	physique	kookaburra
kink	cricket	frisky	magic	plaque	China
kiss	docket	colicky	mechanic	statuesque	kaolin
kit	jacket	finicky	metallic	technique	kapok
kitchen	junket	**-qu- = /k/**	mimic	torque	German
kite	locket	conquer	mosaic	unique	kaiser
kitten	market	croquet	music	***Compound Words***	kaput
kiwi	musket	etiquette	nomadic	*candlestick*	Japan
skeleton	packet	lacquer	panic	*deadlock*	kamikaze
skein	picket	liquor	pathetic	*fiddlestick*	karate
skeptic	pocket	mannequin	phonetic	*haystack*	Jewish
sketch	racket	mosquito	photographic	*henpeck*	kosher
skew	rickets	piquant	picnic	*hunchback*	
ski	rickety		plastic	*potluck*	
skid	rocket		rhetoric	*thunderstruck*	
skill	socket		romantic	*yardstick*	
skillet	thicket		sarcastic	*cornflake*	
skim	ticket		scenic	*daybreak*	
skimp	trinket		scientific	*earthquake*	
skin	wicket		skeptic	*landmark*	
skip	parakeet		specific	*outbreak*	
skipper			static	*overlook*	
skirmish			statistic	*pocketbook*	
skirt			traffic	*snowbank*	
skit			tragic	*turnpike*	
sky			volcanic		
			cardiac		
			maniac		
			shellac		

A Further Study of /k/

ch=/k/		sc=/sk/>a, o, u	and consonants	sc=/s/>i, e, y	sk>i, e, y
chameleon	anchor	ascorbic	scab	abscess	askew
chaos	architect	ascribe	scald	adolescent	Eskimo
chaotic	catechism	cascade	scale	ascent	basket
character	clavichord	conscript	scalp	ascetic	casket
charisma	earache	describe	scallion	ascertain	diskette
chasm	echo	discard	scamp	condescend	frisky
chemical	epoch	discharge	scan	crescent	gasket
chemistry	hydrochloric	disclaim	scandal	descend	husky
chemotherapy	hypochondria	disclose	scant	descent	musket
chiropractor	leprechaun	discontinue	scarce	discern	musketeers
chlorine	ocher	discount	scare	effervescent	muskmelon
chloroform	orchid	discourage	scarf	fascinate	muskrat
chlorophyll	melancholy	discover	scarlet	fluorescent	pesky
choir (kw)	monarch	discreet	scavenger	luminescent	skeleton
cholesterol	monochrome	discriminate	scoff	miscellaneous	skeptic
choral	parochial	discuss	scold	obscene	sketch
chord	psychology	escalator	scoop	obsolescent	skew
choreography	schedule	escape	scoot	rescind	ski
chorus	scheme	escort	scope	scene	skill
christening	schizophrenia	escrow	scorch	scent	skimp
chrome	scholar	fiscal	score	scepter	skin
chronic	scholastic	inscribe	scorn	science	skirmish
chronicle	school	mascara	scotch	scissors	sky
chronological	schooner	mascot	scoundrel	scythe	whisker
chrysalis	strychnine	masculine	scout	susceptible	whiskey
ache	synchronize	obscure	scowl	**Exception**	**Exception**
alchemy	technique	prescribe	scum	facade	sceptic
anarchy		rascal	scuttle	muscle	skate
		vascular			skull
		viscous			skunk

A Study of 'x'

Initial 'x'=/z/	Final 'x'=/ks/	Suffixes added[1]	'ex'=/ks/ (when followed by a consonant)	'ex'=/gz/ (when followed by a vowel)	'x'=/ks/ (with silent 'c')
xerography	ax	axes	exclaim	exact	exceed
xenophobia	box	boxer	exclude	exaggerate	excel
xylophone	fix	fixed	exhale	exalt	except
	flax	flaxen	expand	examine	excess
	flex	flexing	expect	example	
	mix	mixer	expel	exasperate	
Medial 'x'=/ks/	ox	oxen	expend	exempt	
toxin	six	sixes	experiment	exile	
toxic	tax	taxing	expert	exit	**'x'=/gz/ (with silent 'h')**
taxi	coax	coaxer	expire	exotic	
maxi	hoax	hoaxes	explain	exude	exhaust
Dixie	climax	climaxes	explicit		exhibit
epoxy	complex	complexes	explode		exhilarate
galaxy	equinox	equinoxes	explore		exhort
waxy	paradox	paradoxes	express		
	perplex	perplexed	extant		
	relax	relaxing	extinct		
	sphinx	sphinxes	extract		
	suffix	suffixes	extreme		
	transfix	transfixed			

Computer checked.

[1]'x' is never doubled

Chart 60

A Study of Initial 'g' and 'j'

g=/j/ (with e, i, and y)	j=/j/ (with a, o, and u) (only 4 1/2 pages in dictionary)	g=/g/ (e, i, y, 1--2)	j=/j/ (e, i, y, 1--2)
gelatin	jab	Double vowel (for /e/)	Double vowel (for /e/)
gem	jackal	gear	jealous
gender	jade	geese	jean
gene	jail	geezer	jeep
genealogy	jam	Geiger	jeer
general	January	geisha	jeopardy
generous	jar	geyser	Double consonant
genesis	jaunt	Double consonant	jelly
genetic	jaw	gecko	jellyfish
genius	jazz	gibbon	jenny
genteel	jog	giddy	jetty
gentle	joke	giggle	jiffy
ge·ode	jolly	gill	jigger
ge·ometry	jolt	gimmick	jiggle
ge·ography	jostle	gizzard	jimmy
geranium	journey	**Exception**	jitter
gerund	judge	gift	
giant	juice	gig	**Exception**
giblets	jug	gingham	jerk
gigantic	juggle	girdle	jest
gin	jumble	*girl	jet
ginger	jump	*give	jewel (ew=/ü/)
giraffe	junior	*get	jig
gist	junk	Words ending with '-ger' such as:	jilt
gym	jury	hamburger	jingle
Gypsy	just	hunger	jive
gyp	juvenile	younger	
		gu= /g/ (with e, i, and y)	Jewish names:
		guest	Jesus
		guide	Jehovah
		guild	Jeroboam
		guile	Jerusalem
		guilt	Jesuit
		guinea pig	Jew
		guise	Jezebel
		guitar	
		guy	
		Exception	
		[1]ghetto	
		[1]ghost	
		guarantee	
		guard	
		guess	
		guillotine	

Computer checked. *'Everyday Bloopers': Must be memorized. [1]Note: 'gh'=/g/ in initial position.

A Study of Medial and Final 'g' and 'j'

gue=/g/
(Final)
(Entire List)
catalogue
colleague
demagogue
dialogue
epilogue
fatigue
intrigue
league
monologue
plague
prologue
rogue
synagogue
travelogue
vague
vogue
/ng/
harangue
meringue
tongue
g=/zh/
(Entire List)
arbitrage
barrage
bourgeois
beige
camouflage
collage
entourage
fuselage
garage
gavage
lavage
lingerie
massage
menagerie
mirage
negligee
prestige
regime
rouge
sabotage

ge = /j/
(Final)
acreage
adage
advantage
average
baggage
bandage
bondage
carriage
cartilage
cottage
courage
damage
disadvantage
drainage
engage
enrage
exchange
foliage
garbage
language
manage
marriage
message
mileage
orphanage
outrage
package
plumage
postage
rummage
sausage
usage
arrange
orange
challenge
barge
bulge
Exception
allege
besiege
college
liege
privilege
sacrilege

g = /j/>i,e,y
(Medial)
advantageous
agency
allergy
angel
contagious
courageous
danger
detergent
digest
digit
diligent
ecology
eligible
emergency
endanger
engagement
engine
exaggerate
fragile
fugitive
geology
ginger
gorgeous
hygiene
imagine
indigestion
ingenuity
intelligent
legend
legislature
legitimate
logic
magic
manager
nitrogen
original
oxygen
pageant
pigeon
psychology
ranger
refrigerate
refugee
region
religion
stranger
strategy
surgeon
tragedy
urgent
vegetable
virgin
wager

j = /j/> a,o,u
(Medial)
adjacent
adjourn
adjust
ajar
banjo
cajole
conjugate
enjoy
injure
injustice
lockjaw
lumberjack
major
pajamas
prejudice
rejoice
rejuvenate
Exception
majestic
object
inject
project
reject
dge = /j/
abridge
cartridge
dislodge
drawbridge
hedgehog
judgment
knowledge
lodging
midget
partridge
porridge
trudging
du = /j/
(Entire List)
assiduous
arduous
credulous
deciduous
educate
fraudulent
glandular
gradual
graduate
grandeur
incredulous
individual
module
procedure
pendulum
residual
schedule
Exception
cordial
soldier

g = /g/> a,o,u	
(Medial)	
again	ligament
against	luggage
aggravate	magnet
aggressive	magnify
ago	organize
agree	pagoda
agriculture	pedigree
alligator	photograph
angle	pigment
antagonism	pigtail
arrogant	pilgrim
augment	polygon
beagle	pregnant
beggar	program
bingo	progress
brigade	recognize
bugle	rectangle
bungalow	regard
burglar	regret
category	regular
centigrade	resignation
degree	segment
delegate	segregation
diagram	shingle
dignity	single
disintegrate	singular
dragon	slogan
eager	smuggle
elegant	snuggle
figure	straggle
forget	struggle
fragment	sugar
fungus	synagogue
geography	tangle
gigantic	tingle
jungle	toboggan
igloo	triangle
igneous	vigor
ignite	vinegar
ignore	wagon
illegal	wiggle
immigrant	zigzag
inaugurate	**Exception**
ingredient	anger
insignificant	auger
integrate	begin
integrity	finger
interrogative	forgive
investigate	giggle
irregular	hunger
jingle	linger
juggle	logger
kangaroo	target
kindergarten	trigger
lagoon	

Unit 6 Letter Studies

Chart 62

A Study of 've'

/v/	/ā/	/ē/	/ī/	/ĭ/	/ōv/
(Initial)	bravely	achieve	arrival	active	nova
vacant	gravely	aggrieve	rival	adaptive	clover
vacation	depravement	believe	revival	adhesive	drover
vacuum	enslavement	bereave	survival	adjective	over
valid	pavement	conceive	private	aggressive	plover
valley	engraven	deceive	alive	assertive	rover
valuable	graven	disbelieve	connive	attentive	interwove
vanilla	haven	interweave	contrive	collective	/ŭv/
variety	raven	perceive	deprive	conclusive	above
vault	shaven	receive	derive	conductive	cover
vegetable	quaver	relieve	diver	connective	discover
vehicle	shaver	reprieve	driver	conservative	lover
velocity	waiver	retrieve	revive	constructive	shovel
venomous	waver	even	survive	creative	uncover
venture	behavior	achiever		decorative	unglove
verbal	misbehavior	beaver		descriptive	/o͞ov/
verify	savior	cleaver		digestive	approve
versatile	slavish	fever		distinctive	behoove
vertebrate	disfavor	griever		exclusive	disapprove
veteran	favor	lever		expensive	disprove
vexation	flavor	weaver		extensive	improve
vibrate	savor	evil		informative	remove
vicarious	gravy	previous		imaginative	reprove
vicinity	navy			instinctive	'r'
victim	wavy			intensive	observant
victor	/ă/	/ĕ/	/ĭ/	locomotive	servant
vigorous	avalanche	eleven	drivel	motive	harvest
village	gavel	heaven	shrivel	offensive	larva
vinegar	gravel	leaven	snivel	preventive	marvel
vineyard	javelin	seven	swivel	reactive	conserve
violin	travel	bevel	given	respective	deserve
virulent	cadaver	dishevel	deliver	sensitive	observe
visual	cavern	level	giver	suggestive	preserve
vocabulary	tavern	revel	liver	**Exception**	reserve
vociferous	clavicle	clever	river	octave	unnerve
volatile	avid	ever	shiver		curvy
volunteer	gravity	however	sliver		nervy
vowel	lavish	lever	livid		scurvy
vulgar	ravish	never	vivid		
vulnerable		sever	civil		
vulture		devil	weevil		
		endeavor	pivot		

l̊ and n̊

Chart 64 and 65
The Effect of 'l' and 'n' on Vowels. The letters, 'l' and 'n', affect the vowel sounds or their spellings more than any other letter except 'r'.

① Rule for /ā/: **Use 'ai' with 'l' and 'n', that is, unless it is a homonym.** The majority of 'ai' words are with 'l' and 'n'. There are a number of exceptions, but these words are homonyms. Homonyms are two words pronounced the same but with different spellings and definitions (mail/male, pain/pane). Poems to help learn these homonyms: ☛ See page 199-200.

② Rule for /ē/: **Use 'ie' before 'ld'.** For the long 'e' sound followed by 'l' or 'n', 'ea' or 'ee' is used. There is no clear pattern as to when to use one or the other. However, 'ie', which is a rare spelling, is used when followed by 'ld', "field".

③ Rule for /ī/: **'I' is long with 'nd' or 'ld'.** The consonants, 'nd' and 'ld' affect 'i' by making it long, "kind", "child". The 'l' or 'n' by themselves or in any other combination do not make it long.

④ Rule for /ō/: **'O' is long when followed by 'l'.** When 'o' is followed by an 'l', it is long, "roll". The usual spelling for a long 'o' with 'n' is '-one' or '-oan'. However, verbs ending in 'ow' become passive past tense by adding an 'n', "mown".

⑤ Rule for /å/: **'A' says /å/, "all", in front of 'll', 'ld', or 'lt'.** There are a few words with 'aw', "crawl". However, the same sound becomes an 'o' in multi-syllable words—"call">"collar". The /å/ sound in front of a single 'n' is usually spelled with 'aw' and not an 'o'.

⑥ Rule for /ŭ/: **'O' can say /ŭn/ in front of 'n'.** Many words with 'on' say /ŭn/, "son".

⑦ Rule for /ou/: **Use 'ow' before 'l' or 'n' whenever they are not in a blend.** Most /ou/ words are spelled with 'ou' in the middle of a word. However, they are spelled 'ow' when followed by a single 'l' or 'n', "prowl", "brown". Blends with 'n', such as 'nd' or 'nt', use 'ou', "round", "count".

⑧ **Silent 'l' or 'n' may or may not affect the vowel sound.** Silent 'l' may or may not affect the vowel sound, "talk", "half". 'N' is silent in several words ending in 'mn', "hymn". It is also found rarely with several silent letters—'kn',"knot", 'gn', "gnat", 'pn', "pneumonia", and 'mn', "mnemonic". (See Chart 71.)

A Study of 'l' and 'n' with Single Vowels (One-Syllable Words)

	a		e		i		o		u	
☆ **l**	***all***	***small***	bell	shell	bill	drill	***poll***	***droll***	bull	
	ball	***stall***	cell	smell	dill	frill	***roll***	***scroll***	cull	
	fall	***brawl***	dell	spell	fill	grill	***toll***	***stroll***	dull	
	gall	***crawl***	fell	dwell	gill	quill	***old***	***troll***	gull	
	hall	***drawl***	hell	swell	hill	trill	***bold***	***scold***	full	
	mall	***scrawl***	jell		ill	skill	***cold***		lull	
	pall	***shawl***	sell		kill	spill	***fold***	**Silent 'l'**	mull	
	tall	***scald***	tell		mill	shrill	***gold***	***folk***	pull	
	wall	scalp	well		pill	thrill	***hold***	***yolk***		
	bawl		yell		sill		***mold***			
	bald	**Silent 'l'**	held		till		***sold***			
	alp	calf/calves	weld		will		***told***			
	halt	half/halves	elf		***mild***	***child***	***bolt***			
	malt	***balk***	self		***wild***		***jolt***			
		talk	elk		milk					
		walk	help		silk					
		chalk	kelp		hilt					
		stalk	yelp		jilt					
		alms	belt		lilt					
		balm	felt		silt					
		calm	melt		tilt					
		palm	pelt		wilt					
		psalm	welt		film					
		qualm	elm							
☆ **n**	an	clan	den	glen	in	grin	***dawn***	***brawn***	bun	spun
	can	plan	hen	when	din	spin	***fawn***	***drawn***	dun	clung
	fan	bran	men		fin	twin	***lawn***	***spawn***	fun	flung
	man	scan	pen		pin	chin	***pawn***	blond	gun	slung
	pan	span	ten		sin	shin	***yawn***	prong	nun(none)	sprung
	ran	bland	yen		tin	thin	bond	strong	pun	stung
	van	gland	end		win	***sign***	fond	thong	run	strung
	and	brand	bend	blend	***bind***	***blind***	pond		sun (son)	chunk
	band	grand	lend	spend	***find***	***grind***	gong		dung	shrunk
	hand	stand	mend	trend	***hind***	thing	long		hung	clunk
	land	strand	send		***kind***	bring	song		lung	drunk
	sand	clang	vend		***mind***	cling	tong		rung	flunk
	bang	slang	bent	spent	***wind*** *(v.)*	sling	wrong		sung	plunk
	gang	sprang	cent		ding	spring	conk		bunk	slunk
	hang	twang	dent		king	sting	honk		dunk	spunk
	rang	blank	lent		ping	string	***aunt***		hunk	stunk
	sang	clank	pent		ring	thing	***daunt***		junk	trunk
	bank	flank	rent		sing	swing	***gaunt***		punk	blunt
	dank	plank	sent		wing	blink	***haunt***		sunk	brunt
	lank	crank	went		fink	slink	***jaunt***		bunt	(front)
	rank	drank			kink	brink	***taunt***		hunt	grunt
	sank	prank			link	drink	***launch***		punt	stunt
	tank	spank			mink	stink	***staunch***		runt	shunt
	yank	shank			pink	chink				
	ant	thank			sink	think				
	pant	plant			wink	shrink				
	rant	slant			hint	splint				
		chant			lint	squint				
		scant			mint	**Exc:** ***pint***				
					tint					

Chart 64

A Study of 'l' and 'n' with Long Vowels (One-Syllable Words)

	① /ā/	② /ē/	③ /ī/	④ /ō/	⑤ /å/	⑥ /ou/	⑦ Silent 'l'
☆ **l**	ail — (ale) bail — (bale) fail frail Gail — (gale) hail — (hale) jail mail — (male) nail pail — (pale) quail rail sail — (sale) snail tail — (tale) trail wail **Exception** scale shale stale vale whale	field shield wield yield	child mild wild	droll poll — (pole) roll scroll stroll toll troll old bold cold fold gold hold mold sold scold told bolt jolt	all ball — (bawl) fall gall hall mall pall small stall tall wall bald scald halt malt salt bawl brawl crawl drawl scrawl shawl **Exception** *doll haul maul fault	cowl fowl growl howl jowl owl prowl scowl yowl	/å/: balk, chalk, stalk, talk, walk, alms, balm, calm, palm, psalm, qualm /ō/: folk, yolk /ă/ calf/calves half/halves /o͝o/ *could *should *would
☆ **n**	brain Cain — (cane) chain drain gain grain lain — (lane) main — (mane) pain — (pane) plain — (plane) rain slain sprain stain strain train vain — (vane) - - - - - faint paint quaint saint taint **Exception** crane wane	fiend	bind blind find grind hind kind mind wind sign **Exception** pint wind (n.)	<u>blown</u> <u>flown</u> <u>grown</u> <u>mown</u> <u>shown</u> <u>sown</u> <u>thrown</u> <u>known</u> don't won't	[1]aunt daunt flaunt gaunt haunt jaunt taunt launch staunch dawn brawn drawn fawn lawn pawn spawn yawn **Exception** con *gone *on	brown clown crown down drown frown gown town	/ŭ/ son ton won front **Exception** *done *none *one *once

[1]May be pronounced /ånt/ or /ănt/.

Chart 65

Chart 66
Multi-Syllable Words with 'r' = /ŭr/. All of the vowels with 'r' in unaccented syllables tend to say /ŭr/ and 'er', 'ir', and 'ur' can say in any position. This makes the mastery of these words a matter of memorization. There are certain suffixes with the /ŭr/ sound which are consistent in their spelling; '-ture', '-sure', '-ard'. There are also prefixes with the /ŭr/ sound which have consistent spelling; 'sur-', 'per-', 'inter-', and 'circum-'. Single syllable /ŭr/ words may be found on Charts 17, 28, 45, and 46.

Chart 67
Multi-Syllable Words with 'r' (/ār/, /ēr/, /īr/). In multi-syllable words, most words with the /ār/, "carrot", sound medially are spelled with either 'ar' or 'er'. Note how many words have a double 'r' following the 'a' or 'e'. We use an 'a' with the prefix 'para-' and the suffix '-ary'. (Exceptions for the '-ary' words are; "cemetery", "confectionery", "monastery", "stationery".) At ends of words, '-are', '-ear', '-air' are used.

With the /ēr/, "hero", sound, 'e' is used most often with the exception of the prefix 'ir-'.

With the /īr/, "attire", sound, the spelling is most often 'ire. Single-syllablewords may be found on Chart 29.

Chart 68
Multi-Syllable Words with 'r' (/år/, /ōr/). The /år/, "carbon", sound is almost always spelled 'ar'. (Exceptions are: "borrow", "sorrow", "tomorrow".)

The /ōr/, "absorb" is spelled 'or' except when following a 'w' it changes to 'ar', "warden". At ends of words, it is usually 'ore' ("ignore"). Single-syllablewords may be found on Chart 29.

English
Greek
German
Latin
Old English
French

Roots

The letters 'tw' carry the meaning "two": "Twelve" (two more than ten), "twenty" (two times ten), "twice" (two times) and of course—even though we don't hear the 'w'—"two" (two). Then there is "twin" (two that are identical), "between" (in the middle of two), "twilight" (between night and day), and "twine" (two rope strands).

A Study of Multi-Syllable Words with Medial /ŭr/ Sound

ur = /ŭr/

burden
burglar
burgundy
burrow
curdle
currant
current
cursory
curtail
curtain
furlough
furnish
furniture
furrow
furtive
gurgle
hurdle
hurrah
hurricane
hurry
hurtle
jury
murder
nurture
purple
purport
purpose
pursue
pursuit
rural
scurry
sturdy
surcharge
surgeon
surly
surmise
surmount
surname
surprise
surrender
surrogate
surround
surveillance
survey
survive
turban
turbine
turbulence
turkey
turmoil
turpentine
turquoise
turtle
disturb
discourage
hamburger
luxury
nocturnal
perturb
picturesque
restaurant
return
Saturday
suburb
taciturn
usurp
yogurt

-ur = /ūr/

bureau
bureaucrat
curious
diuretic
epicure
failure
insecure
manicure
mercury
mural
obscure
procure
puree

-ure = /r/

aperture
brochure
capture
censure
conjure
creature
culture
denature
erasure
feature
fissure
gesture
immature
lecture
leisure
mature
measure
mixture
moisture
pasture
perjure
picture
posture
puncture
rapture
reassure
rupture
seizure
stature
texture
tincture
torture
treasure
venture
vulture

er = /ŭr/

beret
ceramic
certain
derby
dermatologist
ferment
fertile
ferocious
geranium
gerbil
heredity
hermit
hernia
jerky
kernel (colonel)
mercenary
merchandise
mercy
percale
perceive
percent
perennial
perfect
perform
perfume
perhaps
perimeter
peripheral
perjury
perky
permeable
permit
perpendicular
perplex
persecute
persevere
persist
personal
perspire
persuade
pertain
perturb
pervade
serene
serpent
servant
terminal
terminology
termite
terrain
terrific
veranda
verbal
verdict
versatile
version
versus
adverb
adverse
advertise
allergy
alternate
amperage
artery
asteroid
beverage
camera
caterpillar
cavern
celery
coverage
desert
deserve
detergent
determine
diverse
expert
external
federal
general
governor
hibernate
hyperactive
hypertension
immerse
impersonal
infertile
insert
intercede
intercept
interest
interjection
intermission
internal
interpret
interupt
intersect
intervention
interview
lateral
leverage
liberty
literature
maternity
mineral
misery
modern
numeral
observe
paternal
puberty
referee
reserve
reverent
reversal
several
supervise
tolerant
undermine
understand

ar = /ŭr/

aquamarine
auxiliary
awkward
billiard
blizzard
briar
collard
coward
custard
dastardly
drunkard
dungaree
exhilarate
forward
gizzard
glossary
granary
hazard
inward
jeopardy
leopard
lizard
mallard
margarine
mozzarella
mustard
notarize
orchard
polarize
rosary
salary
separate
Spaniard
standard
stewardess
submarine
summary
tankard
upward
wayward

ir = /ŭr/

circle
circumnavigate
circumspect
circumstance
circumvent
circus
firmament
giraffe
girdle
mirage
sirloin
stirrup
thirteen
thirty
virtue
admiral
affirm
aspirin
respiration
squirrel

our = /ŭr/

courage
journal
journey
nourish
tourist
tourniquet
adjourn
contour
detour
entourage
glamour
potpourri
tambourine
velour

eur = /ŭr/

amateur
liqueur
neuron
neurotic
pasteurize
voyeur

ear = /ŭr/

early
rehearse
research

or = /ŭr/

attorney
calorie
corporal
decorate
deodorize
effort
elaborate
favorite
hickory
history
invigorate
perforate
memory
opportunity
rhetoric
stubborn
temporary
victory
worry
worsen
worship
worthy

Note: u = /ū/ t = /ch/ s = /sh/ s = /zh/ z = /zh/ g = /zh/

Chart 66

A Study of Words with Medial 'r' (/ār/, /ēr/, and /ār/)

/ār/

arr
- barrack
- barracuda
- barren
- barricade
- barrier
- carriage
- carrier
- carrot
- embarrass
- farrow
- garret
- harrow
- marriage
- marrow
- marry
- narrate
- narrow
- parrot

ar
- agrarian
- aquarium
- cesarean
- disparage
- hilarious
- invariable
- mascara
- scenario
- vegetarian
- caravan
- caraway
- carousel
- garish
- karat
- lariat
- marathon
- marigold
- parable
- parachute
- paradise
- paradox
- paragraph
- parallel
- paralyze
- paranoid
- parasite
- parent
- parody
- tariff
- variant
- varicose

ary
- apiary
- aviary
- binary
- canary
- commentary
- contrary
- coronary
- dietary
- emissary
- estuary
- February
- intermediary
- January
- library
- military
- monetary
- mortuary
- obituary
- ordinary
- primary
- salivary
- sanitary
- statuary
- tertiary

are
- aware
- beware
- compare
- declare
- ensnare
- fanfare
- prepare
- warfare
- welfare

ear
- forebear
- outwear

air
- dairy
- prairie
- affair
- despair
- eclair
- impair
- millionaire
- repair
- solitaire

Exception
- aerate
- aerial

err
- ferrous
- terrace
- terrible
- terrier
- terror

erry
- berry
- cherry
- ferry
- merry
- very

er
- cerebellum
- ceremony
- derelict
- gerund
- herald
- heresy
- heritage
- heron
- kerosene
- merit
- peril
- perish
- serenade
- verify

- demerit
- experiment
- generic
- imperil
- imperishable
- inherent

-ery
- cemetery
- confectionery
- millinery
- monastery
- stationery

/ēr/

irr
- irradiate
- irrational
- irreducible
- irrefutable
- irregular
- irrelevant
- irreligious
- irremovable
- irreparable
- irreplaceable
- irreproachable
- irresistible
- irresolute
- irresponsible
- irreverent
- irreversible
- irrevocable
- irrigate
- irritate
- mirror

ir
- delirium
- miracle
- spirit

er
- cereal
- eerie
- hero
- period
- periodical
- serious
- xerography
- zero

- adhere
- coherent
- exterior
- imperial
- inferior
- interfere
- interior
- severe
- superior
- theory

ear
- clearance
- dreary
- spearmint
- appear
- arrears
- endear

Exception
- leery
- theory
- weird

/īr/

ire
- acquire
- admire
- aspire
- attire
- conspire
- desire
- empire
- entire
- expire
- inquire
- inspire
- perspire
- require
- retire
- sapphire
- satire
- umpire

ir
- iron

A Continued Study of Words with Medial 'r' (år/ and /ōr/)

/år/

aardvark
barbaric
barbecue
bargain
barter
carbine
carbohydrate
carbon
carbonate
carburetor
carcass
cardigan
cargo
carnal
carnival
carpenter
carpet
cartel
carton
cartoon
darling
farther
garble
gardenia
gargle
garlic
garment
garnet
garter
harbor
harmonica
harmony
harness
harpoon
jargon
larva
marble
margarine
margin
market
martyr
marvel
narcotic
parcel
pardon
parka
parsley
partial
particular
partition
partner
partridge
party

sarcasm
sarcoma
sardine
tardy
target
tarnish
varnish
varsity
yarrow

bazaar
bombard
debark
depart
department
disarm
disarray
embargo
enlarge
hierarchy
impart
incarnate
malarkey
monarch
matriarch
patriarch
philharmonic
rampart
regard
remark
retard
restart
rhubarb
safari

Exception
borrow
sorrow
tomorrow

/ōr/

or
border
coral
cordial
corduroy
cornea
corner
cornucopia
coroner
coronation
coronet
corporate
corporeal
corral
correct
correlate
correspond
corridor
corrode
corrugation
corrupt
corsage
cortex
cortisone
dormant
dormitory
forage
forbade
forbid
forebear
foreclosure
foreign
forehead
foremost
forest
foretold
forewarn
forfeit
forgive
formal
format
formidable
formula
forsake
fortress
fortune
forty
forum
gorgeous
gorilla
hormone
hornet
horrible
horror
moral
morbid
morning
moron

mortal
morsel
mortgage
mortuary
porcelain
porpoise
porridge
portable
portend
porter
portion
portrait
sordid
torment
tornado
torpedo
torque
torrent
torso
tortilla
torture

abhor
abnormal
absorb
accord
accordion
adorn
adsorb
afford
allegory
aorta
ashore
assorted
auditory
category
chlorophyll
comfort
conform
contort
decorate
deform
demoralize
deplore
deport
discord
distort
divorce
endorse
enforce
engorge
euphoria
exhort
export
factory
fluoride
galore
ignore
import
inborn
incorporate
information
lavatory
metamorphic
misfortune
perform
pictorial
platform
proportion
purport
rapport
record
reform
remorse
report
resort
retort
sycamore
uniform

war
warble
warden
wardrobe
warrant
warranty
warrior
forewarn
reward

Exception
aura
aural
laurel
laureate
aboard
fourteen
gourmet

Chart 69
A Study of 'u'. The 'u' vowel helps quite a few consonants. The main one is 'q'. The sounds of 'qu' are /kw/, "bequest", /k/, "conquer", "plaque". Following 'qu', the 'a' says /å/, "squad". Do not confuse the /kū /, "cute", sound (which is spelled 'cu') with the /kw/, "quit", sound (which is spelled 'qu').

The further study of 'u' shows more of the jobs that 'u' has. It helps keep the /g/ sound of 'g' before 'i', 'e', or 'y', "guest". The '-gue' at ends of words says the /g/, "vague", sound. Several of these words end in '-ogue', "prologue". Many of the other words need the silent 'e' for the long vowel. Since 'ge' says /j/, the 'u' in these words is to maintain the 'g' sound. The majority of words with a 'j' sound are made with a 'g' or 'j'. However, there are several where the 'd' followed by a 'u' says /j/, "educate". The entire list is given.

In the middle of words, 'u' causes the 's' to say /sh/, "assure", and 'u' causes the 't' to say /ch/, "adventure". For a more complete list, see Chart 57.

The vowel team 'eu', /ü/, "neutral", is rare. This list contains the majority of the words with that vowel combination.

Chart 70
A Study of 'y'. Fewer than 50 independent words have 'y' as a consonant ("yard").

The vowel combination 'io' sounds like /yŭ /, "onion".

The letter 'y' also functions as a vowel. At ends of words, 'y' stands in for 'i' and 'e' ("baby", "shy"). The combinations 'ay' and 'oy' are used for the /ā / ,"bay", and /oi/, "boy", sounds at ends of syllables. There are also words where 'y' says /ī /, "style", or /ĭ / "gym". These must be memorized.

Chart 71
There are limited numbers of words with silent letters. The best way to learn these is to learn them as groups. There are several pages in the section on Teaching Helps that will assist in learning these words. For 'kn': ☛ See page 214. For 'wr': ☛ See page 215. For 'mb': ☛ See page 216.

A Study of 'u' with 'q'

'qu'=/kw/ Medial			'qua'=/kwå/ Medial (Entire List)	'qu'=/k/ (Entire List) Final /k/	Medial /k/
acquaint	enquire	sequin	aqua	antique	appliqué
acquaintance	equate	soliloquy	aquamarine	baroque	bouquet
acquiesce	equilibrium	square	aquatic	boutique	communiqué
acquire	equinox	squeak	equal	brusque	croquet
acquit	equip	squeal	hindquarter	clique	marquee
acquittal	equivalent	squeegee	squab	critique	risqué
adequate	esquire	squeeze	squad	discotheque	
antiquate	exquisite	squib	squabble	grotesque	
aquarium	frequent	squid	squadron	masque	conquer
aqueduct	harlequin	squiggle	squall	mosque	conquistador
banquet	inquire	squint	squander	mystique	etiquette
bequeath	liquefy	squire	squash	oblique	lacquer
bequest	request	squirm	squat	opaque	mannequin
colloquial	require	squirrel	squaw	physique	masquerade
conquest	requisite	squirt	squawk	picturesque	mesquite
consequence	requite	squish		pique	mosquito
delinquent	sequel	tranquil		plaque	piquant
earthquake	sequence	vanquish		romanesque	turquoise
eloquent	sequester			statuesque	
				technique	
				torque	
				unique	

A Further Study of 'u'

gu = /g/	gue = /g/ (Entire)	du = /j/ (Entire)	su = /sh/	tu = /ch/	eu = /u/
guard	catalogue	assiduous	assure	actuary	amateur
guess	colleague	arduous	censure	century	grandeur
guest	demagogue	credulous	erasure	creature	saboteur
guide	dialogue	deciduous	fissure	culture	deuce
guild	epilogue	educate	insure	factual	eulogy
guillotine	fatigue	fraudulent	issue	fluctuate	eunuch
guilt	intrigue	glandular	pressure	fortune	euphony
guinea pig	league	gradual	sugar	furniture	feudal
guise	monologue	grandeur	sure	gargantuan	lieutenant
guitar	plague	incredulous	tissue	habitual	maneuver
guy	prologue	individual	**su/zu = /zh/**	mortuary	neutral
beguile	rogue	modulate	casual	natural	neutron
disguise	synagogue	module	exposure	obituary	neuron
roguish	travelogue	procedure	leisure	punctual	pseudo
gu=gw	vague	pendulum	pleasure	puncture	pseudonym
anguish	vogue	residual	treasure	ritual	pneumonia
bilingual	harangue	schedule	visual	rupture	rheumatism
distinguish	meringue	**Exception**	azure	sanctuary	sleuth
extinguish	tongue	cordial	seizure	signature	therapeutic
jaguar		soldier		situation	**Other**
language				spatula	brochure
languish				spiritual	biscuit
linguist				temperature	circuit
					build

A Study of 'y'

'y' as a Consonant (Fewer than 50 independent words)

'y' = /y/

yak
yam
yank
yap
yard
yarn
yatch
yawn
ye
yea
yeah
year
yearn
yeast
yell
yellow
yelp
yen
yes
yesterday
yet
yield
yip
yodel
yoga
yogurt
yoke
yolk
yonder
you
young
youth
yucca
yummy

beyond
canyon
coyote
lawyer
papaya

Compound Words

farmyard
vineyard

-io = /yŭ/

battalion
billion
bullion
bunion
communion
companion
dominion
galleon
medallion
million
mullion
oblivion
onion
opinion
pavilion
pillion
pinion
quadrillion
quintillion
rebellion
scullion
stallion
trillion
union
vermilion
zillion

anterior
behavior
exterior
inferior
interior
junior
posterior
savior
senior
superior
warrior

'y' as a Vowel (excluding ends of words)

ay = /ā/

bayonet
crayon
layette
mayhem
mayonnaise
mayor
payment
rayon
wayward

Exception:

convey
obey

Compound Words

daybreak
daydream
daylight
daytime
hayloft
haystack
jaywalk
layman
layoff
layover
maybe
Mayday
mayflower
mayfly
maypole
paycheck
payday
payload
paymaster
playback
playground
playpen
playroom
playmate
playtime
playwright
swayback
wayfarer
waylaid
wayside

oy = /oi/

annoyance
buoyant
boycott
boyhood
buoy
coyness
foyer
loyal
oyster
royal
voyage

y = /ī/

analyze
asylum
cycle
cyclone
cypress
dehydrate
dryer
dye
dynamic
dynasty
encyclopedia
enzyme
goodbye
gyrate
gyro
hyacinth
hybrid
hydrant
hydroelectric
hydrogen
hyena
hygiene
hyperactive
hyphen
hypochondria
hypothesis
lye
myopia
nylon
paralyze
psyche
pyrite
python
rhyme
rye
scythe
style
thyme
tycoon
tyke
type
typhoon
typhoid
tyrant

Exception:

geyser
kayak

yr = /ŭr/

myrrh
syringe
syrup
zephyr

yr = /ĕr/

lyric
myriad

y = /ĭ/

acrylic
analysis
asymmetrical
bicycle
tricycle
crypt
crystal
cylinder
cymbal
cynic
cyst
dyslexia
dystrophy
gym
gyp
Gypsy
hymn
hypnosis
hysteria
lymph
lynch
lynx
mystery
myth
nymph
Olympic
onyx
oxygen
physical
physician
pygmy
strychnine
sycamore
syllable
symbol
sympathy
symphony
symptom
synagogue
synapse
synchronize
syndicate
syndrome
synonym
synopsis
syntax
system
tryst
vinyl

y = /ē/

embryo
polygon
pollywog

Chart 70

A Study of Silent Consonants

Silent 'b'

bt = /t/
debt
doubt

mb = /m/
bomb (balm)
comb
climb
crumb (crumble)
dumb
lamb
limb
numb
plumb (plum)
thumb
tomb
succumb
womb

Silent 'c'

sc = /s/
scene
scent
science
scissors
descend
excel
muscle
(see Ch. 60)

c = / /
indict
victual

Silent 'd'

dj = /j/
adjacent
adjure
adjust

dg = /j/
(Samples)
abridge
bridge
cartridge
dislodge
hedge
judgment
knowledge
lodge
midget
partridge
porridge
trudge

d = / /
Wednesday

Silent 'g'

gn = /n/
gnarl
gnash
gnat
gnaw
gnome
gnu
align
arraign
assign
benign
campaign
champaign
consign
deign
design
ensign
feign
foreign
impugn
malign
reign
resign
sign
sovereign
bologna (baloney)
lasagna
cologne
poignant
mignon

gm =/m/
diaphragm
phlegm

Silent 'h'

h = / /
annihilate
exhaust
exhibit
exhilarate
exhort
gingham
graham
herb
heir
honest
honor
hour
shepherd
vehement
ah
eh
oh
uh
hurrah

gh = /g/
ghastly
ghetto
ghost
ghoul
spaghetti

ch = / /
drachm
schism
yacht

rh = /r/
rhapsody
rhesus
rhetoric
rheum
rheumatism
rhinal
rhinestone
rhinoceros
rhizome
rhododendron
rhombus
rhubarb
rhumba
rhyme
rhythm
diarrhea
myrrh

Silent 'k'

kn = /n/
knack
knag
knapsack
knar
knave
knead
knee
kneel
knell
knew
knickerbocker
knickknack
knife
knight
knit
knives
knob
knock
knoll
knot
know
knowledge
knuckle

Silent 'p'

pn = /n/
pneumonia
pneumatic

ps = /s/
pseudonym
psyche
psychology
Psalm

pt = /t/
pterodactyl

Silent 'r'

r = / /
February

Silent 'l'

lm = /m/
alms
balm (bomb)
calm
palm
psalm
qualm
salmon

lk = /k/
balk
chalk
stalk
talk
walk
folk
yolk (yoke)

lf = /f/
calf
half

ld = /d/
could
should
would
solder

Silent 'm'

mn = /n/
mnemonic

Silent 'n'

mn = /m/
autumn
column
condemn
damn
hymn (hymnal)
solemn

Silent 's'

s = / /
aisle
apropos
bourgeois
corps
chassis
chamois
debris
island

Silent 't'

st= /s/
apostle
bristle
bustle
castle
epistle
gristle
hustle
jostle
mistletoe
nestle (nest)
rustle
thistle
whistle
wrestle
chasten (chaste)
christen (Christ)
fasten (fast)
glisten
hasten (haste)
listen
moisten (moist)

ft = /f/
often (oft)
soften (soft)

-et = /a/
bouquet
crochet
croquet

Silent 'w'

wr = /r/
wrack
wrangle
wrap
wrath
wreak
wreath
wreck
wren
wrench
wrestle
wretch
wriggle
wring
wrinkle
wrist
write (right)
writhe
wrong
wrote
wrought
wrung
wry
sword
answer

UNIT 7

FOCUS ON: MEANING

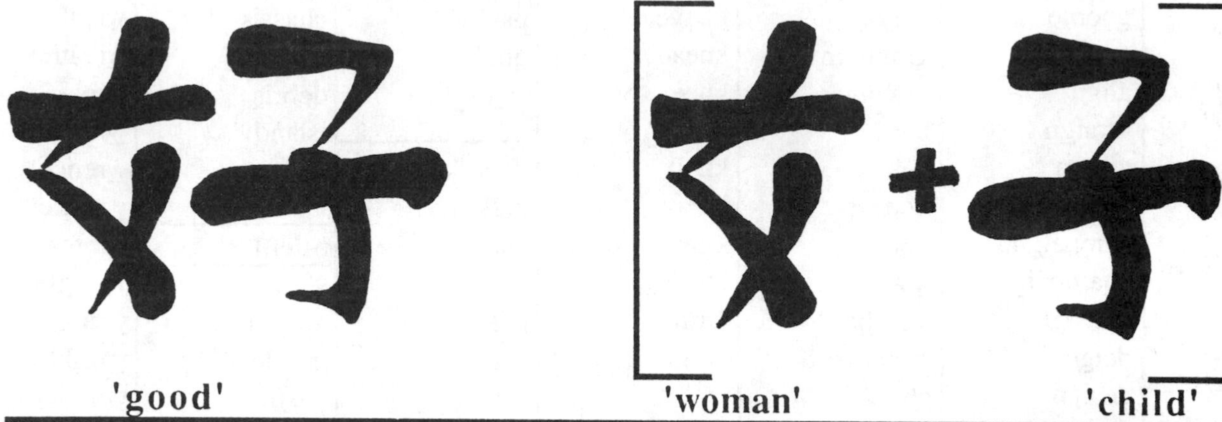
'good'
'woman'
'child'

There is a story told of a young boy who was taught how to read the Chinese script by a wise old gentleman. Patiently the old scholar showed him the symbols for each word. First he showed him the symbols for words like 'woman' and 'child'. Then he put the symbols together, and to the boy's surprise a new word was formed. The old man explained that putting the symbols for woman and child together meant 'good'. What a visual image of peace that projected to the boy—a woman and her child!

"How sad," I thought, at the end of the story, "that our English words don't paint visual images like these."

It was several months later, in researching for this handbook, that I opened a dictionary to do a series on 'roots'. As I began to read, to my amazement the words, just every day words, suddenly became alive, full of visual images. I became so engrossed in my discovery that I could not put the dictionary down until my eyes would no longer focus. It was four a.m.!

May this unit increase your vocabulary and appreciation for your language—not out of a sense of duty, but out of sheer pleasure, as you make your own discoveries in the pages that follow.

Chart 72
Eagle's Wings Select Prefixes. The prefixes on this chart were carefully chosen to include the ones most commonly used. There are twenty-six. The words in each box give examples to use for spelling purposes. Several have the same meaning. For example, 'un-', 'dis-', 'in-' all mean "not", ("unable", "disagree", "incapable").

Chart 73
Eagle's Wings Select Suffixes. This is a list of the suffixes used most often. The words in each box gives examples to use for spelling purposes. There are other suffixes throughout the handbook. Consult the Table of Contents for these.

Chart 74-79
Roots. These charts provide hundreds of roots (the core of the word, passed on from previous generations), their meanings, and samples of words which were derived from them. Scattered through the previous part of this handbook are small examples of where words came from. Use this unit on a regular basis for building vocabulary. ('belli'—means "war". From it we get "belligerent", "bellow", "rebellious", and "rebel". A rebellious person is "at war".)

Chart 80-81
Synonym and Antonym. These two charts give a word, its synonym (word with the same meaning) and its antonym (word with opposite meaning). Use these charts to help in writing exercises by exchanging words of the same or opposite meanings. (The water in the pool was *muddy*. > The water in the pool was *transparent*.) These words can also be used for matching games and are great vocabulary builders.

Chart 82
Homonyms. Homonyms are words that sound the same but have different spellings and different meanings. They are important to know for spelling purposes. Short definitions are included in parenthesis next to each word. ("dear" (beloved), "deer" (animal))

Chart 83
Heteronyms. Heteronyms are two words that are pronounced differently and have different meanings but have the same spelling. (I *dove* into the water. A *dove* flew overhead.) Again, these are for vocabulary building and spelling purposes. Practice saying the words aloud and use them in sentences.

Stumblers. Stumblers are words that are easily confused because of similarities in their spelling. ("dairy" (milk), "diary" (daily record)) Practice these words for spelling and reading, being sure to say the words aloud and use them correctly in sentences.

Contractions. Contractions are two words put together with some of the letters missing. The apostrophe (') shows where the letters were taken out. (can not = can't)

Eagle's Wings Select Prefixes

anti-(against)	**dis**-(not)	**en**-(cause to be)	**ex**- (out of)	**in**-(not)	**inter**- (between)
antibiotic	disagree	enclose	exact	incapable	intercede
anticlimactic	disappear	encourage	excel	incline	intercept
antidote	disbelief	endanger	except	inclosure	interconnect
antifreeze	discharge	enforce	exchange	incomplete	interface
antihistamine	discontinue	engage	excite	inconceivable	interlock
antimatter	discourage	engrave	exclaim	inconsiderate	international
antiseptic	disguise	enjoy	excuse	incorrect	interplay
antisocial	dishonest	enlist	exercise	indefinite	interrupt
antithesis	dismiss	enrage	exit	inside	intertwine
antitoxin	dissolve	entire	express	invisible	intervene

mis-(wrong)	**over**-(beyond, over)	**post**-(after)	**pre**-(before)	**pro**-(forth)	**re**-(repeat)
misfit	overactive	postdate	prearrange	proclaim	react
mishap	overbearing	postdiluvian	precede	procure	recite
misplace	overboard	postgraduate	predestine	profess	reconsider
mispronounce	overcome	posterior	predict	profound	record
misrepresent	overcooked	postpaid	prefer	progress	recover
misspell	overdue	postpone	prefix	project	redeem
mistake	overeager	postmortem	pretend	promote	refresh
mistreat	overshadow	postscript	prevent	pronounce	remember
mistrust	overthrow	postoperative	prepare	protect	reproduce
misunderstand	overwhelm	postwar	present	provoke	require

semi-(half)	**sub**-(under)	**super**-(to be over)	**trans**-(across)	**un**-(not)	**under**-(below)
semiannual	subconscious	superabundant	transcend	unable	underage
semiautomatic	subdue	superb	transcript	unbearable	undercharged
semicircle	subject	superficial	transfer	uncertain	underclassman
semicolon	sublease	superhuman	transfigure	uncover	undercover
semiconscious	submarine	superior	transform	undo	undercurrent
semidetached	submerge	superlative	transfuse	unfinished	underdeveloped
semifinalist	submission	supermarket	transgress	unqualified	underestimate
semipermeable	subscribe	supernatural	translate	unthinkable	underground
semiprecious	subside	supersonic	transplant	unusual	underhanded
semiprivate	substitute	supervise	transverse	unwrap	underwear

uni-(one)	**mono**-(one)	**du**-(two)	**bi**-(two)	**tri**-(three)	**multi**-(many)
unicorn	monochromatic	dual	biannual	triangle	multicolored
unicycle	monocle	duality	bicentennial	triceps	multiform
uniform	monogamy	duel	biceps	tricycle	multimillionaire
unify	monolingual	duet	bicycle	trifocal	multiple
union	monolith	duo	bilateral	trimester	multiplex
unique	monologue	duodecimal	bilingual	Trinity	multiplicity
unison	monopoly	duodenal	bimonthly	trio	multiply
unit	monorail	duplex	binary	triple	multiracial
unity	monotone	duplicate	binocular	triplet	multitude
universal	monotonous	duplicity	bisector	tripod	multivitamin

Chart 72

Eagle's Wings Select Suffixes

-able/-ible (able to)	**-age** (state of or place)	**-ance** (state of) **-ence** (state of)	**-ate** (having to do with)	**-ed** (completed) **-ing** (in process)	**-er** (more than) **-est** (most)
accountable	average	abundance	decorate	allowed/allowing	bigger/biggest
allowable	courage	acquaintance	educate	blessed/blessing	cheaper/cheapest
communicable	damage	annoyance	fascinate	counted/counting	greater/greatest
enable	disadvantage	performance	formulate	helped/helping	higher/highest
likeable	manage	remembrance	illustrate	jumped/jumping	sicker/sickest
loveable	marriage	confidence	integrate	nodded/nodding	-er (person/object)
redeemable	mileage	diligence	isolate	sealed/sealing	leader
horrible	cottage	innocence	moderate	started/starting	hiker
terrible	orphanage	violence	vaccinate	tested/testing	robber
					jogger

-en (state of)	**-ful** (full of)	**-fy** (intensify)	**-hood** (member of)	**-ic** (like)	**-ish** (the act of)
bitten	bashful	amplify	babyhood	arithmetic	anguish
chosen	beautiful	beautify	brotherhood	artistic	cherish
eaten	careful	classify	childhood	autographic	finish
flatten	cheerful	dignify	likelihood	classic	impish
given	colorful	horrify	manhood	drastic	perish
gladden	forgetful	identify	motherhood	humanistic	polish
happen	hopeful	justify	neighborhood	mechanic	relish
madden	houseful	magnify	parenthood	romantic	selfish
sadden	mouthful	qualify	sisterhood	skeptic	vanish
woven	skillful	simplify	womanhood	volcanic	varnish

-ist (person)	**-ive** (inclined to)	**-ize** (practice of)	**-less** (without)	**-ly/-y** (manner)	**-ment** (state of)
balloonist	active	apologize	ageless	clearly	argument
cartoonist	attentive	authorize	blameless	completely	complement
dentist	collective	baptize	childless	deeply	detriment
florist	conductive	capitalize	endless	happily	embarrassment
idealist	defective	criticize	fearless	quickly	government
moralist	effective	fertilize	friendless	crazy	measurement
perfectionist	explosive	memorize	homeless	dizzy	monument
realist	informative	sympathize	odorless	funny	nourishment
specialist	passive	tranquilize	restless	happy	punishment
ventriloquist	submissive	vaporize	weightless	skinny	supplement

-ness (state of)	**-ous** (full of)	**-some** (tends to be)	**-tion/sion** (state of)	**-tude** (state of)	**-ward** (direction)
blackness	cantankerous	adventuresome	action	altitude	downward
cheerfulness	curious	awesome	admiration	aptitude	eastward
closeness	dangerous	bothersome	condition	attitude	homeward
completeness	delirious	burdensome	exhibition	fortitude	inward
dizziness	enormous	cumbersome	introduction	gratitude	onward
joyfulness	generous	frolicsome	compassion	latitude	outward
peacefulness	glamorous	handsome	discussion	longitude	toward
prettiness	humorous	troublesome	expansion	magnitude	upward
respectfulness	jealous	wearisome	permission	servitude	westward
slothfulness	marvelous	wholesome	repercussion	solitude	

Chart 73

Roots

ac/acri	*(sharp, bitter)*	acid, acerbity, acrimony
act	*(to do, act)*	act, activate, action, activity, retroactive
agog	*(leader)*	demagogue, synagogue
agri	*(field)*	agrarian, agriculture
air/aer	*(air)*	aerial, air, airplane, airport, malaria
ali	*(another)*	alias, alienate, alien alibi
angel	*(messenger)*	angel, angelic, evangelist
anim	*(mind, soul)*	animal, animosity, magnanimous, unanimous
anni	*(year)*	anniversary, annual, biennial, perennial, anno Domini (A.D.)
anthrop	*(man)*	anthropology, philanthropist
aqua	*(water)*	aquatic, aquanaut, aquamarine, aquarium, aqueduct
arch	*(ruler, first)*	archbishop, archeology, monarch, anarchy, hierarchy, matriarch, patriarch
audi	*(hear)*	audiovisual, auditory, audible, auditorium, audience
auto	*(self)*	autocracy, automobile, autobiography, automatic, autograph, autocrat, automation
avi	*(bird)*	aviary, aviation, aviator
belli	*(war)*	belligerent, bellow, rebellious, rebel
ben/bon	*(good)*	benefit, benefactor, benevolent, beneficial, bonus, bonanza, bona fide, benign
bibli	*(book)*	Bible, bibliography, bibliographer
bio	*(life)*	biology, biography, biophysics, biopsy
brev	*(short)*	brevity, abbreviate, breve
cant	*(sing)*	accent, cantata, chant, enchant, incantation, recant
cap	*(to seize)*	caption, captive, capture, catch
card/cord	*(heart)*	cardiac, cardiology, cordial, courage, accord, concord, discord
carn	*(flesh)*	carnival, carnal, carnage, carnivorous, incarnate
caust/cast	*(to burn)*	caustic, sarcastic, holocaust, sarcasm
ceed/cede	*(yield, go)*	concede, recede, proceed, antecedent, cease, exceed, succeed
cell/ceal	*(hide)*	conceal, cell
cent	*(one hundred)*	century, centennial, percent, centimeter
chrono	*(time)*	chronological, chronology, anachronism
cian	*(expert)*	beautician, magician, politician, physician
cid/cad	*(die, fall)*	accident, cadaver, cascade, decay, deciduous, incident
cid/cis	*(to cut, kill)*	incision, homicide, suicide
circu	*(ring, circle)*	circle, circa, circumvent, circumstance, search
cise	*(cut)*	scissors, circumcise, concise, incisor, precise, incision
cit	*(start up, call)*	excite,incite, recite
civi	*(citizen)*	civil, civilian, civilize, civilization
claim	*(cry out)*	claim, claimant, clamor, acclaim, declaim, exclaim, proclaim, reclaim
clam	*(cry out)*	clamor, declamation, acclamation
class	*(a group of)*	classic, caste, class, classical, classify, classy
cline	*(lean, bend)*	decline, incline, recline, inclination
contra	*(opposite)*	contrary, countradict, countraband, counter, country, encounter
cosm	*(universe)*	cosmic, cosmology, cosmonaut, cosmopolitan, cosmos

Roots

crat	*(group member)*	autocrat, democrat, aristocrat
cred	*(to trust)*	credence, credential, credible, credit, creed, credit card, incredulous
cres/cret	*(grow, increase)*	crescendo, crescent, decrease, increase, recruit
cumul	*(mass, heap)*	cumulate, accumulate, cumulus
cycle	*(wheel,circle)*	cycle, cyclone, bicycle, tricycle, encyclopedia
deb/du	*(owe)*	debit, debt, due, duty
dec/deci	*(ten)*	decimal, decade, duodecimal
demo	*(people)*	democracy, democrat, demagogue, epidemic, demography
dent	*(tooth)*	dentist, dental, dentin, dentistry, denture, orthodontist, indent
derm	*(skin)*	epidermis, dermatology, pachyderm
dic	*(say, words)*	dictate, diction, indicate, indictment, verdict, dictaphone, dictator, dictionary, benedict, contradict
div	*(separate)*	divide, individual, division, indivisible, divorce, divisive
doc	*(teach)*	document, indoctrinate, doctor, doctrine
dom/dome	*(home)*	domain, domestic, domicile, domesticate
domin	*(rule)*	dominate, domineering, domination, dominion
duc	*(lead)*	viaduct, aqueduct, educate, conduct, conductor, conduction
dupl	*(double)*	duplicate, duplex, duplicity
dur	*(long lasting)*	durable, duration, duress, during, endure, endurance
ego	*(I, self)*	ego, egocentric, egomaniac, egotist
err	*(wander)*	err, erratic, erroneous, error, aberration
eva	*(age, era)*	primeval, medieval, longevity
fall/fal	*(deceive)*	fall, false, fallacy, infallible, falsify
fend	*(ward off)*	defend, defense, fence, offend, offence
fest	*(festive)*	festival, festive, feast, fiesta
figure	*(shape)*	figure, configuration, disfigure, transfiguration
fin	*(end)*	final, finish, finite, infinite
fix	*(fasten)*	affix, crucifixion, fixture, fixative, prefix, suffix
frac	*(to break)*	fracas, fraction, fractious, fracture, fragile, fragment, infraction, infringe, refract
frater	*(brother)*	fraternal, fraternity, fraternize
fric	*(to rub)*	fricative, friction, fry, affricate
gage	*(pledge)*	engage, mortgage, wage, wager
gam	*(marriage)*	monogamy, bigamy, polygamy
gene	*(class, race)*	genus, generic, gender, genetic, genealogy, gene, degenerate, genocide, heterogeneous, indigenous
geo	*(earth)*	geography, geology, geothermal
ghast	*(ghost)*	ghost, aghast, ghastly, poltergeist
gon	*(angle)*	diagonal, hexagon, pentagon
graph	*(writing)*	phonograph, telegraph, epigraph, telegram, diagram, monogram
grat	*(thankful)*	congratulate, grateful, gratitude, gratify, gratis, gratuity, ingrate, ingratitude
greg	*(herd, flock)*	aggregate, congregate, gregarious, segregate
gres	*(to walk or go)*	aggression, congress, digression, progress, regress, retrogress, transgress
hab/hav	*(have, hold)*	habit, habitant, habitation, habitual

Roots

hap	*(chance, luck)*	haphazard, happen, happenstance, happy, hapless
head	*(upper part)*	head, headlight, headliner, headlong, headstone, headstrong, headwater
heart	*(strong emotions)*	heartache, heartbreak, heartily, heartless, heartsick, heart-to-heart, hearty, dishearten
heir	*(orphan)*	heir, heredity, heritage, inherit
hemo	*(blood)*	hemoglobin, hemophilia, hemorrhage, hemorrhoid
hetero	*(different)*	heterogeneous, heterosexual
high	*(superior)*	highbrow, higher-up, highlight, high-spirited, highway
hosp	*(host of guests)*	host, hospice, hospital, hospitality, hostel
hydra	*(water)*	hydrant, dehydrate, hydraulic, hydroplane, hydroelectric, hydrophobia
hyper	*(over)*	hyperactive, hypercritical, hypertension, hyperextension, hypersensitive
hypo	*(under)*	hypochondria, hypodermic, hypothermia
ics	*(knowledge of)*	ethics, physics, politics, tactics
igni	*(fire)*	igneous, ignite, ignition
ject	*(throw)*	projection, eject, trajectory, projectile, injection, reject,
junct	*(join)*	injunction, conjunction, junction
jur	*(swear)*	jury, jurist, adjure, perjury, injury, conjure, perjure, jurisdiction
juv	*(young)*	junior, juvenile, rejuvenate
kine/cine	*(movement)*	kinetic, cinematography, cinema
labor	*(work)*	labor, laboratory, laborious, collaborate, elaborate
lapse	*(slip, fall)*	lapse, collapse, elapse, prolapse, relapse
laud	*(praise)*	applaud, laud
lev	*(lighten, raise)*	leaven, lever, levity, alleviate, elevate, elevator, relieve
lect	*(choose)*	select, elect, election
lex/lect langua	*(tongue)*	language, lingo, linguist, bilingual, tongue, dialect, lexicon, intellect, dyslexia
liber	*(free)*	liberal, liberate, liberty, deliver, libertine
line	*(line)*	line, linear, delineate
liter	*(letter, words)*	letter, literal literacy, illiterate, transliterate
local	*(place)*	local, locale, locality, locate, locator
logy	*(reason, logical)*	logic, logistics, logical, logarithm, biology
long	*(long)*	long, longitude, longevity, elongate, oblong, prolong
lum	*(light)*	lumen, luminary, luminous, illuminate
lun	*(moon)*	luna moth, lunar, lunatic
magni	*(greatness)*	magnificent, magnify, magnitude, magnification
mal	*(evil, ill)*	malady, malaria, malefactor, malicious, malevolence, malformed, malice, malign, malpractice, malnutrition, malignant, dismal, petite mal
man	*(hand)*	manufacture, manuscript, emancipate, manicure, manage, mannerism, maneuver, manipulate
mand	*(order)*	command, commando, commend, demand, mandate, recommend, reprimand

Roots

mar	*(sea)*	maritime, submarine, marine, marina, mariner, aquamarine
matu	*(ripen)*	mature, immature, premature
med	*(cure)*	medical, medic, medicate, medicine, remedy
medi	*(between, middle)*	mean, medial, median, mediate, medium, meridian, intermediate, mediocre, Mediterranean
maj	*(greater)*	major, majority, mayor, majesty, magistrate, master, minister, maestro, maximum
ment	*(bring to mind)*	mind, mental, mania, demented, mention, remember, memory, mind, momento, memorabilia, monument, memorial, comment, reminiscent, mnemonic, memorandum
mes/mit	*(to send off, let go)*	message, missile, mission, missionary, dismiss, admit, emit, commit, omit, permit, submit, transmit
meter	*(measure)*	meter, diameter, centimeter, millimeter, geometry, isometric, semester, trimester
mil	*(thousand)*	million, millipede, millimeter
min	*(smaller)*	minor, minus, minuscule, minimum, minister, ministry
mir	*(cause to smile)*	smile, marvel, miracle, mirage, mirror, admire
mob/mot	*(move)*	mobile, motion, motive, motor, move, commotion, emotion, promote, remote, momentum
mort	*(death)*	mortal, mortuary, mortality, immortal, mortgage, mortify, postmortem, murder, morbid
nat	*(born, naive)*	natal, nation, native, nature, cognate, innate, neonate
nom	*(division or law)*	astronomy, autonomy, binomial, Deuteronomy, number, enumerate, numerous, innumerable
noti	*(get to know)*	notice, notify, notion, notorious
nounc	*(message)*	announce, denounce, enunciate, pronounce, renounce
nova	*(new)*	novice, innovate, renovate, novelty, novel, nova
nur/nour	*(nourish)*	nourish, nurse, nurture, nutrient, nutrition, nutritious
oct	*(eight)*	octane, octave, October, octagon, octopus
ode	*(journey)*	cathode, episode, exodus, method, odometer, period
opt	*(choose)*	opt, co-opt, adopt, option, optimum
ov	*(egg)*	ovum, oval, ovary, ovulate
part/port	*(share)*	parcel, part, compartment, impart, portion, proportion
pater	*(father)*	paternal, patrimony, patron, expatriate, patriot, patriarch
path	*(disease, suffering)*	pathetic, pathology, sympathy, empathy, pathology, homeopathy, pitiful, patient,
pend	*(to hang)*	pendant, appendage, depend, impend, perpendicular, suspend, penthouse, compensate
phone	*(voice, sound)*	phoneme, phonetic, phonograph, telephone, symphony
plus	*(more)*	plural, plus, surplus
polis	*(city)*	police, policy, politic, cosmopolitan, metropolis
port	*(carry)*	portable, porter, deportation, export, report, support, import, portfolio, purport, rapport, transport
posit	*(put, place)*	composite, composition, deposit, impose, oppose, position, posture

Roots

prec	*(value)*	precise, precious, price, appraise, appreciate, depreciate
prehen pred	*(seized before)*	apprehensive, apprehend, comprehend, reprehend, predator (prey), prison
prim	*(first, foremost)*	premier, primal, primary, primate, prime, primitive, primeval
quart quad	*(four)*	quadruple, quadruplets, square, quadrant, quadrilateral, quarter, quarterback, quartet, quart
quest	*(to seek)*	quest, query, inquiry, acquire, conquer, exquisite, prerequisite, require
quo	*(how much)*	quote, quotient, quotation, quota
rad	*(root)*	radish, eradicate, radical
rep	*(to creep)*	repent, repentant, reptile
rex	*(king)*	real, regal, regulate, reign, royal
rota	*(roll, wheel)*	rotund, rotunda, round, roll, rota, rotary, rotate, rote, roulette
rub	*(red)*	rouge, rubella, ruby, ruddy, rubbing, bilirubin, russet
rupt	*(break)*	rupture, abrupt, bankrupt, corrupt, disrupt, erupt, interrupt
sati	*(sufficient)*	satiate, satisfy, satisfaction, saturate
scope	*(a watcher)*	telescope, microscope, horoscope
scend	*(climb)*	ascend, condescend, descend, transcend
scien	*(discern, know)*	science, conscience, conscious, omniscient
scrib	*(scratch, write)*	scribble, scribe, script, Scripture, ascribe, circumscribe, conscript, describe, inscribe, manuscript, postscript, prescribe, subscribe, transcribe
se/solo	*(on your own)*	secede, seclude, secret, secure, sedition, seduce, segregate, select, separate, sole, solitary, solitude, desolate, sullen
sect	*(to cut)*	section, sector, segment, dissect, expect, insect, intersect, resect
sed	*(settle, sit)*	sedentary, sediment, sedate, settle, saddle, seat
seque	*(follow)*	sect, sequel, sequence, suitor, consequence, ensue, execute, persecute, prosecute, pursue, subsequent
sent	*(to feel)*	scent, sense, sentence, sentiment, ascent, consent, present, resent
serv	*(slave)*	serf, serve, sergeant, service, servile, servitude, deserve
sex/hex	*(six)*	six, sextet, sextant, semester, hexagon, hex
sign	*(sign, label)*	seal, scarlet, sign, assign, consign, designate, insignia, resign
snof	*(make noise)*	sneeze, snore, snorkel, snort
socio	*(follower)*	sociable, social, society, associate, associate, dissociate
sol	*(sun)*	solar system, solar, solarium, insulate, parasol
son	*(sound)*	sonic, sonar, sonnet, sound, unison, sonata, consonant, dissonant, resound
spine	*(thorn)*	spine, porcupine, spike
spir	*(breath)*	spirit, aspirate, conspire, expire, inspire, perspire, inspiration, transpire
spect	*(to look)*	specimen, spectator, spectacle, spectrum, speculate, aspect, circumspect, conspicuous, despise, expect, inspect, introspect, perspective, prospect, respect, perspective, suspect, species
spon	*(solemn pledge)*	sponsor, spouse, despond, espouse, respond, responsible
statu	*(stand erect)*	stage, stance, stanch, stanza, statue, stature, status, statistics, stable
stella	*(star)*	stellar, constellation, aster, astronaut, asterisk, astronomy, asteroid, astral, astrology, disaster
string	*(draw tight)*	string, strain, strict, stringent, astringent, constrain, restrict

English

Greek
German
Latin
Old English
French

Roots

struct	*(build)*	structure, construct, destruction, destroy, instruct, obstruct
stupi	*(stunned)*	stupefy, stupid, stupendous
super	*(over)*	sovereign, superior, supreme, superb
tang	*(touch)*	tangent, tangible, taste, tactile, attain, contact, intact
tech	*(skill, craft)*	architect, technician, technical, technology, technique
tect	*(to cover)*	detect, protect, tile
tele	*(distant)*	telecast, telegraph, telephone, telescope, telethon, television
tempo	*(time)*	contemporary, extemporaneous, temporal, temporary, tempo
tend	*(stretch)*	tendon, tense, contend, extend, pretend, intend
term	*(limit)*	term, terminate, exterminate, determine
terra	*(dry land)*	terrain, territory, Mediterranean
test	*(witness)*	test, testament, testimony, testify, attest, contest, detest, protest
text	*(weave/fabricate)*	textile, text, tissue, context, pretext, texture, textual
therm	*(warm)*	thermal, thermograph, thermometer, thermonuclear, thermos, thermostat, thermosphere
thri/tri	*(three)*	three, thrice, thirteen, thirty, tricycle, triturators, triplet, triangle, trilogy, trimester, Trinity, trio, triplicate, tripod
thun/tor	*(thunder)*	thunder, detonate, stun, astonish, tornado, torpedo
tom	*(cut)*	anatomy, atom, diatom
tort	*(twist)*	torch, torment, contort, distort, extort, retort, torture
tract	*(pull)*	tractable, traction, trail, train, tractor, abstract, extract, protract, retract, subtract
turb	*(tumult)*	trouble, turbine, disturb, perturb
turn	*(circle)*	turn, contour, detour, return
vad	*(to go)*	vamoose, evade, invade, pervade
val	*(strong)*	valiant, valid, valor, value, avail, prevail, convalescent
vapor	*(steam)*	vapor, evaporate, vaporize, vaporous
vect	*(carry)*	vector, vehicle, convection, eviction
vent	*(to come)*	advent, adventure, avenue, circumvent, convent, convention, event, intervene, invent, prevent
verd	*(truth)*	verify, very, verdict
vers	*(move around one place)*	versatile, vertebrae, vortex, adverse, anniversary, controversy, convert, divert, introvert, revert, universe, vice versa, transverse
vio	*(forceful)*	violent, violate, vim, vehement, violation
vin	*(wine)*	vine, vinegar, wine, vineyard, vintage
vis/voy	*(to see)*	view, visible, visa, visit, visitor, visual, vision, vista, evidence, advice, review, survey, supervise
viv	*(alive)*	viper, viviparous, viva, vivacious, vivid, revive, survive, viable, vital, vitamin
voc	*(to call, voice)*	voice, vocal, vowel, advocate, evoke, invoke, provoke, revoke, vociferous
vol	*(to roll)*	volume, evolve, involve, revolve
vot	*(pledge)*	vow, vote, devote, devout
ward	*(guard)*	warden, wardrobe, award, ward, reward
wr	*(twist)*	wreath, wrath

Synonym (same as) and Antonym (opposite of)

Key Word	Synonym	Antonym	Key Word	Synonym	Antonym
above	over	below	day		night
abundant	plentiful	rare	dear	loved	unloved
achieve	accomplish	fail	deep		shallow
add	sum up	subtract	delight	joy	sorrow
after	behind	ahead	desert	wasteland	oasis
aid	help	hinder	die	perish	live
alike	similar	different	dingy	dull	bright
anger	rage	peaceful	dirty	soiled	clean
argue	dispute	agree	disturb	annoy	avoid
arrive	reach	leave	doubt	suspicion	certainty
avoid	shun	seek	drain	empty	fill
awful	terrible	wonderful	draw	sketch	erase
beautiful	lovely	ugly	dry	arid	wet
before	precede	after	dull	stupid	clever
beg	ask	give	early		late
begin	start	end	easy	simple	hard
benefit	help	destroy	elastic	flexible	rigid
better	improve	worsen	emotion	feeling	indifference
bland	mild	harsh	empty	vacant	full
blind	unseeing	sighted	enlarge	expand	reduce
bold	brave	timid	enough	sufficient	inadequate
bright	shining	dull	entertaining	amusing	boring
brisk	quick	slow	equal	same	different
busy	industrious	lazy	error	mistake	correction
calm	smooth	ruffled	esteemed	valued	underrated
care	concern	neglect	eternal	everlasting	temporary
cease	stop	continue	evaporate	vaporize	solidify
certain	true	questionable	evil	sinful	holy
cheap	inexpensive	costly	expense	cost	profit
clear	transparent	muddy	extravagant	wasteful	economical
clever	smart	dull	fact	truth	lie
collect	gather	dispose	famous	celebrated	unknown
common	ordinary	exceptional	fast	rapid	slow
complain	murmur	rejoice	fat	stout	thin
complete	finished	partial	father	daddy	mother
comprehend	understand	misunderstand	fear	terror	trust
conceal	hide	reveal	fill	replenish	drain
confident	certain	unsure	find	discover	lose
consider	think about	ignore	finish	complete	start
copy	imitation	original	first	leading	last
correct	right	false	fix	mend	break
costly	expensive	cheap	flat	level	slope
courage	bravery	cowardice	flood	overflow	drought
damp	wet	dry	forget	unlearn	remember
daring	brave	timid	forward	advanced	backward

Chart 80

Synonym (same as) and Antonym (opposite of)

Key Word	Synonym	Antonym	Key Word	Synonym	Antonym
frail	weak	strong	laugh	chuckle	cry
freedom	liberty	restriction	left		right
frequent	often	occasional	level	smooth	rough
fresh	new	stale	lie	fib	truth
friend	companion	enemy	lie	(lay down)	rise
front	anterior	back	light	not weighty	heavy
fulfill	complete	neglect	light	beam	dark
funny	comical	serious	liquid	fluid	solid
gave	donated	took	little	small	big
gain	get	lose	live	survive	die
gentle	tame	rough	lost	misplaced	found
gift	present	purchase	love	affection	hate
glad	happy	sad	memorize	remember	forget
go	depart	stop	move	go	stop
good	right	bad	narrow	thin	wide
gradual	slow	sudden	new	fresh	old
grieve	sorrow	rejoice	near	close	far
group	crowd	individual	on	engaged	off
guess	suppose	prove	open	uncover	close
guide	direct	mislead	perfect	faultless	imperfect
handsome	good-looking	ugly	praise	honor	blame
happy	merry	sad	pretty	attractive	plain
hard	firm	soft	proud	arrogant	humble
harm	hurt	help	pull	drag	push
haste	quick	slow	punish	discipline	reward
heat	warm	cool	question	inquiry	answer
heavy	weighty	light	quiet	still	noisy
help	aid	hinder	real	true	false
hide	conceal	expose	right	correct	wrong
hold	grasp	drop	sad	depressed	happy
honor	respect	contempt	save	rescue	abandon
hope	trust	despair	secret	hidden	known
horrible	awful	wonderful	sharp	pointed	dull
huge	enormous	tiny	short	brief	long
humble	modest	proud	shy	timid	bold
humorous	funny	serious	simple	plain	complex
hurt	harm	heal	single	one	plural
idle	lazy	industrious	slow	sluggish	fast
ignorant	uneducated	smart	sour	tart	sweet
illusion	dream	reality	stop	halt	go
imply	hint	state	strange	odd	familiar
important	significant	trivial	strong	powerful	weak
in		out	superior	better	inferior
inferior	lesser	superior	yes	positive	no
innocent	blameless	guilty	young	immature	old

Chart 81

Unit 7 Meaning

Homonyms (Same sound, different spelling and meaning)

ad (advertisement)	add (total)	hall (corridor)	haul (carry)	ring (circle)	wring (squeeze)
air (atmosphere)	heir (inheritor)	hear (listen to)	here (at this place)	right(correct/direction)	write (compose)
aloud (spoken)	allowed(permitted)	heel (part of foot)	heal (make well)	road (way)	rode (traveled)
ate(consumed)	eight (8)	higher (nearer top)	hire (employ)	rote (repetition)	wrote (composed)
ant (insect)	aunt (relative)	hoarse (scratchy voice)	horse (animal)	rung (sounded)	wrung (squeezed)
aught (none)	ought (should)	holy (sacred)	wholly(completely	sail (canvas)	sale (bargain)
bail (to empty)	bale (bundle)	hour (time)	our (pronoun)	scene (view)	seen (looked at)
bait (lure)	bate (lessen)	hymn (song)	him (male pronoun)	scent (odor)	sent (gone)/cent (coin)
ball (round object)	bawl (cry)	in (opposite of out)	inn (hotel)	sealing (covering)	ceiling (of room)
base (support)	bass (voice)	isle (island)	aisle (passageway)	seam (a joint)	seem (appear to be)
be (to exist)	bee (insect)	knead (mix)	need (require)	sea (ocean)	see (view)
bear (animal)	bare (uncovered)	knew (understood)	new (recent)	sell (barter)	cell (a unit)
beet (vegetable)	beat (win, hit)	knight (soldier)	night (dark time)	session (meeting)	cession (surrender)
berry (fruit)	bury (cover)	knot(twisted string)	not (no way)	sew (stitch)	sow(scatter)/so (therefore)
blew(push with air)	blue (color)	know(understand)	no (negative)	shoot (fire gun)	chute (trough)
board (lumber)	bored (uninterested)	lane (road)	lain (lie down, pt)	shown (demonstrated)	shone (appeared shiny)
bowled (knock over)	bold (brave)	lead (metal)	led (directed)	side (a location)	sighed(expeled breath)
braid (to twist)	brayed(horse sound)	leased (rented)	least (fewest)	sight (vision)	site (location)
brake (slow down)	break (crack)	lone (only one)	loan (borrowed)	slay (kill)	sleigh (snow vehicle)
buy (to purchase)	bye (goodbye)	made (created)	maid (house help)	soar (fly)	sore (painful)
capital (city)	capitol (building)	mail (letter)	male (man)	some (several)	sum (the total)
carrot (vegetable)	carat (weight)	main (primary)	mane (hair)	son (male child)	sun (star)
council(assembly)	counsel (advise)	meet(to come upon)	meat (food)	stair (step)	stare (look closely)
course (subject)	coarse (rough)	might (strength)	mite (small insect)	stake (marker)	steak (meat)
creak (a sound)	creek (small river)	miner (digger)	minor (underage)	steel (metal)	steal (take unlawfully)
dear (beloved)	deer (animal)	oar (paddle)	ore (mineral)	tale (story)	tail (hind part)
desert (leave)	dessert (sweet food)	one (1)	won (achieved victory)	taught (instructed)	taut (pulled tight)
dew (moisture)	do (perform)	pain (hurt)	pane (panel)	time (clock)	thyme (herb)
die (stop living)	dye (color)	pail (bucket)	pale (wan)	their (pronoun)	there (at that place)
doe (female deer)	dough (bread)	pair (2 things)	pear (fruit)	threw (tossed)	through (by way of)
earn (to gain)	urn (vase)	peace (calm)	piece (a section)	tow (pull)	toe (part of foot)
eye (organ of sight)	I (pronoun)	pedal (part of bike)	peddle (to sell)	to (toward)	too (also) / two (2)
fair (lovely)	fare (price)	pistil(part of flower)	pistol (gun)	vain (conceited)	vein (blood vessel)
feat (accomplishment)	feet (body part)	plain (flat region)	plane (airplane)	vale (valley)	veil (covering)
find (discover)	fined (charged)	pray (petition)	prey (victim)	wade (walk in water)	weighed (measured heaviness)
fir (tree)	fur (animal skin)	prints (copies)	prince (king's son)	waist (middle)	waste (squander)
flea (insect)	flee (go away)	principal (man)	principle (rule)	wait (postpone)	weight (measure of heaviness)
flew (to fly, pt.)	flu (influenza)	quarts(measurement)	quartz (stone)	waive (give up)	wave (flutter)
for (preposition)	four (4)	rain(drops of water)	reign (to rule)	ware (goods)	wear (have on)
foul (offensive)	fowl (bird)	rap (tap)	wrap (cover)	way (course)	weigh (measured heaviness)
gait (motion)	gate (opening)	rays (beams)	raise (lift up)	weak (feeble)	week (7 days)
great (large)	grate (framework)	read (understand writing)	reed (grass)	whole (complete)	hole (cavity)
groan (moan)	grown (adult)	real (actual)	reel (spool)	wood (tree)	would (will, pt.)
guessed (figured out)	guest (visitor)	red (color)	read (read, pt)	you (pronoun)	ewe (sheep)
hail (frozen rain)	hale (healthy)	rest (quiet)	wrest (grab)	yolk (yellow of egg)	yoke (join)
hair (threadlike growth)	hare (rabbit)	retch (vomit)	wretch (miserable one)	your (possessive pronoun)	you're (you are)

Heteronyms

(two meanings, two pronouciations, with same spelling)

dove
live
tear
read
lead
close
bow
sow
row
wind
wound
accent
combat
compact
compress
concrete
conduct
console
content
contest
contract
convert
convict
digest
defect
minute
present
produce
progress
project
protest
rebel
record
reflex
refuse
slough
subject
suspect
tear
upset

Stumblers (easily confused)

accept (receive)	except (exclude)
accent (speech)	ascent (rise)
access (admittance)	excess (extra)
adapt (adjust)/adept (skillful)/adopt (take in)	
addition (add)	edition (publication)
adjoin (next to)	adjourn (disperse)
affect (cause)	effect (result)
allowed (permitted)	aloud (spoken)
ally (friend)	alloy (metallic compound)
altitude (height)	attitude (viewpoint)
angle (perspective)	angel (celestial being)
annual (yearly)	annul (cancel)
assistance (help)	assistant (helper)
attain (gain)	attend (present)
bazaar (market)	bizarre (odd)
bean (seed)	been (be, pt)
bellow (bray)	below (under)
bridle (restrain)	bridal (wedding)
cease (stop)	seize (capture)
cloths (pieces of cloth)	clothes (clothing)
command (order)	commend (praise)
conscience (moral awareness)	conscious (aware)
conservation (protect nature)	conversation (talk)
confidant (friend)	confident (sure)
costume (clothing)	custom (habit)
cymbal (percussion instrument)	symbol (emblem)
currant (berry)	current (recent)
dairy (milk)	diary (daily record)
deceased (dead)	diseased (ill)
decent (proper)	descent (go down)
decree (law)	degree (measure)
depravation (corruption)	deprivation (loss)
desert (arid land)	dessert (sweet food)
diagram (sketch)	diaphragm (filter)
either (one of two)	ether (drug)
empire (dominion)	umpire (referee)
expand (enlarge)	expend (spend)
lessen (decrease)	lesson (study)
parish (governing unit)	perish (to die)
personal (private)	personnel (staff)
prophecy (prediction)	prophesy (to predict)
propose (suggest)	purpose (aim)
soldier (man)	solder (welding flux)
statue (figurine)	statute (law)
weather (climate)	whether (if)
worship (praise)	warship (ship)

Contractions

not
aren't
can't
didn't
doesn't
hadn't
hasn't
haven't
weren't
won't
couldn't
shouldn't
wouldn't

am
I'm

are
we're
you're
they're

is
it's
he's
she's
who's
that's
what's
here's
there's

will
I'll
you'll
he'll
she'll
we'll
they'll

would
I'd
you'd
he'd
she'd
we'd
they'd

Chart 83

UNIT 8

FOCUS ON:
PENMANSHIP, WRITING AND BOOK REPORTS

Unit Eight brings together the skills of being able to correctly form the letter (in manuscript and cursive) and the ability of being able to communicate thoughts on paper (creative writing). Reading books and making reports of them helps bridge the gap in this process.

There was once a village which sat on the top of a tall mountain which was nearly flat at its pinnacle. How the village had come in to existence no one knew for sure. There were no written records of the history of the village.

The village also had no roads which travelled in or out linking them with other people or villages. And yet, if you stood at the edge of the village which was also the mountain's edge, you could see for miles. There were trails and other villages visible in the mist of the distance. Yet no one had dared to consider them too closely for fear that they would develop a longing to go and see. And since there were no bridges to the opposite cliffs and no roads down the mountain, what would be the use?

But there was one boy who would go each day and strain to see all that he could. His friends and the other villagers began to shun him. They thought he was developing an unhealthy obsession. But this did not stop the boy from dreaming of what might lie in the worlds beyond his village.

One day, quite suddenly in fact, the boy resolved to do something about his problem. Taking a strong cord, he tied it to a heavy wooden stick. Then he went to the edge of the village. As others gathered to watch, he paced off some steps. Then with a running start, the boy hurled the stick across the crevasse, as he held fast to one end of the cord.

In a flash the stick landed in a tangle of bush at the edge of the opposing cliff. The boy pulled. The stick was securely trapped. He then tied the cord to a tree stump. In this manner, the boy had created a bridge to the rest of the world.

As he prepared to leave, a village elder stepped forward.

"Son,", he said, "Your path to the rest of the world lies within your reach. Go. Then return. Come back and tell others what you have seen and how they too might go out and discover new worlds."

--Mike Klumpp

Letter Formation

LETTER FORMATION: On a blackboard draw a base line, upper line and dotted middle line with 'L' on left-hand side and 'R' on right-hand side. If at all possible, use a permanent marker for drawing these lines, since they will be used daily. Talk with the student about each line: Top line—sky (picture of star), middle line—flower, base line—the ground, and below that—water (picture of fish). The *teacher* then demonstrates formation of letter. She is careful to work at the student's eye level, and makes the letter at least 12" in size. She says the appropriate poem for the formation of the letter (page 166-167), while tracing over the letter, and then discusses the direction in which the letter is made (left/right) and its orientation to a base line, upper line and middle line. The *student* then practices the formation of the letter in two ways: 1. He draws the letter in the air with full arm and shoulder movement while saying the poem five times with his eyes open and five times with his eyes closed. 2. He traces teacher's letter on the blackboard while saying poem ten times.

In addition to this, the teacher should have a daily review of the previous letters studied, using the formation poems and practicing writing them on wide-lined paper. Make sure the lines have a middle line to insure correct and uniform letter and number formation. Prepare the page by adding a star on the top line, a flower from the base line to the middle line, and a fish below the base line. (The symbols are simple enough for students to add by themselves after they have learned them.) When introducing the capital letters, have student match them with the corresponding lowercase letter. Capital letters are used at beginning of sentences and for proper names.

AUDIO DISCRIMINATION: In order for students to learn audio discrimination of each letter, use the word lists on **Chart 51**. Have the students hold up a "Tell-a-Phone" card of the sound or write it down. Randomly choose words from only the letters that have been studied. Write down the answers yourself to use as the answer sheet.

Number Formation

Teach the student how to count and make numbers. The following poems will help to teach the formation of numbers. Introduce only one at a time.

0	Circle around just so, Now you've made a zero.
1	Straight down the slide and you have won, You just made the number 1.
2	Circle right to make a 2, Now back with a line and you are through.
3	A balancing act is number 3, Curve back, curve back carefully.
4	Go down and over as you soar, Then down with a line and you have a 4.
5	Down with a line and a stomach big and fat, You have a 5 when you add his hat.
6	We want 6 to roll a hoop, A nice big curve with a tight little loop.
7	Go across the sky to make a 7, Now add a ladder coming down from heaven.
8	Starts with an "S" to make an 8, Now close it up and don't be late.
9	Circle round then down with a line, Now you have the number 9.
10	10 is easy, don't you know, First a 1 and then a zero.

Cursive

Cursive is a form of writing that is actually easier than printing. A command of cursive increases writing speed, which is helpful when trying to capture a train of thought or dictation. There are several basic strokes that can transform printed letters into cursive. These individual parts should be practiced separately and then added as directed. By adding small changes, each person's handwriting can be distinctive and meet with their personal taste. A slant of approximately 45 degrees is generally added. The charts, on page 169 and 170 are arranged by groups of letters that contain similar strokes.

Formation Poems

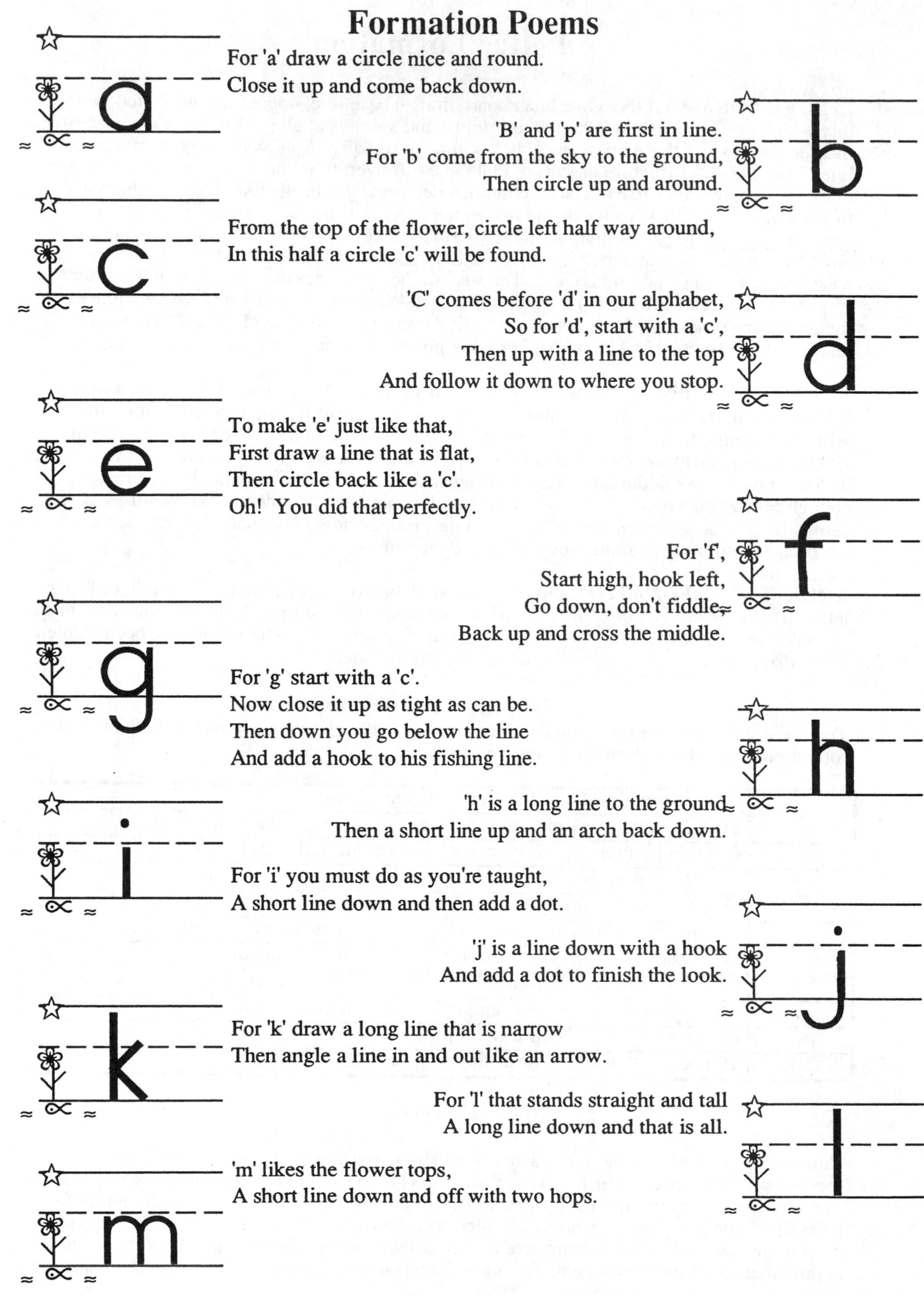

a
b
c
d
e
f
g
h
i
j
k
l
m

For 'a' draw a circle nice and round.
Close it up and come back down.

'B' and 'p' are first in line.
For 'b' come from the sky to the ground,
Then circle up and around.

From the top of the flower, circle left half way around,
In this half a circle 'c' will be found.

'C' comes before 'd' in our alphabet,
So for 'd', start with a 'c',
Then up with a line to the top
And follow it down to where you stop.

To make 'e' just like that,
First draw a line that is flat,
Then circle back like a 'c'.
Oh! You did that perfectly.

For 'f',
Start high, hook left,
Go down, don't fiddle,
Back up and cross the middle.

For 'g' start with a 'c'.
Now close it up as tight as can be.
Then down you go below the line
And add a hook to his fishing line.

'h' is a long line to the ground
Then a short line up and an arch back down.

For 'i' you must do as you're taught,
A short line down and then add a dot.

'j' is a line down with a hook
And add a dot to finish the look.

For 'k' draw a long line that is narrow
Then angle a line in and out like an arrow.

For 'l' that stands straight and tall
A long line down and that is all.

'm' likes the flower tops,
A short line down and off with two hops.

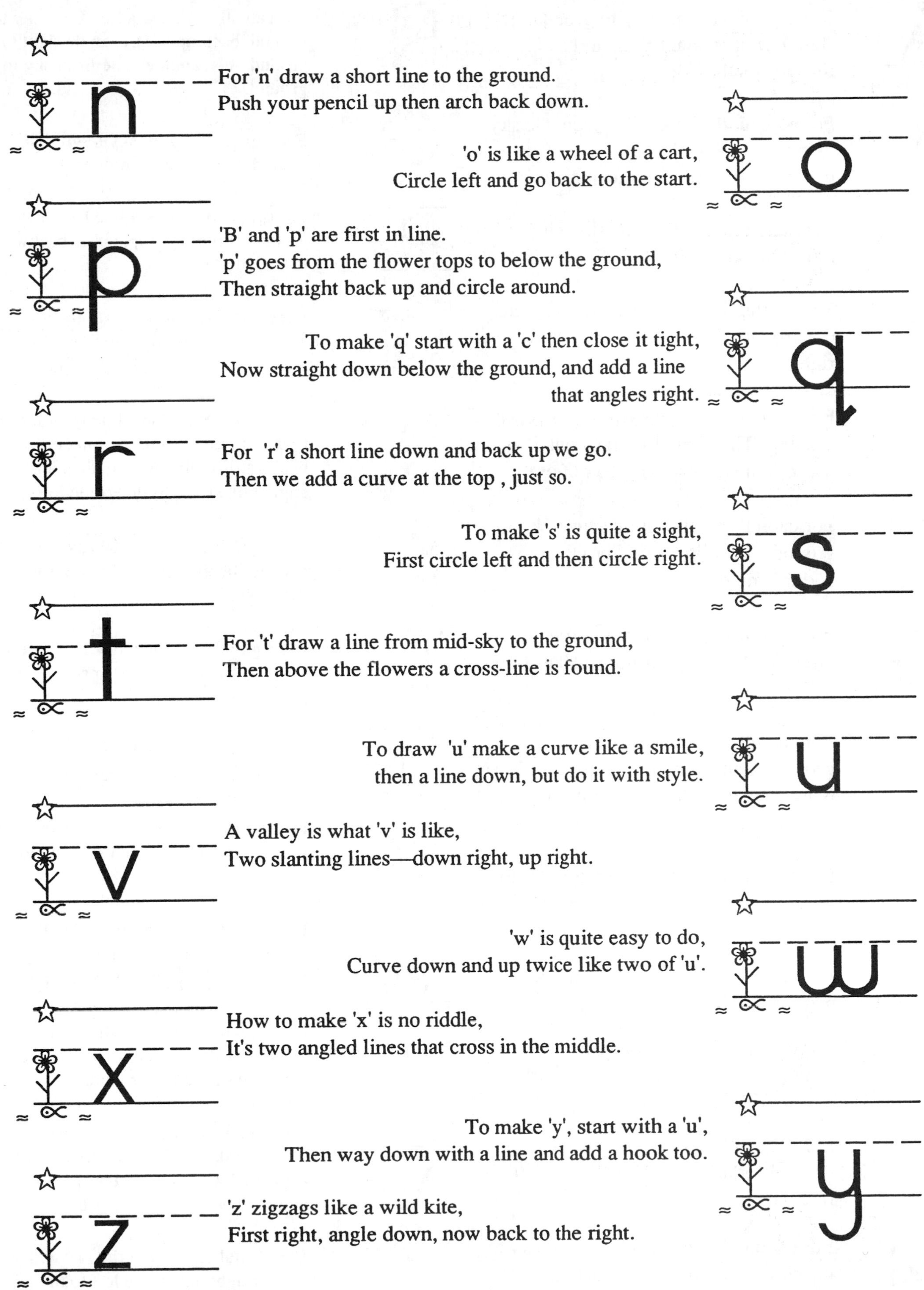

For 'n' draw a short line to the ground.
Push your pencil up then arch back down.

'o' is like a wheel of a cart,
Circle left and go back to the start.

'B' and 'p' are first in line.
'p' goes from the flower tops to below the ground,
Then straight back up and circle around.

To make 'q' start with a 'c' then close it tight,
Now straight down below the ground, and add a line
that angles right.

For 'r' a short line down and back up we go.
Then we add a curve at the top , just so.

To make 's' is quite a sight,
First circle left and then circle right.

For 't' draw a line from mid-sky to the ground,
Then above the flowers a cross-line is found.

To draw 'u' make a curve like a smile,
then a line down, but do it with style.

A valley is what 'v' is like,
Two slanting lines—down right, up right.

'w' is quite easy to do,
Curve down and up twice like two of 'u'.

How to make 'x' is no riddle,
It's two angled lines that cross in the middle.

To make 'y', start with a 'u',
Then way down with a line and add a hook too.

'z' zigzags like a wild kite,
First right, angle down, now back to the right.

A

For capital 'A' from sky to ground slant left, then slant right and add a line across the middle.

B

For capital 'B' draw a line from the sky to ground, then a backward 'c' on a backward 'c', just like the number '3'.

C

For capital 'C' start at the sky, circle left to the ground.

D

For capital 'D' draw a line from sky to the ground. Now a large half circle right.

E

For capital 'E', draw a line from sky to ground. Three parallel lines out from the top, the middle and the bottom.

F

For capital 'F', draw a line from sky to ground. Two lines out from the top and the middle.

G

For capital 'G', from sky to ground draw a half circle left then a short line in .

H

For capital 'H', draw a line from sky to ground, then a parallel line next to it. Now connect with a short line across the middle.

I

For capital 'I', draw a line from sky to ground. Then a short line across the top and bottom.

J

For capital 'J', draw a line from sky to ground and hook left.

K

For capital 'K', draw a line from sky to ground, angle in to middle, then angle out to ground.

L

For capital 'L', draw a line from sky to ground and then on the ground, a short line out.

M

For capital 'M', draw a line from sky to ground. From top slant short right down and short right back up. Now another line from sky to ground.

N

For capital 'N', draw a line from sky to ground, back up to sky, angle right to ground, then another line from sky to ground.

O

For capital 'O', from sky to ground, circle left all the way around.

P

For capital 'P', draw a line from sky to ground. From the top, circle backwards to the middle.

Q

For capital 'Q', from sky to the ground, circle left all the way around. Now add a short line in the right bottom corner.

R

For capital 'R', draw a line from the sky to the ground. From the top circle backwards to the middle, then an angled line right to the ground.

S

For capital 'S', start at the sky, circle back to the middle, now curve right to the ground.

T

For capital 'T', draw a line from the sky to the ground. Top with a short line across the sky.

U

For capital 'U', from the sky to the ground, hook right then up to the sky .

V

For capital 'V', from the sky slant right to the ground, then slant right up to the sky.

W

For capital 'W', from the sky to the ground, slant right, then a line angled up right, down right and back up right.

X

For capital 'X', angle right from the sky to the ground then cross with angle left from the sky to the ground.

Y

For capital 'Y', a short angle right right from the sky to mid way, then angle right back up. Now at the tip of the angle, draw a line to the ground.

Z

For capital 'Z', start at the sky with a line straight out, angle left to the ground. Now draw a line straight out.

Cursive Lower Case Letters

BASIC STROKE	LETTER	DIRECTIONS
	i i	Short up/Sharp point down/ Connective curve/Dot
i	t t	Long up/Sharp point down/Connective curve/Cross
	u u	Short up/Sharp point down/Curve up/Sharp point down/ Connective curve
	w w	Short up/Sharp point down/Curve up/Sharp point down/ Curve up/Line out
	n n	Arch up and down/Arch up and down/Connective curve
n	m m	Arch up and down/Arch up and down/Arch up and down/ Connective curve
	v v	Arch up and down/Curve back up/Line out
	x x	Arch up and down/Connective curve/Cross
	l l	Curve way up and back/Straight down/Connective curve
	e e	Curve short up and back/down/Connective curve
l	h h	Curve way up and back/Straight down/Arch up and down/ Connective curve
	k k	Curve way up and back/Straight down/Arch up/Tight circle in/ Come down/Connective curve
	b b	Curve way up and back/Straight down/Curve up/Line out
	f f	Curve way up and back/Straight way down/Loop right, in and out
	j j	Short up/Straight way down/Loop left, over and up/Dot
j	p p	Short up/Straight way down/Straight back up/ Circle up around/Connective curve
	y y	Short up/Sharp point down/Curve up/Straight way down/ Loop left, over and up
	z z	Arch up and down/short curve /Straight way down/Loop left, over and up
	c c	Curve around up/Curve back around
	a a	Curve around up/Curve back around/Sharp point down/ Connective curve
c	o o	Curve around up/Curve back around/Tight loop left, over/ Line out
	d d	Curve around up/Curve back around/Curve way up/ Straight down/Connective curve
	g g	Curve around up/Curve back around/Straight down below the line/Loop left, over and up
	q q	Curve around up/Curve back around/Straight way down/ Loop right, in and out
r	r r	Short up/Sharp point out/Straight down/Connective curve
	s s	Short up/Curve in, down, and out

Cursive Capital Letters

BASIC STROKE	LETTER	DIRECTIONS
	H H	High hook/Come down/Another line down/Loop up and over first line/Cross second line
	K K	High hook/Come down/Curve into middle/Loop up and down/ Connecting curve
	N N	High hook/Come down/Follow up/Large Arch down/Connective curve
	M M	High hook/Come down/Follow up/Large Arch down/Follow up/ Large Arch down/Connective curve
	P P	High Hook/Come down/Follow up/Loop up around to middle
	R R	High Hook/Come down/Follow up/Loop up around to middle/ Curve down/Connective curve
	D D	High Hook/Come down/Follow up/Loop up, around to ground/ Connective curve
	B B	High hook/Come down/Follow up/Loop up around to middle/ Another loop to ground/Connective curve
	U U	High hook/Come down/Curve way up/Straight down/Connective curve
	V V	High hook/Come down/Curve way up/Line out
	W W	High hook/Come down/Curve half way up/Straight down/Curve up/Line out
	Y Y	High hook/Come down/Curve way up/Straight down below the line/Loop left, over and up
	Z Z	High hook/Come down/Small arch up/Down below the line/Loop left, over and up
	X X	High hook/Come down/Connective curve/Cross left
	A A	Curve back around/Straight up/Straight down/Connective curve
	O O	Curve back all around/Small loop down and out
	Q Q	Curve back all around/Small loop down and out/Add short line
	C C	High loop/Curve back around
	E E	High loop/Small curve back around/Small curve back around
	T T	High hook/Straight across/Come down/Curve left/Straight line out
	F F	High hook/Straight across/Come down/Curve left/Straight line out/Cross
	J J	Start at ground/Curve way up left/Come down below the line/ Loop left, over and up
	I I	Start at ground/Curve way up left/Come down/Loop left/Line out
	S S	Start at ground/Curve up and back/Short loop middle/Curve in, down and out
	G G	Start at ground/Small loop over line and up/Curve in down/ Line out
	L L	High loop/Come down/Loop left, over and out

Eagle's Wings 600 Sight Words

Good spelling is a matter of habit. A good speller always checks to make sure words are correctly spelled. A poor speller has often been allowed to be careless. After a word has been spelled incorrectly several times, it begins to look "right" and it is difficult to relearn it with the correct spelling.

In order to insure that our students get off to a good start, we prepare the Eagle's Wings 600 Sight Words by coloring the 'color' boxes and then laminating them. This sheet is then either glued to the back of their phonics workbook or taped to their desks. Instantly their writing improves. They have more confidence, are more concerned with the contents in their creative writing, and take more pride in their finished product. As teachers, our time can be more effectively used to encourage creativity when we can encourage the students to look up the word they need on their sheet. When a student needs to know the spelling of a word, tell them where to find the word on the page. This means that we all have to become very familiar with the layout of the page. Use the list of Eagle's Wings Sight Words for reading and spelling words (see Unit 9, **Focus On: Activities,** page 193-194) and talk about how the words are spelled versus how they sound. Point out that almost all of the 'wh' words on the page are question words and use teaching helps to reinforce the 'igh' and 'family' words. (See Unit 10, ***Focus On: Fun Forms.***) By spending some time learning these words, the students are gradually 'weaned' away from the lists. They are soon looking up their words less often, but the sheet is still available as a reference when necessary. There is no excuse for misspelling a word that is on the list.

There has been no problem with the students using the list as a 'crutch'. Until third or fourth grade, a student has not been exposed to enough spelling to know all these sight words. Many of these words are not spelled according to phonetic rules and are called 'Everyday Bloopers' (common words that break the rules). What these children are learning is pride in spelling words correctly.

Eagle's Wings 600 Sight Words were carefully chosen and presented in an orderly and useable manner to include the majority of words used most often. A large portion of any text will be words from this page. In fact, in the lower grades, these words may comprise up to 90% of the text. Memorizing this list as sight words for reading (this means being able to instantly recognize the word without sounding it out) will also dramatically improve the students' reading abilities. Memorizing this list for spelling purposes will improve the students' spelling. (This would be a great summer project!) And having the list handy to check their spelling as they write will give them freedom in writing creatively as well as help them make correct spelling a matter of habit and pride.

Eagle's Wings 600 Sight Words

pronouns

pronouns	it/its	**he/him/his**	**she/her/hers**	
I	**me**	mine	**my**	I'm (I am)
we	**us**	ours	**our**	we're
you		yours	**your**	you're

little words

little words		a/an	**all**	**any**	**and**
are	**as**	**at**	**be**	**but**	**by**
can	**did**	**do**	**done**	**feel**	**fine**
for	**fun**	**get**	**had**	**has**	**have**
how	**if**	**into**	**is**	**just**	**keep**
let	**lot**	**may**	**most**	**much**	**must**
need	**none**	**not**	**now**	**of**	**oh**
only	**or**	**put**	**so**	**some**	**since**
such	**to/too**	**try**	**use**	**yet**	**very**

verbs

verbs	talk	say/says	**said**
call	ask	tell/told	**know**
speak	hear	listen	sing
read	spell	**write**	wrote
look	**see**/saw/seen		fall
walk	**run**	stand	**sit**
jump	wake	sleep	ride

all

almost
already
also
although
altogether
always
all right

opposites

yes	**no**	on	off
in	**out**	fast	slow
over	under	first	last
top	bottom	start	**stop**
up	**down**	early	late
front	back	lead	follow
near	far	stay	leave
here	**there**	**go**	**come**
big	**little**	**to**	**from**
		give	**take**
huge	small	lost	found
tall	short	rent	own
long	short	quiet	noisy
fat	thin	**make**	break
wide	narrow	buy	sell
round	square	show	hide
wet	dry	open	close
dirty	clean	hope	fear
hot	**cold**	**love**	hate
soft	hard	**like**	dislike
full	empty	real	pretend
more	less	truth	lie
many	few	right	wrong
good	**bad**	dangerous	safe
nice	mean	**happy**	**sad**
young	**old**	awful	wonderful
pretty	ugly	live	die
(beautiful)		eat	drink
new	used	sour	sweet
strong	weak	**hello/good-bye**	
help	hurt	forget/remember	

uh!

about
above
across
again
ago
agree
ahead
allow
along
alone
aloud
among
another
apart
approve
arise
around
asleep
away
awake

body

face
eye
ear
nose
mouth
hair
arm
leg
hand
foot/feet

w

wait
want
warm
was/wasn't
water
watch
way
well (sick)
went
were/weren't
will/won't
with
word
work (play)
world
worn
worth
worst (best)

th

the
this
that
than
then
these
those
they
them
their
they're
there/here
think
thank/please
thing
something
other
bother
either
neither
rather

ev

even
event
ever
every
everything
everywhere
never

© 1990 S.M.

wh?

what?
where?
why?
when?
which?
who?
whom?
whose?
while
whole (half)

gh

caught
taught
bought (sold)
brought
fought
ought
sought
thought
through
thorough
enough
tough
laugh (cry)
high (low)
sigh
bright (dim)
fight
fright
light (dark)
might
night
right (left)
sight
slight
tight (loose)
height (width)
weight
straight (turn)

be

because
become
before (after)
begin (**end**)
behind
believe
belong
below
beside
between
could
should
would

people

people	family	children	parent	**baby**
dad	**father**	husband	man	Mr.
mom	**mother**	wife	woman	Mrs.
girl	daughter	sister	niece	Miss
boy	son	brother	nephew	Dr.
grandpa	grandma	cousin	uncle	aunt
friend	neighbor	**teacher**	**name**	

place

place	**sun**	**moon**	**star**	earth
mountain	hill	valley	plains	country
ocean	lake	pond	river	stream
desert	jungle	forest	prairie	field
city	**street**	**house**	home	**school**

plant	**tree**	bush	**flower**	**grass**
animal	**dog**	**cat**	fish	bird
horse	cow	lion	elephant	bear

time

time	hour	minute
today	tomorrow	yesterday
morning	afternoon	evening
breakfast	lunch/dinner	supper

day **week** month year **date**

Sunday	1 January	Jan.	31
Monday	2 February	Feb.	28/29
Tuesday	3 March	Mar.	31
Wednesday	4 April	Apr.	30
Thursday	5 May	May	31
Friday	6 June	June	30
Saturday	7 July	July	31
winter	8 August	Aug.	31
spring	9 September	Sept.	30
summer	10 October	Oct.	31
fall/autumn	11 November	Nov.	30
	12 December	Dec.	31

color

❑ red ❑ yellow
❑ blue ❑ orange ❑ green
❑ purple ❑ brown ❑ pink
❑ white ❑ black ❑ gray

number

number	count	question	answer
(+) add	(plus)	(-) subtract	(minus)
(x) multiply	(times)	(÷) divide	sum

1 one	1st first	11 eleven	**once**
2 **two**	2nd second	12 twelve	20 twenty
3 **three**	3rd third	13 thirteen	30 thirty
4 **four**	4th fourth	14 fourteen	40 forty
5 **five**	5th fifth	15 fifteen	50 fifty
6 **six**	6th sixth	16 sixteen	60 sixty
7 **seven**	7th seventh	17 seventeen	70 seventy
8 **eight**	8th eighth	18 eighteen	80 eighty
9 **nine**	9th ninth	19 nineteen	90 ninety
10 **ten**	10th tenth		100 hundred
1,000 one thousand		1,000,000 one million	

Creative Writing: The End Result

The story on the opening page of this unit (page 164) tells of a boy yearning for worlds beyond his realm. We, in our own way, are limited to our own little world. But new worlds and new sights are all within our reach through the avenue of the written word. Writing enables us to share experiences, adventures and insights with people who are far away. Insights written down hundreds or even thousands of years ago are as fresh and meaningful as the day they were written. Historical drama, letters, poems, stories and the Scriptures are timeless examples of the value and impact of the written word.

Do not let words like "literature" and "creative writing" strike fear and anxiety in your heart. It is an illusion that creative writing is lofty, stuffy, and beyond your grasp. For creative writing is just as simple as enjoying writing a letter to a friend. It is as easy as leaving a witty "post-it" note on a friend's locker or windshield. It's the telling of stories, the making of dramas, the writing of a song or the sharing of a rhyme.

This text offers a fresh perspective on creative writing, coupled with some ideas for developing these skills. Your thoughts, ideas and experiences can be captured on paper where others, by reading them, can share them with you. Through your words, they can feel your feelings, share your thoughts and even be moved to action. Writing is a powerful tool. Your link to the rest of the world is not a cord fastened to a stick. It is your ability to read and write. So go and learn to use it well. Chin up. Here you go. Keep your eyes straight ahead and your feet on the ground. You're on the right path!

GETTING STARTED

What you think can be said. What you say can be written. And what you write can be read and understood. Therefore, writing really begins with your ability to put ideas into language. Anyone who can conceive an idea, imaginary or concrete, is capable of placing that idea, at some stage of personal development, onto paper.

It is helpful to begin this process with verbal expression. This will be most effective for encouraging creative communication with younger children who are not yet able to wield a pencil. In fact, while encouraging writing whenever possible, verbal exercises may be an excellent change of pace for even experienced writers.

Creative writing is a dynamic and vital form of art. However, in order to be a competent creative artist (regardless of the medium) you must have a firm grasp of the fundamentals of your trade. In order to be able to use form and structure in dynamic ways to enhance ideas or explore new concepts, you must have a firm grasp of spelling, vocabulary, grammar, style, sentence structure, and form. Only then can you use these tools to paint pictures, create images, or project emotions and ideas.

☞ THE CONCEPT: OBSERVATION

Only God creates from nothing. We, on the other hand, create from what already exists. Therefore, our creativity involves becoming observant students of our world. As students of life, writers need to develop their senses to observe carefully the structure and content of life in order to use the structure and content in creative expression.

Just as an artist has to have an understanding of line, color, form, shading, and light in order to paint, he also needs a subject. Whether the subject is disassembled and represented as the sum of various parts or whether the subject is duplicated in a portrait, in order to use the medium of paint and canvas to present an idea, there has to be something concrete. Therefore, this section will offer some ideas for the development of observation.

✍ **Putting it into practice.**

1) Find an object such as an old shoe, camera, teapot, virtually any item with character, and hold it up for a moment for all to see. Then remove the item from sight and using memory have everyone describe the object in detail. (Remember, the description may be verbal or written)

Now take the object out and compare the description with the object. Note new details. See how much more detail can be discovered.

2) Take an item, or a scene and list 15 observations about the item being viewed. Then after reviewing the list, repeat the process listing 15 new observations. Continue on until you have completely exhausted the observing of the item being viewed. (The number of observations required may be adjusted according to the particular situation. However, push your observations beyond what is obvious or easy to see.)

3) Go to an area where there are several different noises going on at once. (i.e. on the street you may hear engines, sirens, talking, horns etc. or in a field, rustling of wind, birds, airplane overhead, nearby roads) Identify as many sounds as you can. Spend the time and energy to absorb all there is to hear.

4) Observe a scene through a window, in a photograph, or out of doors. How many different colors are visible? Examine the lighting—what time of day is it?

5) Observe a scene or action and describe it in detail after looking away. Then compare and search for more detail. One method of viewing an action which may be helpful is to use a video recorder and play a scene. Then with the set off, describe what you saw. Now run it back and see what was missed or what needs to be corrected. (For example, you might have thought you saw three cars in a chase scene where there were actually only two.)

6) Read a passage from a story and observe as many details as possible about the passage.

☞ THE CONCEPT: VOCABULARY.

Essential to language are words. Sounds form the words. Words transmit ideas. Therefore, continually work to develop your vocabulary.

Vocabulary development comes through interaction with new words. Unit 7, **Focus on: Meaning** is packed full of various ways to learn words. Words from these charts will help in the following exercises.

✍ **Putting it into practice.**

1) Take a sentence and replace a word with its synonym or antonym (Chart 80-81). See how that creates a different visual picture. (The water in the pond was clear.—The water in the pond was muddy.)

2) Look up the definition of a new word and write a sentence with it.

3) Use homonyms (Chart 82) or heteronyms (Chart 83) together in a sentence. (They went to see the sea.)

4) Read literature and look up a definition of each new word and discuss the meaning. Study its roots, prefixes and suffixes (Chart 72-79).

5) Create some new words. Define them. Have them sound like what they are. Have them be totally innovative. Write a sentence, paragraph, story, or poem using them.

☞ THE CONCEPT: PERSPECTIVE.

The way we hear, see, or otherwise sense depends a great deal on perspective. When we look at an object from one side, certain details may be evident which go unnoticed when we look from the other. Perspective makes all the difference.

Therefore, as writers, part of observing is to learn to look at things from new or different perspectives. In a story about a conflict between a Father and Son, an understanding of each character's point of view or perspective is needed in order to represent their arguments.

✍ Putting it into practice.

1) Look at an object from one side then describe it. Look at it from another angle and describe what you see. Again from another angle. For example, if we look at a teapot from the side we might see a round pot with a spout on one side and a handle on the other. Then if we look at it from the bottom we might see a large sphere with a ring on its surface and an inscription. Turn it over and tea might run out on the floor.

2) Take a short tube like the cardboard from a paper roll and look through it as though it were a camera. Use different angles and describe what you see. Or do this same operation looking through the lens of a camera or through your hands.

3) Describe a room from sitting in a chair in the room and again from looking in at the room through the window.

4) Describe a scene as if you were flying overhead or looking out of a hole in the ground.

☞ THE CONCEPT: STORY TELLING.

There are a number of ways and reasons to tell a story. When you write a letter to a friend telling about what's going on in your life, you are writing a story. When you tell a group at a party about what you saw that morning on the way to the park, you are spinning a yarn, that is, telling a story. People tell and write stories all the time and yet if asked to write a story, they will tell you it can't be done. They will tell you that it is a task beyond their abilities. That, you see, is a fallacy. Almost everyone is an accomplished storyteller.

While a story can be done as a play, a poem, a newspaper article, or any other literary form, the style will most often be narrative. A narrative is simply telling a story as it happened. Wherever there is a person, there is a story. All that is needed is for the person to tell what they see, hear or otherwise sense and the story has begun.

The story can be about real events or made up events. The only limitations are those of the imagination. Stories are most commonly told from either first person (I went to the store) or third person (John went to the store). The choice is up to the writer and determined by the perspective of the story.

Let your young writers ramble on the creative lines of their story. As they develop they will naturally formalize their communication into more disciplined arrangement. At this age, encouraging story telling outweighs literary form and structure. Begin with fact and move to fiction. Good creative writers are often good story tellers. For this reason, encourage them to develop stories.

✍ Putting it into practice.

1) Begin a story and let your student finish it.

2) Pass a story along. One person begins the story and others continue the story in turn.

3) Take a familiar story then say "What if . . .?" and finish the story.

4) Take three words or ideas and turn them into a story. (i.e. bear, house, sandwich—now tell a story using these elements)

5) Take three things observed that day and create a story.

6) Record the story as it is told. Then transcribe the story from the tape. Make corrections or shorten as needed.

7) Adapt stories such as popular fairy tales, "Little Red Riding Hood" or "Humpty Dumpty", into plays. Simply take the characters and give them lines. The storyline is already in place by following the story. If a video camera is available, you may want to include the filming in your production.

☞ THE CONCEPT: FIGURES OF SPEECH.

A figure of speech is a word, sentence, or phrase which captures one idea in an alternate form. Exploring figures of speech is necessary for the competent critique of literature, and using these literary devices adds color, attracts attention, transforms abstract ideas into concrete ideas, aids in retention, and encourages reflection. So encourage the definition and exploration of figures of speech.

Here is a list of some of the common figures of speech and their definitions. In each of these literary devices is a world of fun with words!

Figures of Speech	Definition	Example
Simile	A comparison in which one thing resembles another by using "like" or "as".	Your eyes are like pools of water. "I send you out as lambs in the midst of wolves"
Metaphor	A comparison in which one thing is or acts or represents another thing from which it is essentially different.	"You are the salt of the earth" His legs were pillars.
Personification	Ascribing of human characteristics to inanimate objects, ideas or animals.	The trees nodded with approval at the cool breeze and refreshing rain.
Apostrophe	A direct address to a thing or non-present entity.	Oh Sea! What will you do with those you have swallowed?
Hyperbola	An exaggeration for effect or to add emphasis.	The teacher gave me a ton of homework.
Irony	A kind of ridicule in which the statement means the opposite of what has been said.	John loved it when the teacher called on him and he wasn't listening. It gave him the chance to show everyone what a fool he was.
Paradox	A statement which is seemingly absurd or contrary to received opinion.	"Whoever wants to be great among you must be your servant..."
Onomatopoeia	The use of words which sound like what they represent.	The rock plopped into the pond.
Rhyme	The use of words, sentences, or phrases with the same terminal sounds.	"Beauty is but a flower Which wrinkles will devour:"
Allegory	The figurative treatment of one subject or idea under the guise of another.	*The Chronicles of Narnia* *The Little Prince* Symbolic narrative
Alliteration	Corresponding sounds between nearby initial consonants.	She shook the shimmering curls of her hair.

✍ **Putting it into practice.**

1) Personification is an easy device for promoting imagination. Point out an object like a barbecue pit and personify it. "He was a short squatty character with a cigar and a derby who always seemed ready to devour whatever food we placed on his grill."

Perhaps a teapot would be better. "He was short and stout but always ready for action whenever it was teatime." And the exercises can be expanded. Start by identifying the teapot as a person. Then give that person a function. Then tell how that teapot feels. Next take the teapot through an action as if it were a person. Then tell what the teapot did on a given day. And before long the student has created an entire story.

2) Using allegory. In order to encourage creativity in developing a story and begin to grow a concept of imagery put together a story in allegory. Take a historical event or and event from your own experience. Then construct a fictional account which mirrors the original.

3) "To seem rather than to be" - Take an object like a wooden fence and describe it in a representative but different form. The slats might be teeth in a row or pencils in a pack neatly bundled together. Whatever the object, try to see it as what it **could** be.

4) Choose a sentence from a novel or other story, write it down, then write a parallel account. ("There was a village on the top of a mountain." "There was a man at the top of a tower." In these two accounts the differences are obvious. The man is an allegory for the village. The tower parallel the mountain.)

5) Write sentences or stories using the other figures of speech in the above chart.

☞ THE CONCEPT: POETRY.

Another form of creative writing which is easily explored is poetry. A poem is simply a composition in verse. Although poetry is often highly developed in imagery, it can be nothing more than a simple idea.

Poetry uses rhyme, rhythm, meter, or an acute sense of words and the power of word combinations and word pictures. Poetry can be lyrical, formal in design, or free form resting solely on the power of words and their placement on the page. There are many forms of poetry such as; ballad, couplet, blank verse, free verse, Haiku, limerick, ode, and sonnet. [For an in depth analysis of poetry you might consider using *Prosidy Handbook*, by Shapiro and Beum.]

✍ **Putting it into practice.**

1) Work with the idea of rhyme. Take a word and see how many different words you can find that rhyme with it. (Most of the word charts in the first two units are set up to use for finding word families, that is, words that end with the same sound and which rhyme.)

2) Have your students construct various poems using different rhythms. Then have the student couple these rhythms in various rhyme schemes. For example:

a a	first and second lines rhyme is a couplet	The clouds float **by** High in the **sky**.
a a a	three rhyming lines is a triplet	***Please Don't Give Me*** Clouds without **sun**, Work without **fun**, Start without **done**.
a ***b*** **a** ***b***	first and third lines rhyming and second and fourth is a ballad	The pilgrims came across the sea In search of land and *freedom.* Their efforts blessed both you and **me** For that's where America came *from.*

3) Find examples for the different forms of poetry and make a booklet of your own efforts.

☞ THE CONCEPT: CLUSTERING.

One way to get all your thoughts out on paper quickly with minimal effort is to 'cluster'. 'Clustering' does several things that cannot be done in the confines of an outline approach. Thoughts can be put down in random order, and any new ideas or thoughts can be added easily. In clustering, paragraphs are formed almost automatically. And best of all, 'clustering' takes only a few minutes to do.

Get started 'clustering' by putting your main topic in the center of the page and circling it. Around that circle, write down all the areas you want to cover and circle them. Attach these smaller circles by straight lines to the center circle. These will be the beginnings of your paragraphs. Write any additional thoughts that relate to each of the smaller circles, circle them and connect them with straight lines to the appropriate smaller circle.

When all your thoughts are explored and on paper in front of you, decide which order you want to arrange them in. Each circle coming from the main circle and all its satellites will be a paragraph. The writing of the paper will flow easily.

With younger students, it may be necessary to help them with their 'clustering'. Ask them directed question to help them pull their thoughts out and write down the ideas for them. In this way, many of the major words will be spelled for them when they actually begin to write so that they can concentrate their efforts in maintaining their train of thought. Included are several forms with 'cluster' designs complete with ready-made questions to think about. These will help you get started. There is a form for a student's first story (page 180), a friendly letter (page 182), and setting/character development for a short story (page 183). You may copy these forms for your use only.

The main thing to remember is that 'clustering' need not be sophisticated or complicated. Here is a rough sketch to show you how to do 'clustering' anytime, anywhere.

✍ Putting it into practice.

1) Use the "My First Story" form (page 180) for beginning story writing. Help choose a topic. Use the numbered questions to prompt thinking. Write down the answers for the beginning student. Then write the story, using the top section as the first paragraph and the bottom section as the second paragraph. Use complete sentence. Allow the student to do as much of this process as he is capable of doing.

2) Write a friendly letter following the directions for "Beginning Letter Writing" (page 181) and using the form for "Friendly Letter" (page 182).

3) Develop the setting and characters for a short story using the form for "Setting/Character Development" (page 183). Cluster some ideas for the story line and events. Then incorporate them into a short story.

☞ THE CONCEPT: BOOK REPORTS.

Writing about the books you have read can be an important aspect of creative writing. It gives an opportunity to analyze the elements of good literature as well as to develop a sensitivity to what an author is trying to say 'between the lines'. Reports should always include the title and author (for future reference) but should not be limited to a summary of the story. "50 Book Report Ideas" (page 184) keep book reports from becoming tedious and boring.

✍ **Putting it into practice.**

1) Use page 184 for ideas for writing book reports.

2) Read a variety of books by one author. Then research the author's life and background and see how it relates to his writing.

3) Read a wide variety of literature including fiction, non-fiction, nature, biography. Choose a selections from each category. Below is one way to set up a reading schedule. (The categories may be adapted for skill level of reader.)

Student's Name: **Date:**

Nature/Science Title: Author:	**"How to"** Title: Author:	**Biography** Title: Author:	**Historical Novel** Title: Author:
Adventure Title: Author:	**Mystery** Title: Author:	**Animal Stories** Title: Author:	**World Awareness** Title: Author:
Poetry Title: Author:	**Plays** Title: Author:	**Classics** Title: Author:	**Free Choice** Title: Author:
Science Fiction Title: Author:	**Inspirational** Title: Author:	**Magazine** Title: Author:	**Newspaper** Title: Author:

Date: # My First Story by:

2.
Who or what

3. Describe it (who with, how it looks, feels, smells, its size, location, speed, what it reminds me of, why I like to go)

4. Tell what happens (what is said, done, seen, felt, heard, how it is used, what it does, how it works, what I do with it)

5. Tell me more (what happened next, what was the result, did something else happen)

Ending (what happens at the end, is there something to lear

6. How it makes me feel (wonderful, worried, shy, upset, comfortable, cheerful)

Ideas for Story: (May be dictated to Teacher)
1. What is fun?
2. What makes me: happy, sad, mad, scared, excited.
3. My favorite: animal, food, activity, person, sport, holiday, memory.
4. All about my: mom, dad, brother, sister, friend, teacher.

1. My story is about: (Topic)

7.
Who or what

8. Describe it (who with, how it looks, feels, smells, its size, location, speed, what it reminds me of, why I like to go)

9. Tell what happens (what is said, done, seen, felt, heard, how it is used, what it does, how it works, what I do with it)

10. Tell me more (what happened next, what was the result, did something else happen)

Ending (what happens at the end, is there something to lea

11. How it makes me feel (wonderful, worried, shy, upset, comfortable, cheerful)

BEGINNING LETTER WRITING

Letters are very personal and can be written many different ways. There is not just one way to write a letter that will work all the time. A **thank-you note** would contain more about **why** and **what** you liked about what was given. It would also say **how** and **where** it was used. A **love letter** would deal more with how much you **miss**, **love** and **think about** the other person and may not touch on much else. To certain friends you would only write about **other friends** and **your thoughts**. Whatever you write, make sure you cover what why when and most important how you feel. The same goes for writing about work or play. Tell what happened, who was with you, and how you feel about it.

To help you get started and to have a well-rounded letter, fill in the blanks on the "Friendly Letter Format" (page 182).

First write in the person you are writing to (#1). Then write in your name. Put the date in the box at the top of the page (#2). Now think about all the things you need to answer: Did you get a letter, call, gift, money? You need to write "Thank you for . . ." these things. Were there particular questions asked or not resolved the last time you talked or were together? Write briefly about them in the boxes provided (#3). Now, what questions do you want to ask your friend about his health or feelings? Has anything happened lately to make him feel strongly one way or another? How is he physically? What would you like to find out about his school, church, or work? Are there other activities that you want to find out more about? Don't be afraid to ask. Do you know or want to know about any of his friends? Find out more by asking more questions (#4).

If you know a specific family member or friend, find out what he is doing, where he is going or how he feels by asking about him.

(#5) Refresh your friendship by recalling memories either good or bad. Tell how you feel about the person—do you miss him or love him? Think out what you would like to do with him if he was with you. And think about your hopes or wishes about seeing him again.

(#6) Now write about things you want to tell your friend. What is happening in your life at school, church or clubs? Who does it involve and how do you feel about it?

The next step is to write the letter. Start by putting the date in the right-hand corner. Next, on the left-hand side, leaving at least the space of one line, write: "Dear ___ (the friend's name). Drop down to the next line, leave about the space of five letters (this is called 'indenting') and start your first paragraph, using what you wrote under #3. Make complete sentences from the thoughts that you have jotted down in each category. Make sure to capitalize the beginnings of sentences and names, and so forth. Whenever you get to a circle on the outline, start a new paragraph by going down to the next line and indenting. When you have finished writing about all the things you wanted to say, drop down a line from the last paragraph, indent and write a closing such as: Write back soon, Love you, Your Friend, Miss you, Have to run, or I'm thinking about you. Then sign your name. If you have any more thoughts you want to add, write P.S. (post script or afterthought) at the bottom of the page and write what you want to say.

Finally, fold the letter in half and then in thirds, and place it in an envelope. Address the envelope with your address in the upper left-hand corner (the return address), your friend's address in the center of the envelope, and the stamp in the upper right-hand corner. Drop it in the mail and wait for a letter to come back to you!

P.S. You may want to include a "Friendly Letter Format" to help your friend write back to you!

Friendly Letter

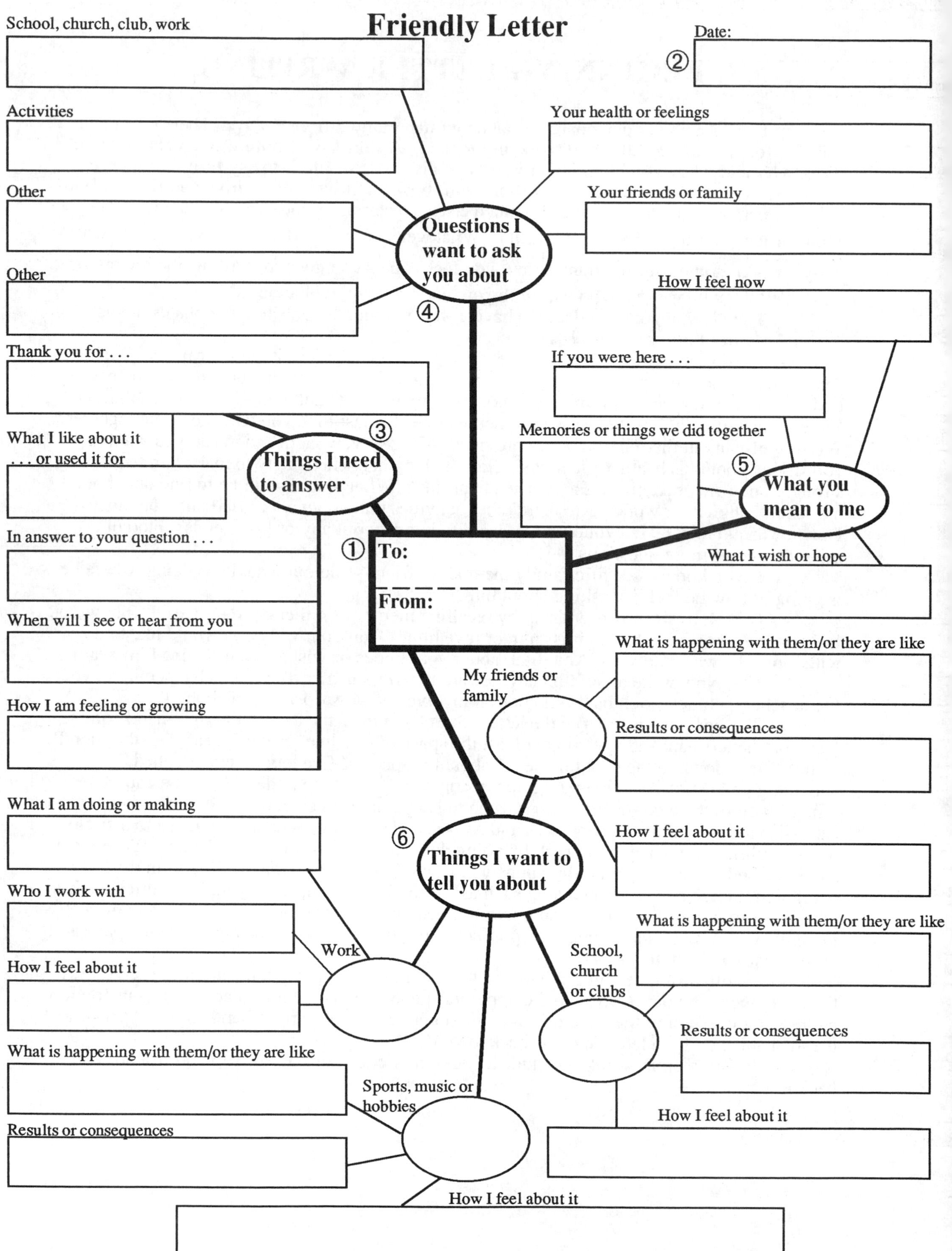

School, church, club, work
Date:
②
Activities
Your health or feelings
Other
Your friends or family
Questions I want to ask you about
Other
How I feel now
④
Thank you for . . .
If you were here . . .
What I like about it . . . or used it for
③
Things I need to answer
Memories or things we did together
⑤
What you mean to me
In answer to your question . . .
① To:
From:
What I wish or hope
When will I see or hear from you
What is happening with them/or they are like
How I am feeling or growing
My friends or family
Results or consequences
What I am doing or making
How I feel about it
⑥
Things I want to tell you about
Who I work with
What is happening with them/or they are like
Work
School, church or clubs
How I feel about it
What is happening with them/or they are like
Results or consequences
Sports, music or hobbies
How I feel about it
Results or consequences
How I feel about it

Setting/Character Development

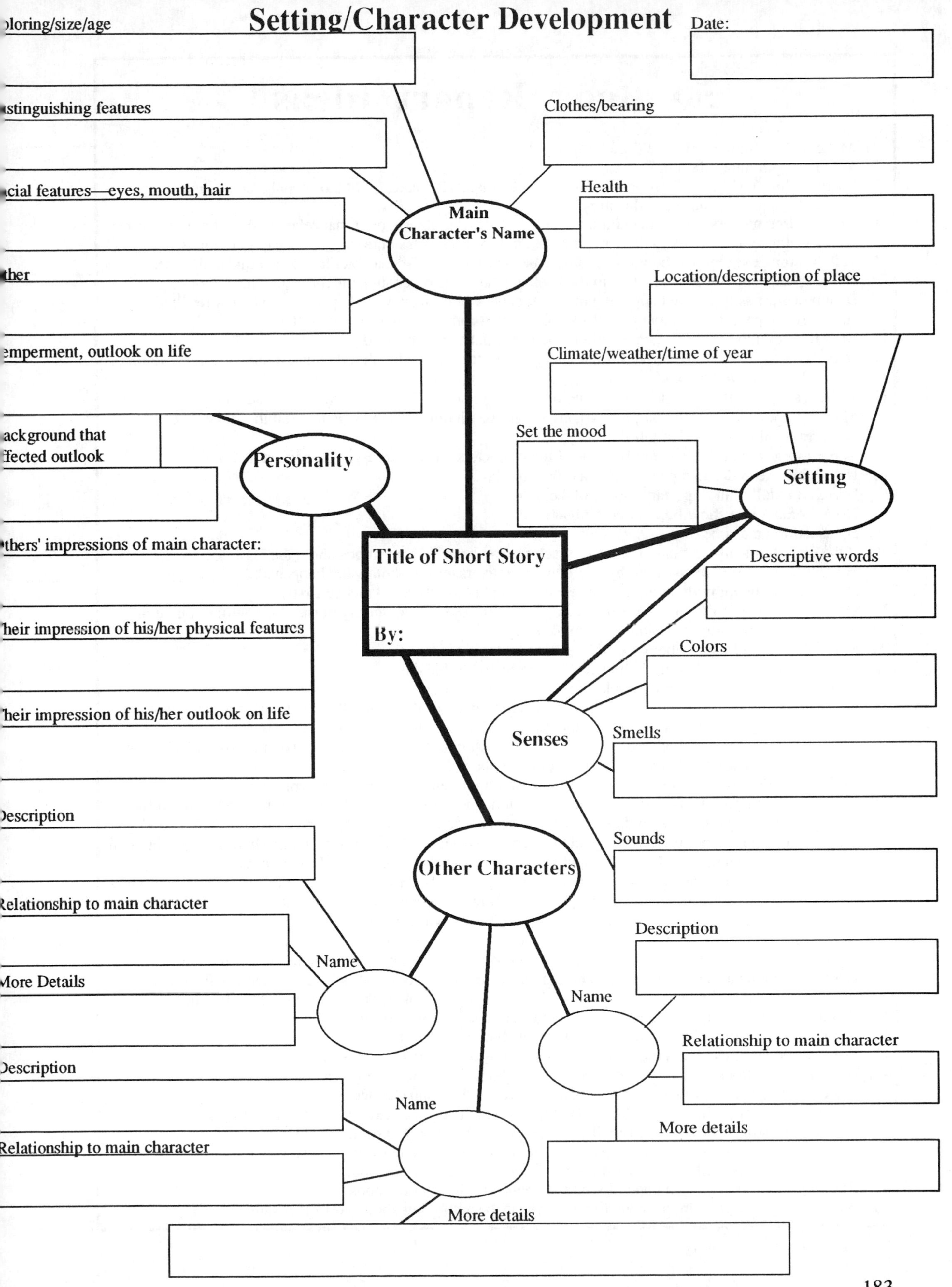

Date:
oloring/size/age
istinguishing features
Clothes/bearing
acial features—eyes, mouth, hair
Health
Main Character's Name
ther
Location/description of place
emperment, outlook on life
Climate/weather/time of year
ackground that ffected outlook
Set the mood
Personality
Setting
thers' impressions of main character:
Title of Short Story
By:
Descriptive words
heir impression of his/her physical features
Colors
heir impression of his/her outlook on life
Senses
Smells
Description
Sounds
Other Characters
Relationship to main character
Description
Name
More Details
Name
Relationship to main character
Description
Name
More details
Relationship to main character
More details

50 Book Report Ideas

1. Make a TV commercial to sell the book.
2. Write a poem about the book.
3. Read a "How To" book. Demonstrate what you learned. (Pet care, build a fire, make bread, and so on.)
4. Make up your own ending to the story.
5. Create a flag on paper for some character in the book. Put objects on it that relate to that character. (For instance, if he likes to read, put a book on it; or if he rides horses, put a horse on it, and so on.)
6. Tell the story and then tell how it would have been different if the character had been blind and/or deaf.
7. Dress up like one of the characters in the book and have the other students interview him.
8. Do a newscast as if it were happening today. Include where, who, what happened, and what resulted.
9. Have several people who have read the book take parts and act out a section of the book.
10. Do a finger puppet show. (Or any other type of puppets could be used.)
11. Make a cereal box into the cover of the book. Cover the box with colored paper. Glue a short write-up of the book on the back.
12. Write a song about the book. Use a tune from another song. Then teach the class your song.
13. Make a photo album with real photographs, magazine pictures or drawings that tell the story.
14. Do a series of cartoons that tell the story.
15. Make a large paper doll to look like one of the characters. Then write your report on its body.
16. Use a video recorder to tape your puppet show or play.
17. Make a model of an important aspect of the book.
18. Do a diorama in a show box about the book.
19. Dress a doll up as one of the characters.
20. If the class has read the same book, have each student write five questions about the book for a test.
21. Write a letter as if it was written by one of the characters telling about what happened.
22. Do a chalk drawing with colored chalk as you tell about the story. (Practice first!)
23. Do a pantomime of the story. Introduce the characters and tell the setting of the story before you begin.
24. Make a clay sculpture of an animal from the story.
25. Make a scrapbook about the book from pictures cut out of magazines.
26. Rewrite a section of the story in a different time period or location.
27. Make a map of where the book took place.
28. Read a few paragraphs from one of the most exciting parts of the book. Be sure to tell enough about the story beforehand so that the audience knows what is going on and who the characters are.
29. Make a food that was talked about or is from the location or time of the book. Tell the story and let the class taste the food. (Make enough for everyone to have some!)
30. Make a mobile about the book. Have different important items and characters represented.
31. Make a curved time line and draw pictures of what happened first, second, and so forth, on the "time trail".
32. Create a radio show, using sound effects from things around (door closing, horses running, and so on.).
33. Make a card file. Write title, author, publisher, and two sentences about the book. Then tell why the book should or should not be read. Sign your name and keep in a class file box for class reference.
34. Give a report of the book and then tell five words and their meanings used in the book that you didn't know before. The teacher will pick words from several students for a spelling test.
35. For science or history book reports, make a poster of what was learned.
36. Act out a dialogue between two characters in the book. Set the scene before you begin.
37. Do a shadow play of the book. Have actors stand between a hanging sheet and a bright light source.
38. With a telephone as a prop, pretend to be a character from the book and talk about what is happening.
39. Pretend you are a character from the book who is now old. Look back on your life and tell about it.
40. Tell about the story up to the climax. Have the audience write their own endings.
41. Draw an illustration of something from the book and tell about it.
42. Write several entries in a diary as if it were written by a character in the book.
43. Write five questions to ask the audience about the book after you have given your report.
44. Read two or three biographies and compare the lives of the main characters.
45. Tell what you might have done differently than the character in an exciting part of the story.
46. Tell how the story would have been different if one detail/action had been changed.
47. Make a certificate of achievement for a character in the book and tell why he deserved it.
48. Do a group report, with each person responsible for a portion of the book.
49. Have a three or four person panel discussion about a topic from the book.
50. Write three paragraphs in the same literary style as the author but about a different subject.

UNIT 9

FOCUS ON: ACTIVITIES

Page	Title	Description
186	Alphabet Soup	alphabetizing skills
186	Color/Number Match	recognition of color/number words
186	Rhyme Time	word family and rhyme
186	Word Memory	matching words
187	Vowel Bingo	recognizing vowel sounds
187	Opposite "Go Fish"	synonyms and antonyms
187	Telephone Spelling	spelling "gossip"
187	Build a Word	making words from letters
188	Holiday Word List	making words from words
188	Bee to the Flower	team spelling bee
188	Banana Split	spelling bee
188	Star Shine	spelling/reading race
189	Scrambled Eggs	figuring out mixed-up words
189	Instant Recall	memory concentration
189	Ink-Pink Rhyming Game	figuring out rhyme word
189	Pie-Eating Contest	team spelling bee
190	Dictionary Drill	dictionary skills
190	Harder than Ever	spelling stretcher
190	Act or Draw	reading skills
190	Missing Letters	spelling words from clues
191	Simple Syllables to Read and Spell (Chart 1-8)	reading/spelling skills
192	Simple Syllables to Read and Spell (Chart 9 +)	reading/spelling skills
193	Eagle's Wings Sight Words for Reading and Spelling (Beginning)	sight words to read and spell
194	Eagle's Wings Sight Words for Reading and Spelling (Advanced)	sight words to read and spell

Alphabet Soup

Ability: Beginning
Preparation: Each player gets a piece of paper and randomly places every letter of the alphabet on the sheet.
Procedure: The players then exchange papers and try to connect the letters alphabetically.
Goal: Correct alphabetization.
Time: 5-10 minutes.

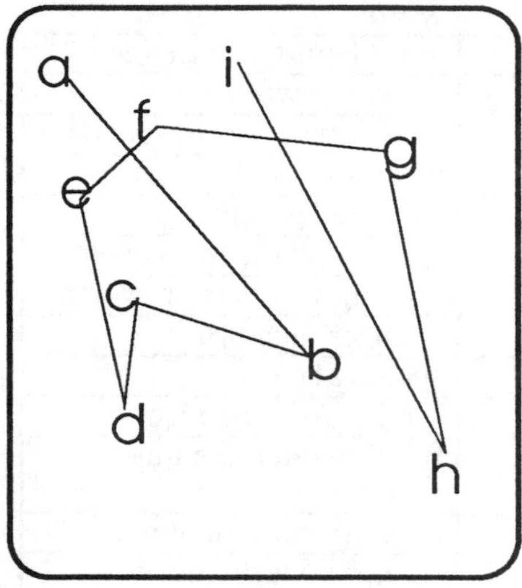
a
i
f
g
e
c
b
d
h

Color/Number Match

Ability: Beginning
Preparation: Write the names of colors on 3x5 cards and color corresponding cards. Also write the name of the numbers on cards and the corresponding symbol on other cards. Use only the cards that have been studied.
Procedure: Mix cards up. Then have students match the color cards to the correct color and the number cards to the correct numbers symbol.
Goal: Number and color familiarization.
Time: Variable

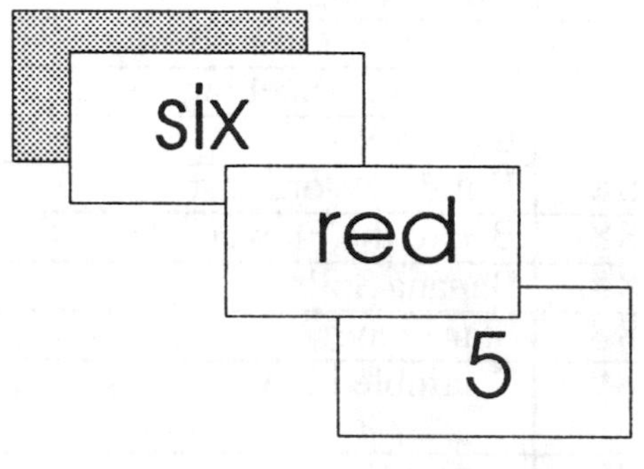
six
red
5

Rhyme Time

Ability: Beginning
Preparation: Draw simple pictures of up to four words on the blackboard.
Procedure: Say a word and have students come up to spell theword under the picture that it rhymes with.
Goal: Understanding rhyme patterns and word families.
Time: Variable.

ox
fox
king
sing

Word Memory

Ability: Beginning/Intermediate
Preparation: Prepare two copies each of 10 to 20 words on 3x5 cards. Choose 2 to 4 players.
Procedure: Turn the cards face down. Have players take turns turning over two cards at a time. If they match, the student reads the word and keeps them. He also gets another turn. If the words are different, they are turned back over and the next player takes a turn.
Time: Variable.

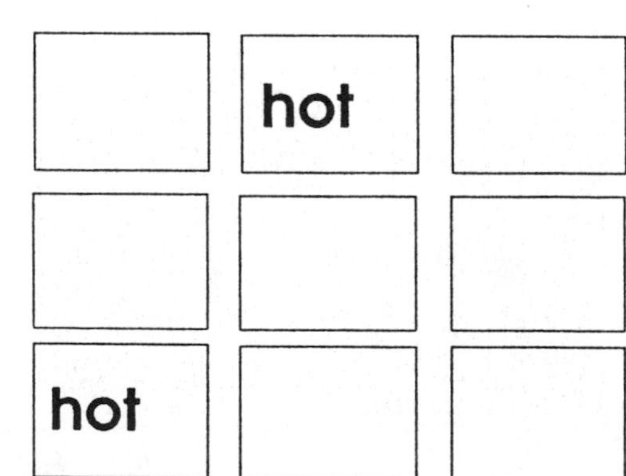
hot
hot

Vowel Bingo

Ability: Beginning

Preparation: Have students fold their paper into 16 squares. Write the short and long vowels on the blackboard. (Do not use long 'e' until it has been studied.) Have students randomly fill their boxes with vowels.

Procedure: Read one-syllable words aloud with a short or long vowel sound in them. Have students put an 'x' (or write the word) in the box with that vowel sound.

Goal: Winner is the first to have four in a row.

Time: 5-10 minutes.

Variations: Use blends, 'cliffs', digraphs, "Everyday Bloopers", or "Everyday Words".

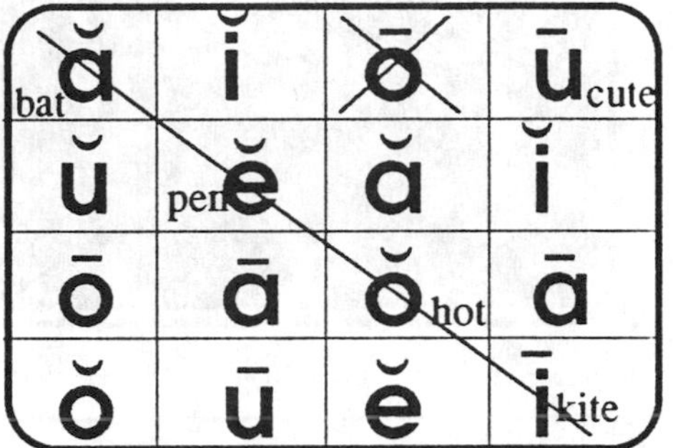
bat ă
ō
ū cute
pen ĕ
ŏ hot
kite

Opposite "Go Fish"

Ability: Multi-level

Preparation: Use list of opposites on Charts 80-81. Write one word in the center of a 3x5 card, with its opposite in the corner. Using the same two words, reverse the positions for the next card.

Procedure: Deal 7 cards to each player. Each player checks for matching 'sets' (two words that are opposite), and sets them down. Then, taking turns, each asks all players for a specific card that will make a 'set' with one of theirs. A turn continues until no one has the requested card, and the player then draws another card from the deck.

Goal: The winner is the player with the most 'sets'.

Time: Variable

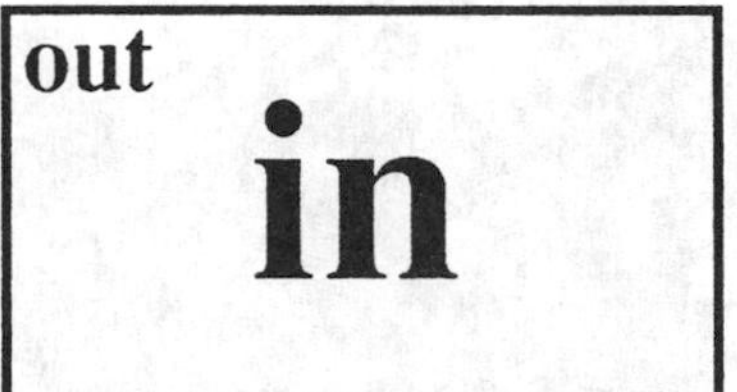
out
in

Telephone Spelling

Ability: Multi-level

Preparation: None.

Procedure: Whisper the spelling of a word into a student's ear. He then whispers what he hears to the student next to him. And so on until the "message" has been sent around the room. The last student goes to the blackboard and writes what he heard and tries to figure out what the word was. Alternate where the "message" begins so that the ending person changes.

Goal: To figure out what a word is.

Time: Variable.

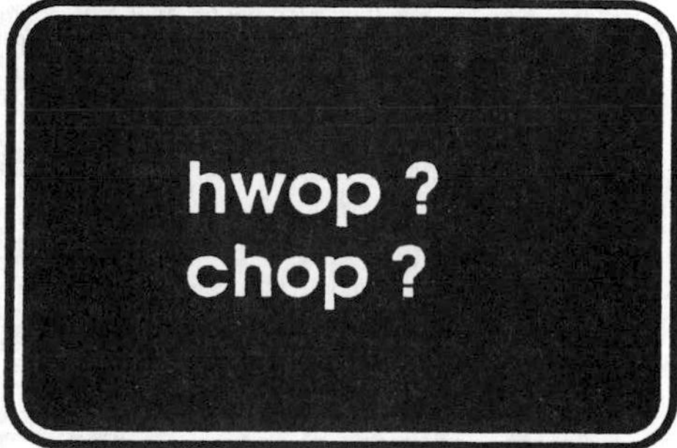
hwop ?
chop ?

Build a Word

Ability: Multi-level

Preparation: Write the following catagories and letters on the blackboard.

Procedure: Have the students build words, using letters from each catagory.

Goal: To get the most correct words.

Time: 5 minutes.

Variation: Use blends and affixes in place of individual letters.

Beginning	Vowel	End	Optinal
b c d f g	a e	d g	Silent e
h j k l m	i o	m n	
n p r s t	u	p t	
v w y z		x	

Holiday Word List

Ability: Intermediate
Preparation: Write the name of a holiday on the blackboard. [Easter, Valentine, Christmas, Lincoln (birthday), etc.]
Procedure: Have students spell as many words as they can, using only the letters in the word on the blackboard.
Goal: Winner is one with most correctly spelled words.
Time: 5-10 minutes.

Easter

Answers: eat, east, star, sat, rat, rest, etc.

Bee to the Flower

Ability: Multi-level.
Preparation: Draw a flower with seven petals and a bee with seven dots to get to the flower.
Procedure: Divide students into the "Flower Team" and the "Bee Team". Team members take turns spelling words. If the word is spelled correctly by "Flower Team", they can erase a petal on the flower. If it is spelled correctly by the "Bee Team", they can erase one of the dots leading to the flower.
Goal: The idea is to see if the bee can get to the flower before the flower wilts.
Time: Variable.

Banana Split

Ability: Multi-level
Preparation: Draw one banana split per team on the blackboard. Each banana split has one banana, three scoops of ice cream, and three cherries.
Procedure: May have as many teams as possible. Taking turns, as in a spelling bee, the students will spell a word correctly orally or on the blackboard. For each correct spelling, a student can "eat" one item on the banana split by erasing it.
Goal: The team to "eat" their banana split first wins.
Time: Variable.

Star Shine

Ability: Multi-level
Preparation: Draw 20 or more stars on the blackboard (Depending on time alotted.)
Procedure: Taking turns, have students correctly read or spell given words.
Goal: For every correct answer the student may make a star "shine" by coloring it.
Time: 5-10 minutes.

Scrambled Eggs

Ability: Multi-level
Preparation: Mix up letters of each word on blackboard. (Up to 20 words.)
Procedure: Have students figure out as many words as they can in 2-5 minutes.
Goal: Winner is one with most correctly spelled words.
Time: 2-5 minutes.

1. klabc
2. epho
3. dlto

Answers: 1. black, 2. hope, 3. told.

Instant Recall

Ability: Multi-level
Preparation: Write 10-20 words on the blackboard. (Be sure to have a copy of the words on paper.)
Procedure: Let students look at the words for 1 minute. Erase them completely. Have the students write as many as they can recall on paper.
Goal: The winner is the one with the most correct words.
Time: Variable

write train
frog sleep
apple book

Ink-Pink Rhyming Game

Ability: Multi-level
Preparation: Write three to five words on the blackboard.
Procedure: Have students write as many rhyme words as they can on paper or on the blackboard.
Goal: Winner is one with the most correct words.
Time: Variable.

ran
hat
hop

Answers: ran: tan, van, can, man, etc.
hat: cat, sat, fat, mat, etc.
hop: cop, mop, stop, top, etc.

Pie-Eating Contest

Ability: Multi-level
Preparation: For each team, draw three circles representing pies on the blackboard.
Procedure: Divide students into teams. (The more teams, the more practice per student.) Have students spell given words on the blackboard. For each correct word, a "pie" may be "eaten" by erasing one circle. Each student must eat all his pies before sitting down. The next student will need three new "pies".
Goal: Continue until every team member has had a turn.

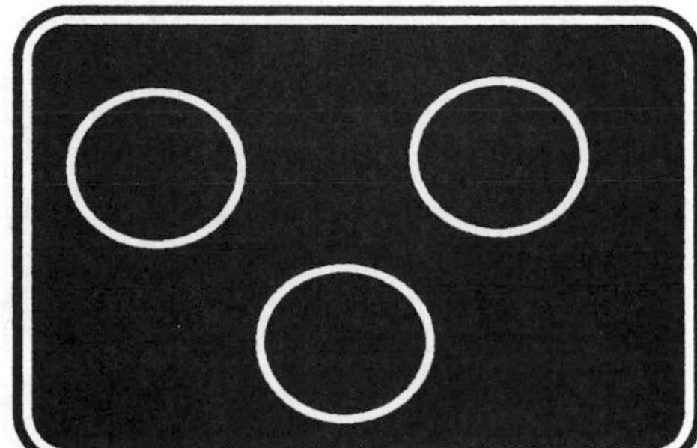

Dictionary Drill

Ability: Intermediate/Advanced
Preparation: Have as many teams as you have dictionaries.
Procedure: Have students hold dictionary closed on their desks. Teacher will say a word. (Younger students may need to have the word written on the blackboard.) At the word "go", each student will find it in the dictionary. Then he will go to the blackboard and spell it in syllables.
Goal: Winning team is first to find/spell word correctly.
Time: 5-10 minutes.

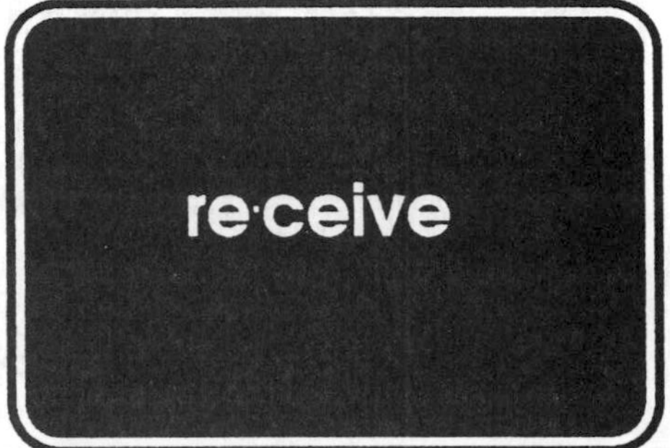
re·ceive

Harder than Ever.

Ability: Multi-level
Preparation: Divide students into two teams.
Procedure: Have the first student of each team come to the blackboard. The teacher will say a different word for each team that is several levels above their spelling ability. The first players will write the first letter and the teacher will tell them if it is correct. If it is correct, it is left on the blackboard. If it is incorrect, the student erases it. Then he goes to the end of the line. The next student adds the next letter, the teacher checks it, and the process continues.
Goal: The first team to correctly spell their word gets a point and then they start on a new word.
Time: Variable

econom

Act or Draw

Ability: Multi-level
Preparation: Choose words that can be easily pantomimed or represented by a simple drawing.
Procedure: Have student silently read a word, then go to the front and either draw a picture of it on the blackboard or act it out. The rest of the class gets to guess what the word is. The student who guesses the word gets to act or draw the next word.
Goal: Demonstrates reading comprehension.
Time: Variable.

Answer: cat

Missing Letters

Ability: Multi-level
Preparation: Divide into two teams. The teacher chooses a word the class has studied, writes a few letters of it on the blackboard, and putslines in the appropriate spaces for the other letters.
Procedure: The teacher gives a short clue. Then a student from the first team goes to the blackboard and writes in the missing letters. If it is correct, their team gets a point. If not, the other team gets a turn.
For example, the word is "black". The teacher writes _ _ac _ on the board. The clue is : "a color".

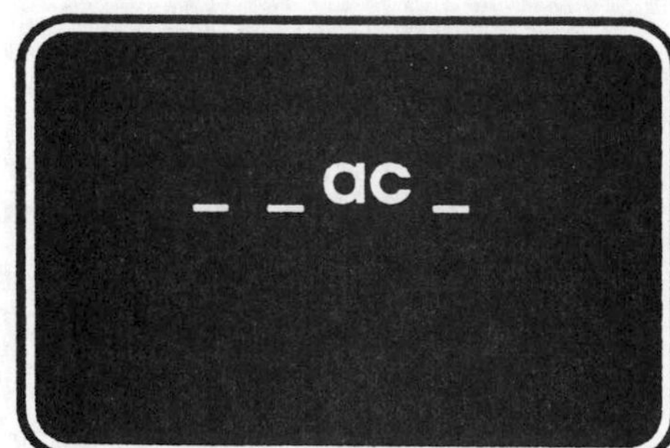
_ _ ac _

Answer: black.

Simple Syllables to Read and Spell

Chart 1	Chart 2	Chart 3	Chart 4	Chart 6	Chart 7
tom cat	up hill	ex pose	trum pet	ab sent	wind mill
ham per	pon tiff	bag pipe	trip let	hand bag	hand bill
up set	hap less	dis robe	spec trum	in tend	stand still
cat gut	un less	fox hole	trin ket	ex pand	grand ness
jun ket	can vass	pan cake	drag net	un mask	ink well
em bed	god less	pot hole	splen did	com pact	sub class
pop gun	un lock	cos tume	stop gap	sand bag	trans gress
sun tan	dis cuss	ex cuse	dog trot	in sist	soft ness
tan dem	wit ness	man date	blan ket	un just	self less
in set	pot luck	bed side	tran sit	con duct	dark ness
sub let	dis miss	bed time	hun dred	ex tent	un dress
but ton	job less	cas cade	bob sled	sub ject	wind sock
mag net	pad lock	in vade	prob lem	in vest	ham string
nap kin	ran sack	mis name		in sult	bed spring
com bat	wed lock	in hale	**Chart 5**	sus pect	gang plank
ban dit	hen peck	dis pose	ex plode	hus band	ob long
ad mit	dis till	am pule	mem brane	pump kin	wing span
nit wit		up date	slap stick	sus pend	up swing
can did		es cape	dis close	in sect	ring side
nut meg		con cave	trom bone	mid land	ink stand
pom pom		con fide	trans cribe		ring let
hob nob		in side	en close		mis print
ram rod		dis like	con trite		con tract
gob let		com bine	em press		en trust
up set		ig nite	mis quote		ab stract
hot rod		con fine			in flict
sun set		in vite			mis trust
cat nip		con dole			im print
bob cat		ob tuse			in spect
sun lit		con sole			trans plant
		cut rate			un clasp
		con done			sub tract
		es tate			

Simple Syllables to Read and Spell

Chart 9	More	Practice	Syllables	to Read
bath tub	tu lip	fe male	re pent	stu dent
fish net	be gun	re sale	de pend	pro tract
fresh men	re run	e vade	tri dent	re ject
whip lash	o pen	do nate	bro ken	re tract
bath robe	re fit	de bate	de frost	tri pod
chip munk	hu man	po lite	re cast	pro test
ship ment	o mit	re fine	va grant	ro bust
chest nut	cli max	u nite	re flect	re cant
slip stitch	si ren	ro tate	re plant	pu trid
un latch	ma trix	fe line	pre tend	pro pane
fish pond	ra ven	re bate	va cant	de grade
rash ness	be gan	de fine	ro dent	ni trate
chil dren	re cap	be came	mo ment	de prave
ship mate	e mit	va cate	re sent	pro vide
thick ness	gra ven	ca nine	pre test	re cline
rich ness	re lax	se nile	de funct	de prive
hunch back	re mit	be have	pru dent	pro voke
ship shape	stu pid	re take	ro tund	pre lude
with stand	e ven	re late	pro ton	
hot shot	re fill	de file	de ject	
pub lish	ti gress	re side	re sist	
nut shell	re gress	de cide	re fund	
cat fish	re press	e rode	be long	
thank less	re buff	re sume	pri mate	
gun shot	pro fess	re buke	re print	
cam shaft	be fall	e voke	de tect	
am bush		e lope	re flex	
chit chat		o zone	slo gan	
clam shell		e lude	re vamp	
		de vote	pre mix	
		de note	de tract	
		re pute	pre vent	
		mi nute	re spect	
		re fute	si lent	
		re mote	re lent	
			pre sent	
			po tent	
			re spond	

Eagle's Wings Sight Words for Reading and Spelling (List 1)

Row 1	Row 2	Row 3	Row 4	Row 5	Row 6
I	but	any	color	late	could
we	into	feel	number	last	three
you	may	just	one	ride	begin
are	of	much	that	fall	green
can	put	ask	why	half	think
for	was	some	moon	mom	end
it	try	yet	wet	dad	many
a	has	most	tree	first	over
at	give	away	dog	best	hope
do	all	have	two	say	short
get	oh	keep	white	tell	work
go	make	must	sleep	won't	high
to	need	very	when	your	fast
she	off	her	father	fine	tall
and	only	want	friend	since	mine
by	look	way	jump	write	play
let	such	new	star	there	street
yes	read	went	house	nice	face
in	love	good	happy	hello	stay
up	cat	help	than	also	bird
big	here	were	then	I'm	while
no	like	bad	blue	call	son
hot	him	old	six	top	live
me	my	will	they	long	open
sit	how	with	mother	fat	count
us	our	hers	name	wide	hour
as	be	this	nine	round	low
did	done	what	four	dirty	eat
fun	had	place	ever	soft	eight
if	man	sun	girl	full	cold
lot	now	time	yellow	more	should
the	so	day	ten	talk	walk
or	use	week	them	hear	before
he	said	their	thing	spell	animal
see	know	thank	who	yours	stand
run	stop	out	grass	school	less
his	come	from	five	far	plant
not	sad	take	leg	small	seven
is	red	mean	saw	city	every
boy	few	date	other	black	hundred

Eagle's Wings Sight Words for Reading and Spelling (List 2)

Row 7	Row 8	Row 9	Row 10	Row 11	Row 12
speak	you're	whom	allow	week	teacher
front	listen	well	arm	tomorrow	forty
near	seen	although	bother	children	once
huge	first	even	everywhere	taught	sixty
young	start	between	believe	fifty	flower
drink	early	sweet	weight	January	always
die	lead	wrong	tight	height	thought
safe	lost	lie	left	September	another
pretty	rent	seventy	dark	afternoon	good-bye
strong	family	dislike	fight	jungle	October
ours	quiet	July	sold	daughter	twenty
wake	buy	hate	fought	neighbor	around
bottom	show	altogether	ugly	grandma	remember
back	truth	fear	please	November	slight
we're	right	close	they're	brown	below
thin	awful	hide	worth	subtract	enough
dry	sour	sell	August	minute	sight
clean	forget	break	grandpa	yesterday	question
hard	almost	noisy	ocean	valley	through
empty	add	own	desert	pond	Wednesday
hill	wait	tough	horse	forest	laugh
under	warm	April	breakfast	parent	brother
light	across	found	Friday	nephew	morning
slow	June	leave	winter	plains	caught
lake	asleep	uncle	purple	river	autumn
today	ear	bought	square	prairie	behind
pink	mouth	follow	bright	husband	answer
spring	never	neither	mountain	February	sister
ago	event	whole	cow	tenth	thousand
eye	agree	become	Monday	wife	worse
Sunday	May	night	lunch	niece	multiply
aunt	where	Saturday	December	Tuesday	thorough
gray	thank	world	woman	home	elephant
ought	rather	aloud	orange	earth	bear
cry	ahead	because	plus	country	divide
sing	watch	March	third	fourth	fifth
water	might	approve	hand	loose	narrow
beside	straight	month	hair	real	Thursday
already	summer	second	feet	pretend	belong
which	minus	hurt	year	thirty	wonderful

UNIT 10

FOCUS ON:
"FUN FORMS"

Alphabet Island
Phonics
Teacher's Guide
Revised & Expanded
CIRCUS
Photo
© 1987, 1988, 1994 Mortimer and Smith
by Susan Mortimer and Betty Smith

Alphabet Island Phonics

Created and Illustrated by Susan Mortimer

Most of the teaching helps included in this unit are taken from ***Alphabet Island Phonics,*** a phonics program designed specifically to be used with ***Eagle's Wings Comprehensive Handbook of Phonics for Spelling, Reading and Writing. Alphabet Island Phonics*** provides many activities, songs, and games to enhance the learning process. Detailed Teacher's Manuals and Workbooks are included. For more information, please contact:

Eagle's Wings Educational Materials
PO Box 502, Duncan, OK 73534
www.EaglesWingsED.com

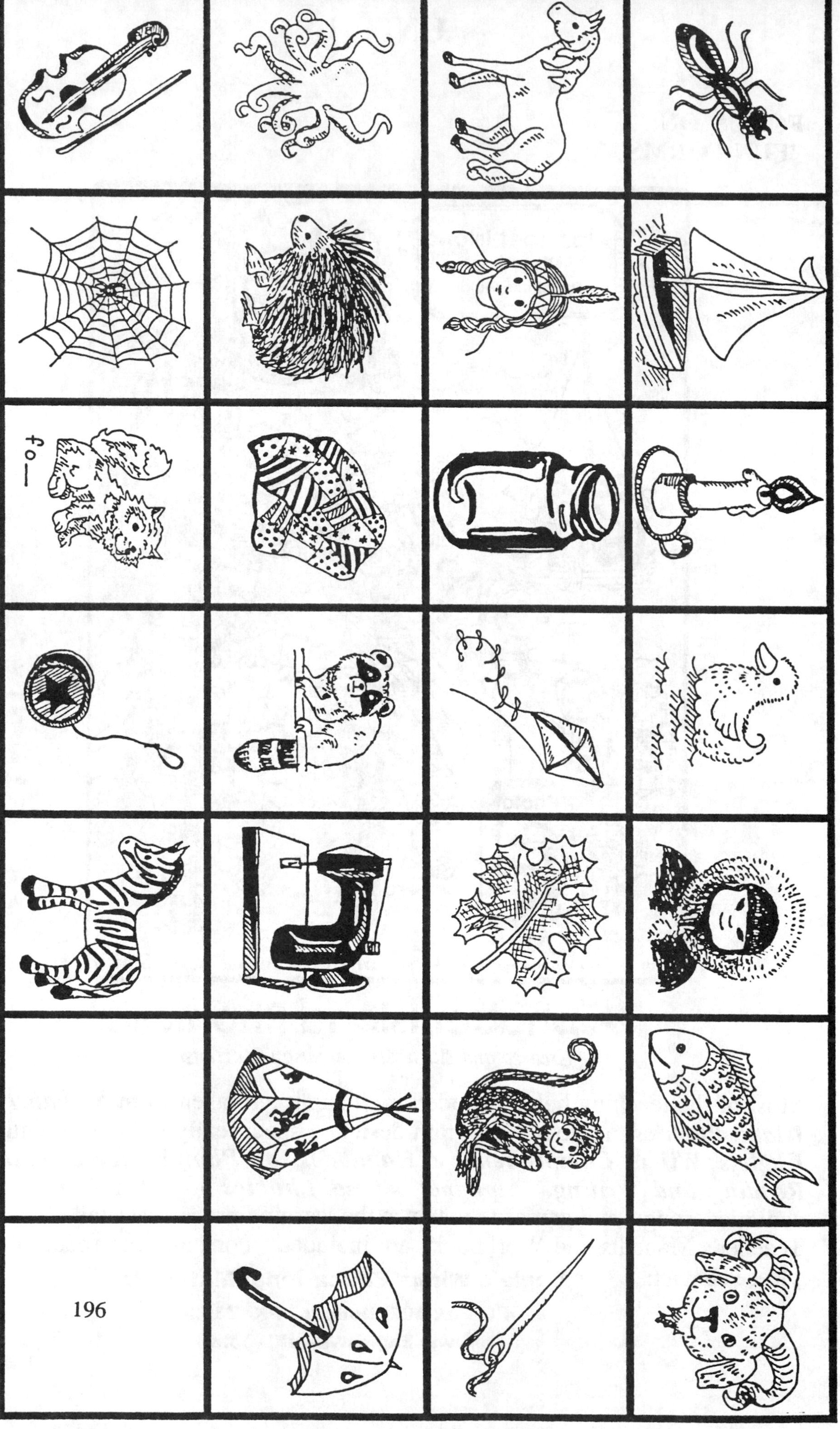

Clever C's Two Sounds

k
s
c
a
o
u
Consonants
c
e
i
y

The letter 'c' says /s/, "cent", in front of 'e', 'i', or 'y'. Elsewhere, (before 'a', 'o', 'u', or a consonant) it says /k/, "cat".

Goofy G's Two Sounds

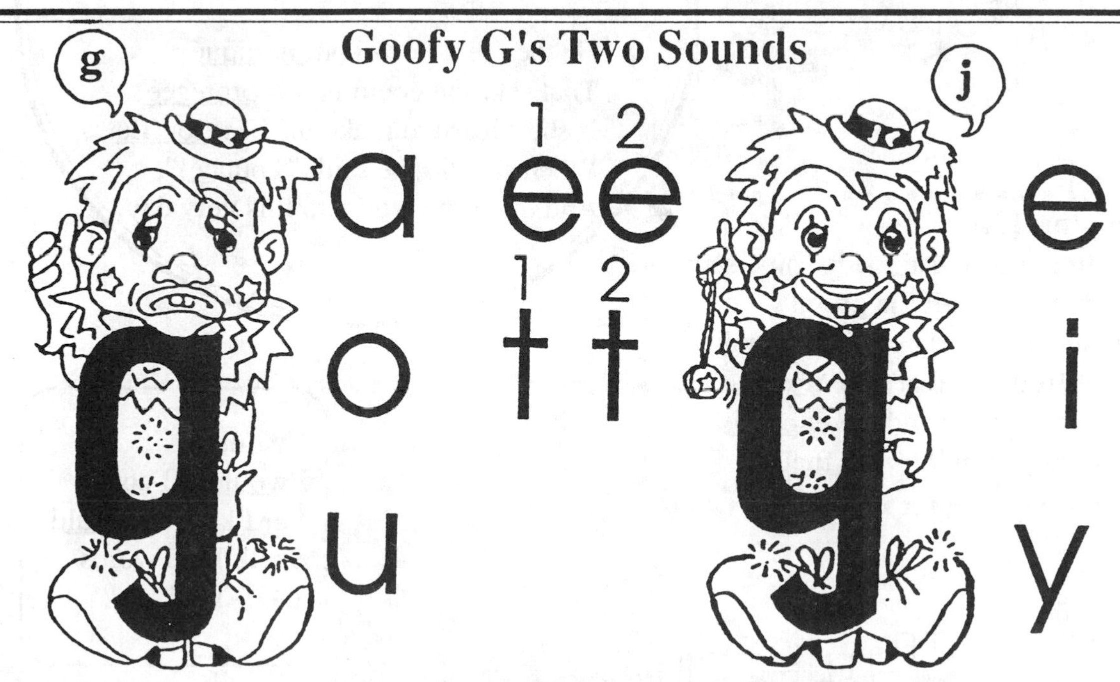
g
j
a
1 2
ee
o
1 2
tt
u
g
e
i
y

The letter 'g' says /g/, "goat", in front of 'a', 'o', 'u', and in front of two vowels or a vowel followed by two consonants. 'G' says /j/, "gem" in front of a single 'i', 'e', or 'y', followed by a single consonant.

A Potpourri of Poems!

Don't twang the string or you'll tweak the sparrows.
(A tongue twister!)

Twelve and twenty stars twinkled
As the twin birds twitter twice.
Then the wind twirled twine between the two,
And now they need help and advice.

A dwarf came by all dressed in tweed
"Don't worry," he said, "and don't twinge.
("God knows where you dwell and He's in control.
"Your lives in His balances hinge.")[1]

"I will twist the twig in twain with my tweezers
"And then you can merrily tweet."
"The gloom you will thwart as you twitch yourselves free,
"And before twilight dwindles you'll eat."

[1]Note: These two lines optional.

The Soufflé Protegée
René sewed appliqués on new negligées,
Until she sent off her complete resumé,
To a bald headed man who wore a toupée
And owned a popular small café.

He then sent her a communiqué
That said she could be his protegée
If she'd learn to make the best soufflé.
When she did, he said, "Touché!",
And there she works to this very day.

The Camping Trip
On the camping trip, dad made some soup
And had enough for all the group.
"Suit yourselves," said one small youth,
"But I want fruit and that's the truth.
"Still, since I am kind and never cruel,
"I'll tie my shoe then look for fuel."

I would
I would if I could
For I know I should,
Spell these words
'o'-'u'-'l'-'d'.

To send the sleigh straight by freight by eight,
You must pay more for its weight.

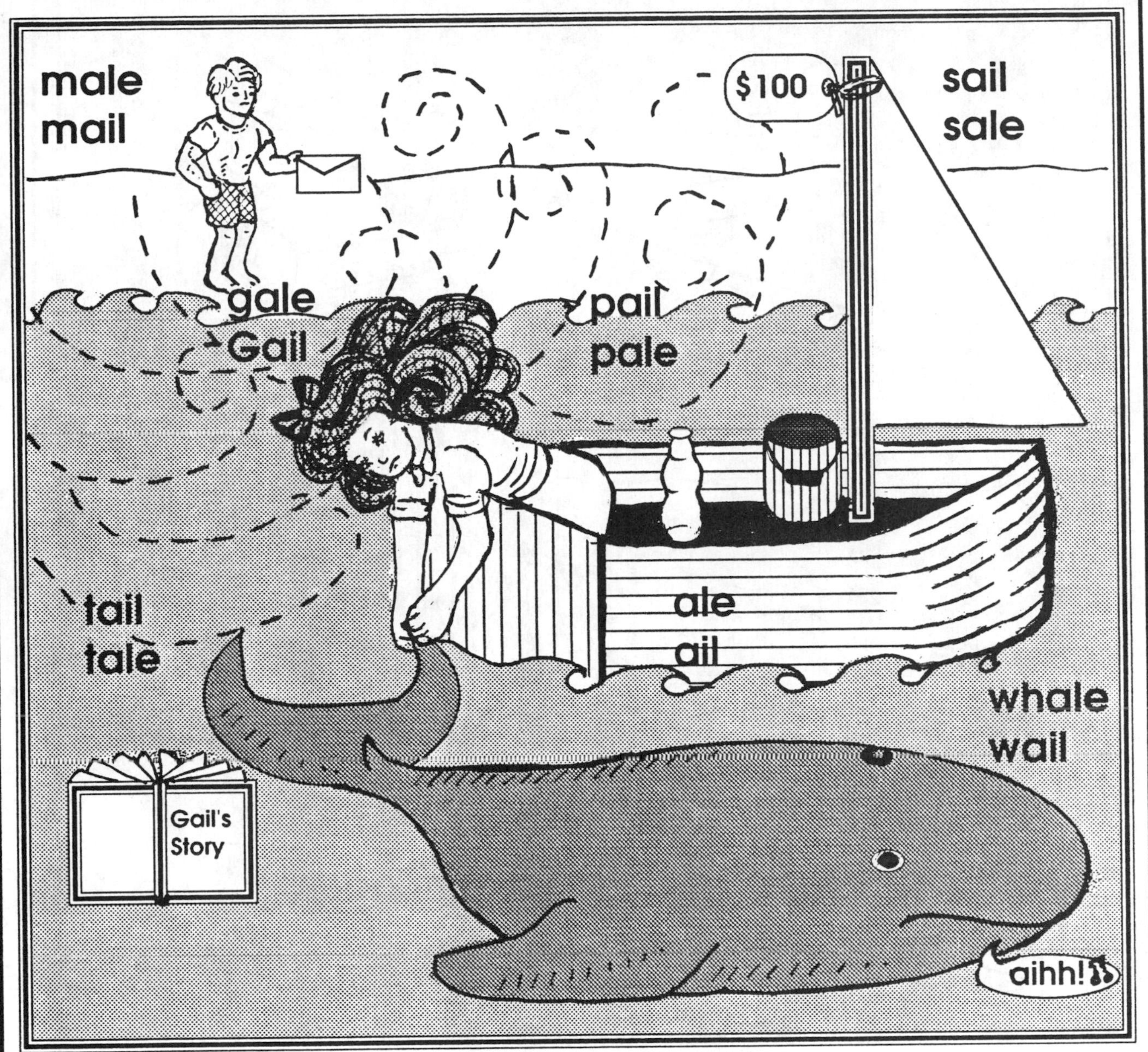
male
mail
$100
sail
sale
gale
Gail
pail
pale
tail
tale
ale
ail
whale
wail
Gail's
Story
aihh!

Gail's Tale

She got some mail from a male
That said to buy a sailboat on sale.
But a gale of wind made Gail turn pale
As she mopped the deck with suds from a pail.

She took ginger-ale for what made her ail,
Then caught the tail of a wailing whale.
Now no one quite knows what became of Gail,
For this is the end of her sad little tale.

mail sail Gail pail ail tail wail

pane
plane
cane
lane
mane

A Lion in Pain

From the window pane of his two engine plane
The ranger could see, for it was plain,
A lion who was in a whole lot of pain.
There was blood on the lane where the lion had lain,
So he landed his plane by some sugar cane.
The golden-maned lion was his main concern,
And he saved his life with the first aid he'd learned.

afraid
maid
braid
raid
50¢
paid
band aid
laid

Cookie Raid

The maid with a braid
For baking cookies got paid.
But she was afraid
There would be a cookie raid.
So she got the dog to come to her aid
And growling, in front of the cookies, he laid.

maid braid paid afraid raid aid laid

Fun with 'ee' (Farm, town, people)

sheep	steed	weed
cheep	deer	beet
peep	bee	green
beef	seed	tree
flee	queen	meet
creep	meek	greet
glee	cheer	teen
speed	steep	kneel
wheel	feet	feel
street	heel	steel
jeep	knee	week

Sunday
Monday
Tuesday
Wednesday
Thursday
Friday
Saturday

Fun with 'ee' (Fish,odds and ends, and face)

fleet	breed	reef
deep	wee	feed
creek	reel	reed
eel		

bleed	fee	peel
tee	tweed	sweet
greed	sheet	deed
free	sweep	screen

cheek	sleep	seep
need	keen	seek
speech	weep	peer
see	reek	peek

'ee' and 'ea' Homonyms

1	see	8	feet
	sea		feat
2	creek	9	heal
	creak		heel
3	reed	10	reel
	read		real
4	meet	11	flea
	meat		flee
5	peak	12	cheep
	peek	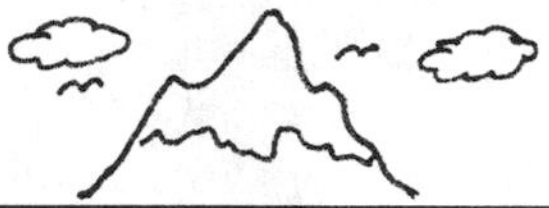	cheap
6	deer	13	weak
	dear		week
7	tea	14	beet
	tee		beat

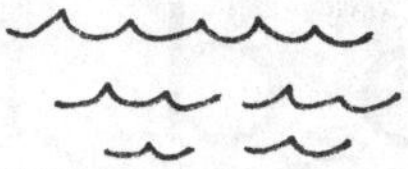

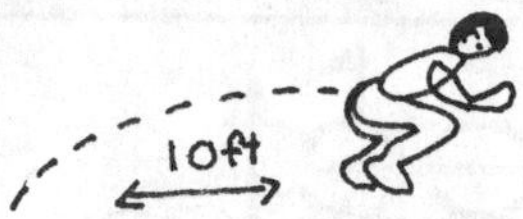

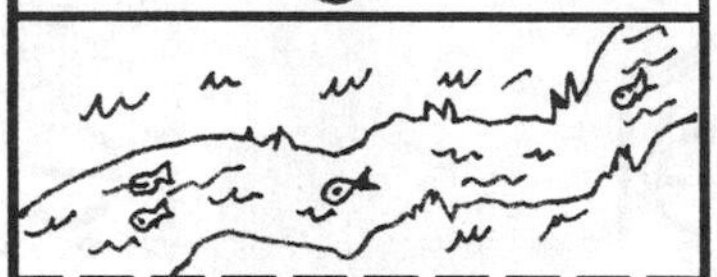

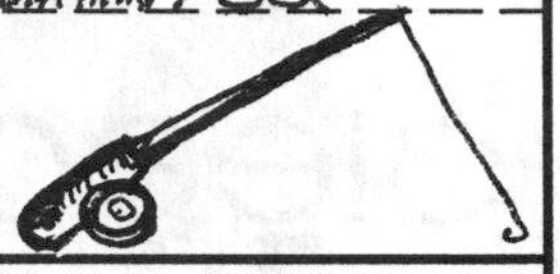

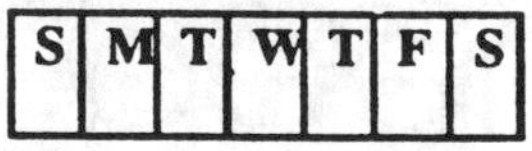

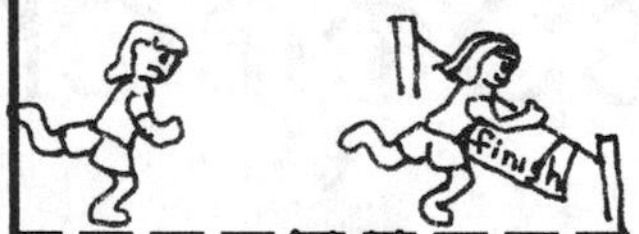

flight
night
bright light
high
slight
fright
right
sigh
sight
height
knights
fight with
might
thigh
held tight
because of
plight
nigh

The Knight's Plight

Under a bright light two knights did fight with all their might.
It was a sight when, at its height, one had a slight fright.
Because of his plight, to his horse he held tight
As he took flight right into the night.

Then riding his horse and sitting up high
His foe came nigh and giving a sigh,
He pulled out the sword that hung by his thigh,
Threw it down and waved good-bye.

Fun with 'oa' words!

toad	foam	foal
croak	soap	goat
throat	moat	loaf
groan	float	load
moan	soak	road
boast	boat	coal
gloat	coast	coat
coach	roam	cloak
bloat	oat	toast
goal	oak	roast
		loan

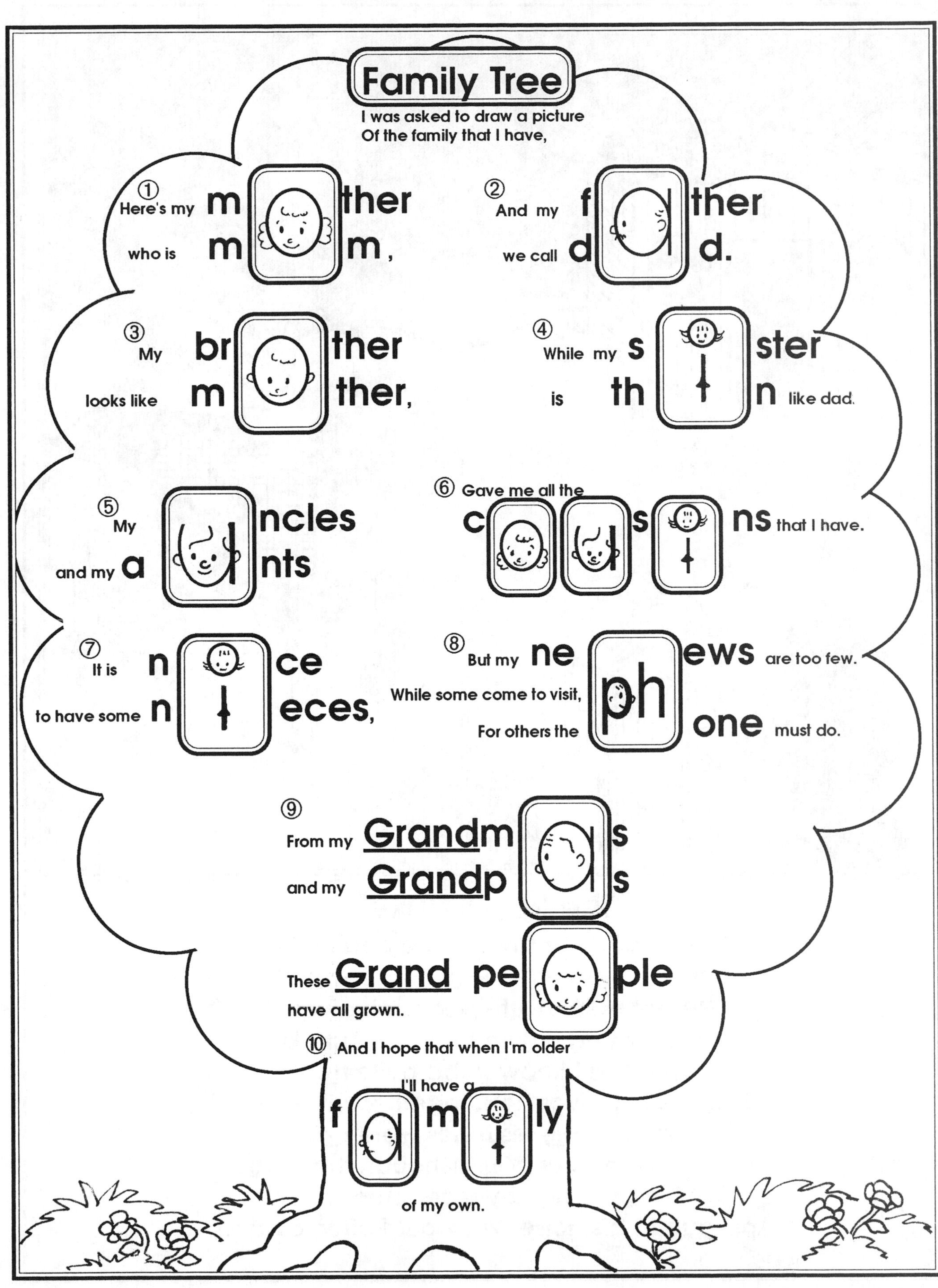
Family Tree
I was asked to draw a picture
Of the family that I have,
① Here's my mother
who is mom,
② And my father
we call dad.
③ My brother
looks like mother,
④ While my sister
is thin like dad.
⑤ My uncles
and my aunts
⑥ Gave me all the
cousins that I have.
⑦ It is nice
to have some nieces,
⑧ But my nephews are too few.
While some come to visit,
For others the phone must do.
⑨ From my Grandmas
and my Grandpas
These Grand people
have all grown.
⑩ And I hope that when I'm older
I'll have a
family
of my own.

Teaching Helps/Fun Forms

Unit 10

The Royal Duke

The royal <u>duke</u> always dressed in <u>blue</u>
When he rode his <u>huge</u> old gray <u>mule</u>.
His hat had a <u>cute</u> peacock <u>plume</u>,
And he played a <u>flute</u> that was out of <u>tune</u>.
And this I know to be quite <u>true</u>,
That his <u>flute</u> was held together with <u>glue</u>.
And as a <u>rule</u> his tunes were <u>crude</u>
So we covered our ears although that is <u>rude</u>.
But the <u>clue</u> he never seemed to take
And <u>due</u> to his noise, we would often awake.

third
first
birds chirp in birch
fl irt
I don't squirm or smirk, or a hard job shirk.
fir
birthday
thirst
whirl
twirl
dirt on shirt
skirt
girl
Sir

'I am a Girl'

"I, sir, am a girl. I whirl and twirl, until I'm dying of thirst.
Then I listen to the chirp of the birds in the fir and birch.
I don't squirm or smirk, or a hard job shirk.
But I'm the first to dust dirt off a brand new skirt.
I have a birthday on the third, and I hope I'm not a flirt,
I want you to come, but please wear a clean shirt."

blurt out
but not curt
I don't splurge.
I resist the urge.
church
curl
turtle
burn
hurt
hurl
curve ball
left in
lurch
purse
purr
fur
nurse cur

You are a Boy

You are a boy with a single curl,
A fast curve baseball **you** can hurl.
You don't burn matches so **you** won't get hurt.
You blurt out **your** feelings, but **you're** never curt.
You curb **your** spending, and rarely splurge,
If **your** purse is empty, **you** resist the urge.
You have a small turtle, **you** nurse the stray cur,
And when **you** brush **your** cat's fur, she loves to purr.
(When **you** see someone who was left in the lurch,
On the spur of the moment, **you** invite them to church.)

12
9
3
6
U'R
R

The object of this game is to learn to quickly associate the correct sounds with the correct letter combination. Lay out the large cards and have the players place the smaller cards on the lower half of the picture card that says its sound. (Answers on back.)

are care	ēør fear	ore more	ire fire
ure cure	oar soar	our sour	air hair
eer steer	oor poor	ĕør learn	ur curl
ir girl	or corn	ar car	er fern
øār bear	(w)ar warm	(w)or worm	211 **The 'R' Game** © 1988 S.M.

air

air-hair
are-care
ear-bear

oar

(of a boat)
ore-more
oar-soar
oor-poor
or-corn
(w)ar-warm

ŭr-ŭr-ŭr

ur-curl
ir-girl
er-fern
(w)or-worm
ear-learn

ear

ear-fear
eer-steer

hour*

(on a clock)
our-sour
*'h' on hour is silent

iron

ire-fire

R

sounds like 'are'*
ar-car
*'are' is an exception

'U' R

sounds like 'your'*
ure-cure
*'your' is an exception

drought
bough
thought
I'm thoroughly beat. I ought to take a furlough
cough
slough
bought
SOLD
Land Sale $1.00
dough
laugh
ha!
naught in trough
rough and tough enough
fought
brought
taught
through
sought
caught
Farm

The Taming of the "ough"/"augh"

He thought he was rough and tough enough
When he sought to tame this land.
Though he fought to farm as his father had taught,
The drought turned his fields to sand.
He stood under a bough and coughed back a laugh
That caught and tickled his throat.
Then he sat on the trough and sadly said,
"I'm through and thoroughly beat.
"For the land I bought has brought me naught,
"No dough is left to my name.
"I ought to take a furlough
"And go back to the slough where there's rain."

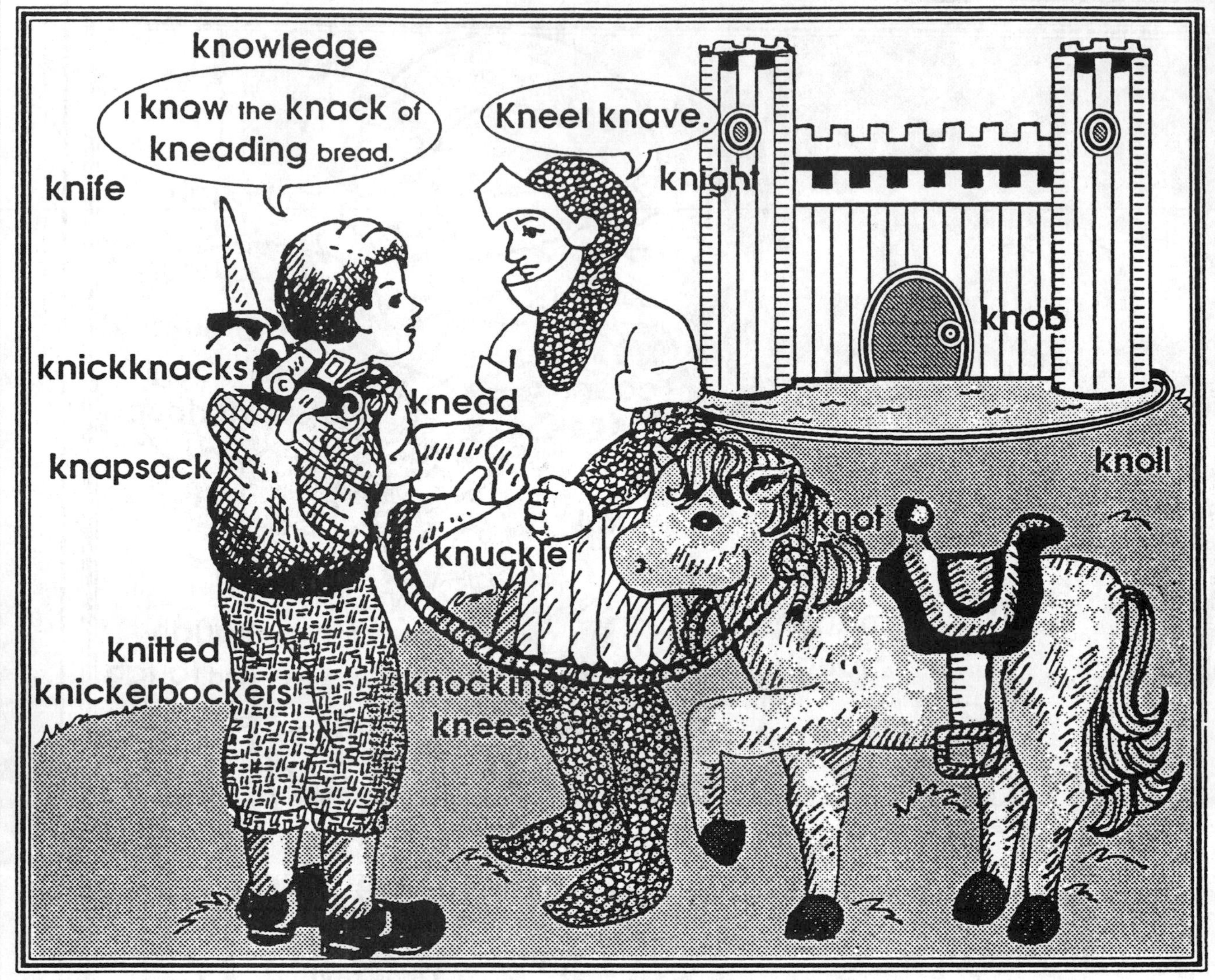
knowledge
I know the knack of kneading bread.
Kneel knave.
knife
knight
knob
knickknacks
knead
knapsack
knoll
knot
knuckle
knitted
knickerbockers
knocking
knees

The Bread-Kneading Knave

I knew the knack of kneading bread
Was all the knowledge that I had.
But I hoped to my fortune it would lead,
So in my knitted knickerbockers I mounted my steed,
And knowing with knickknacks my knapsack was full.
I headed to the castle on top of the knoll.
With trembling knees and a knot in my throat,
I knocked with my knuckles at the door past the moat.
Then the knob turned and I saw a knight.
He said, "Kneel, knave, or prepare to fight."
"I'll use a knife," I said, standing brave.
"But only to cut the fresh bread I've made."
All ended well as you can see now,
My life was spared for my baking knowhow.

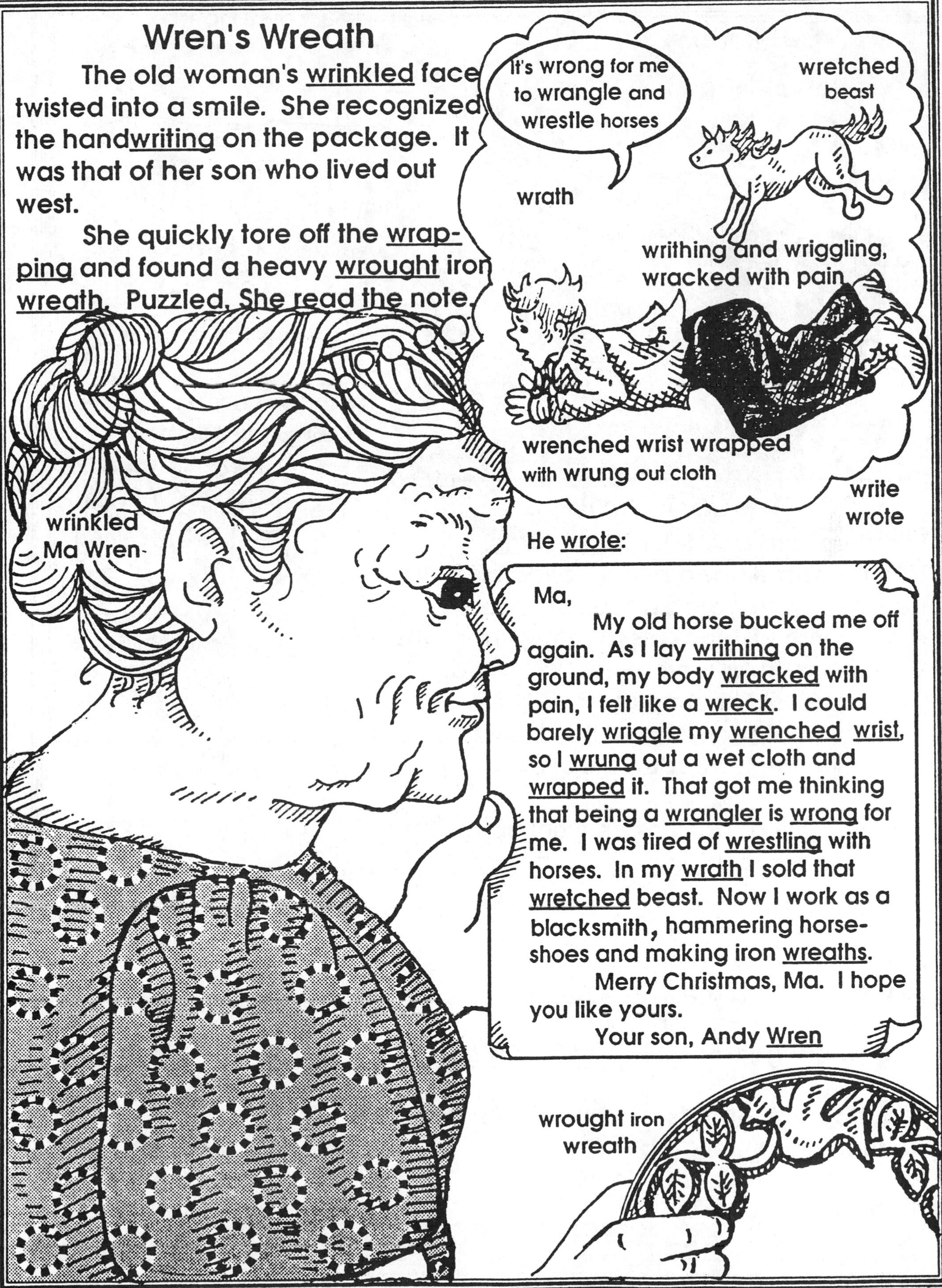
It's wrong for me to wrangle and wrestle horses
wretched beast
wrath
writhing and wriggling, wracked with pain
wrenched wrist wrapped with wrung out cloth
write
wrote
wrinkled Ma Wren
wrought iron wreath

Wren's Wreath

The old woman's wrinkled face twisted into a smile. She recognized the handwriting on the package. It was that of her son who lived out west.

She quickly tore off the wrapping and found a heavy wrought iron wreath. Puzzled, She read the note.

He wrote:

Ma,

My old horse bucked me off again. As I lay writhing on the ground, my body wracked with pain, I felt like a wreck. I could barely wriggle my wrenched wrist, so I wrung out a wet cloth and wrapped it. That got me thinking that being a wrangler is wrong for me. I was tired of wrestling with horses. In my wrath I sold that wretched beast. Now I work as a blacksmith, hammering horseshoes and making iron wreaths.

Merry Christmas, Ma. I hope you like yours.

Your son, Andy Wren

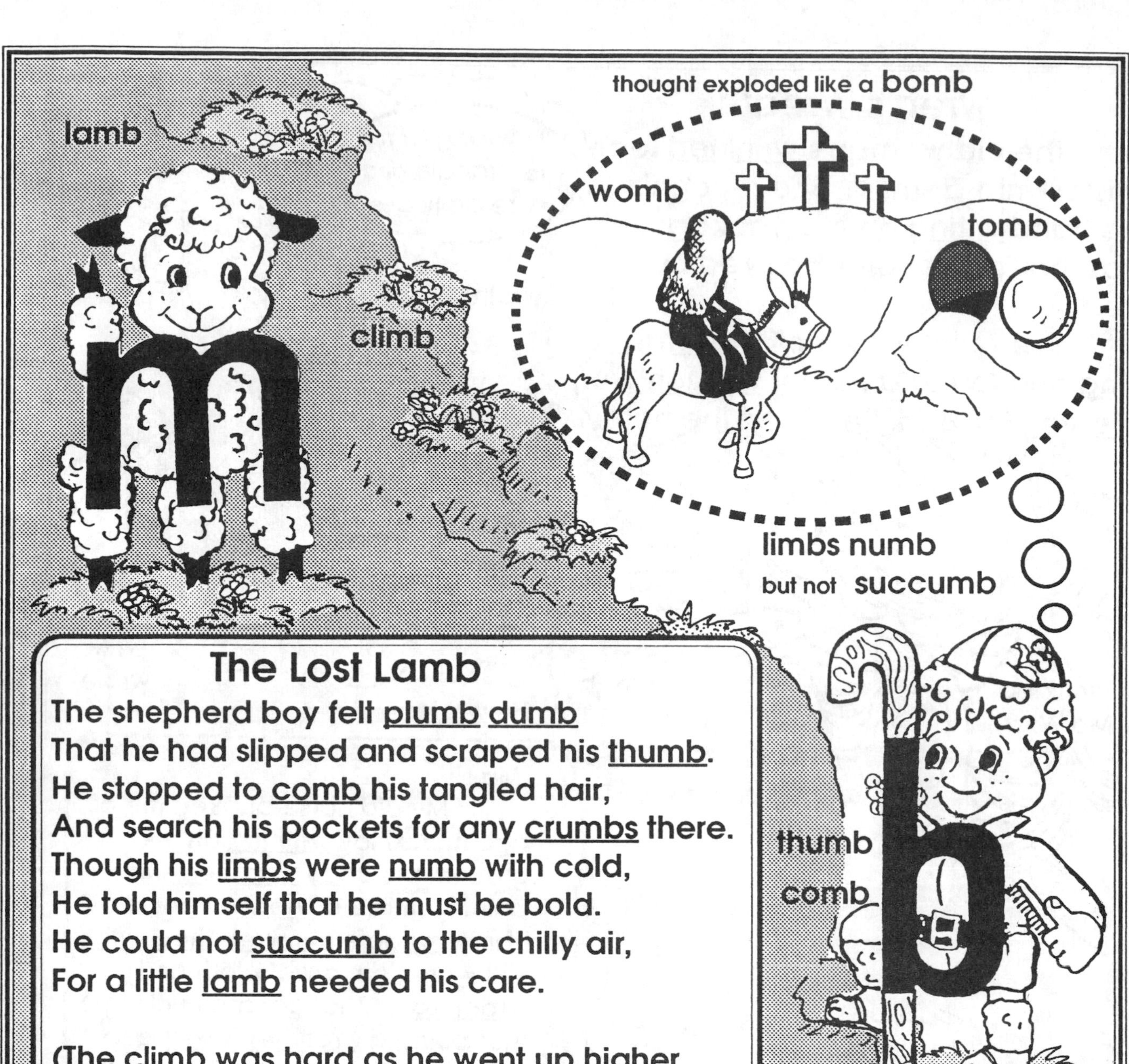
thought exploded like a bomb
lamb
womb
tomb
climb
limbs numb
but not succumb
thumb
comb
plumb
dumb
crumbs

The Lost Lamb

The shepherd boy felt plumb dumb
That he had slipped and scraped his thumb.
He stopped to comb his tangled hair,
And search his pockets for any crumbs there.
Though his limbs were numb with cold,
He told himself that he must be bold.
He could not succumb to the chilly air,
For a little lamb needed his care.

(The climb was hard as he went up higher,
Then a thought exploded like a bomb of fire.
He remembered his own good Shepherd
Who had come from Mary's womb,
And how He had loved His sheep enough
To die and be placed in a tomb.
But, best of all He had come back to life
And would gather his sheep to Him soon.)

With happy thoughts to warm his heart,
He found his little lamb.
Then, gathering her up in his arms,
He headed home again.

Eagle's Wings /shŭn/ Check List

1. Use **ci** + an

    —/shŭn/ for a person

    A musi**cia**n, physi**cia**n, or beauti**cia**n can say, "See, I'm human." (**C I**'m hum**AN**)

2. Use **si** + on

    —/zhŭn/

    If it says /zhŭn/ there's no revi**si**on if your deci**si**on is '-**si**on'.

    —/shŭn/ following '**l**'☆ and sometimes '**n**'☆.

    Feel no ten**si**on if you have a compul**si**on to use '-**si**on' with 'l' and sometimes 'n'.

3. Use **ssi** + on

    —/shŭn/ following short 'e' or short 'u'.

    With /ĕ/ or /ŭ/ you'll have the impre**ssi**on of seeing double with 'double **si**on' (-ssion).

    —/shŭn/ with mission.

    You have per**mission** to use double 's' with '-mi**ssi**on'.

4. Use **ti** + on

    —/shŭn/ **everywhere** else

    Remember there is a na**TION** of words with '-**ti**on'.

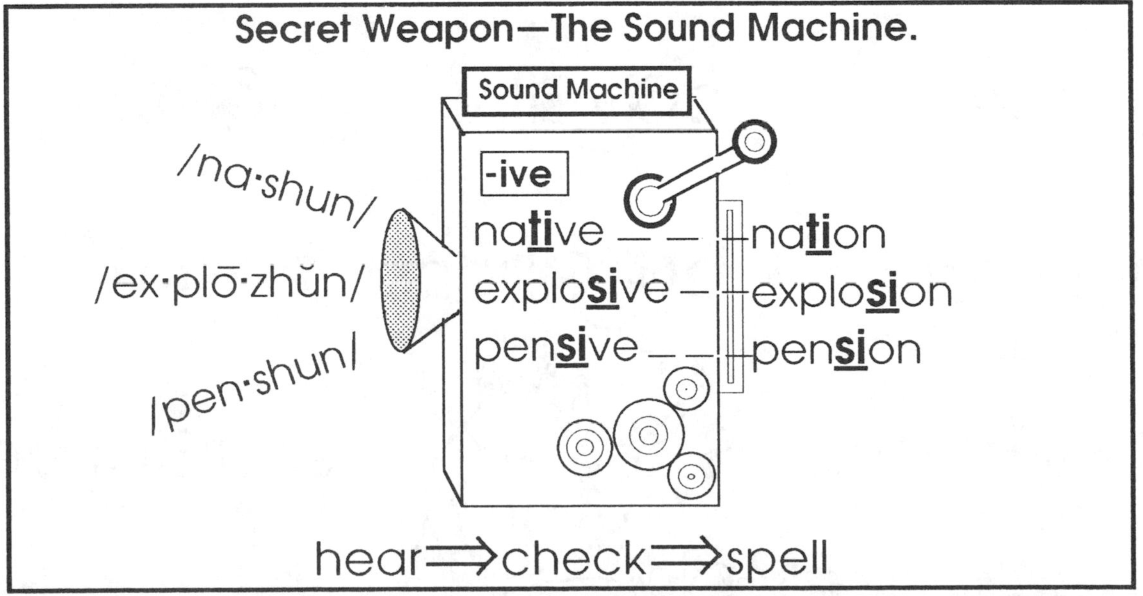
Secret Weapon—The Sound Machine.
Sound Machine
-ive
/na·shun/
/ex·plō·zhŭn/
/pen·shun/
native
explosive
pensive
nation
explosion
pension
hear⟹check⟹spell

When in doubt, use the secret weapon to determine whether to use '**si**' or '**ti**'.
Directions: Change the 'ion' to '-ive' and instantly you can hear the '**si**' or '**ti**'.

Private! We have our eyes on you!

general		military
sergeant	captain	insignia
defense	admiral	brigadier
veteran	seaman	combat
regiment	airman	commander
deferment	aviator	company
bootcamp	parachutor	decorate
colonel	cavalry	major
corporal	battalion	armor
commodore		squadron
platoon		pentagon

"Tell-a-phone" Cards (1)

d /d/ dad **-ed (past tense)** /t/ packed following 'c', 's', 'ch', 'f', 'p', 'x' /ed/padded following 't', 'd' /d/ called elsewhere	**c** /s/ cent before 'i', 'e', or 'y' /k/ cat elsewhere ↧ '-ck'/'-ce' at ends of words '-c' ends of multi-syllable words	**b** /b/ bib	**a** /ă/ apple closed syllable /ā/ ate silent 'e'/open syllable /å/=/ŏ/ all after 'w' and 'u' and in front of 'l', 'r' /a̮/=/ŭ/ America unaccented syllable, often at beginnings and endings of multi-syllable words
h /h/ hope	**g** /j/ gem before 'i', 'e','y' except 'ee' or 'ea' or 'i', 'e' or 'y' followed by two consonants /g/ got elsewhere	**f** /f/ farm ↧ **'-ff'/'f' at ends of words**	**e** /ĕ/ bed closed syllable /ē/ be open syllable / / apple "silent e" at ends of words
l /l/ ladle ↧ **'-ll'/'-le' at ends of words**	**k** /k/ kick ↧ **'-ck'/'-c'/'-que' at ends of words**	**j** /j/ jam only at beginnings of syllables ↧ **'-ge'/'-dge' at ends of words**	**i** /ĭ/ bit closed syllables /ī/ bite silent 'e'/open syllables /ē / antique, Indian preceding '-que' and '-an'
p /p/ pop	**o** /ŏ/ rod closed syllable /ō/ rode, hello, corn, silent e, open syllable, ends of words, before l and r /o̮/ love — with v, th, and sometimes n /ü/ move	**n** /n/ nun	**m** /m/ mom

a b c d

e f g h

i j k l

m n o p

"Tell-a-phone" Cards (2)

t /t/ tot	**s** /s/ sips /z/ please between vowels ↧ '-ss'/'-se' at ends of words	**r** /r/ roar	**qu** /kw/ queen /k/ plaque ends of words ↧ '-que' at ends of words
x /x/ fox ends of syllables	**w** /w/ well functions as a consonant at beginnings of syllables	**v** /v/ valve ↧ '-ve' at ends of words	**u** /ŭ/ up closed syllable /ü/=/o͞o/ flute silent 'e'/open syllable /ū/ cute silent 'e'/open syllable
tch ↧ /ch/ catch at ends of words, following a short vowel	**ck** ↧ /k/ back at ends of words following a short vowel	**z** /z/ zap	**y** /y/ yellow functions as a consonant at beginnings of syllables /ē/ baby ends of words, unaccented syllables /ī/ shy ends of words, accented syllables (all one-syllable words) /ĭ/ gym medially
ch /ch/ church /k/ school /sh/ chef (French words)	**sh** /sh/ shush	**dge** ↧ /j/ judge ends of words, following a short vowel	**ge** ↧ /j/ cage ends of words, not following a short vowel **gue** ↧ /g/ plague ends of words, not following a short vowel

qu r s t

u v w x

y z ck tch

ge
gue dge sh ch

"Tell-a-phone" Cards (3)

ea /ē/ beat /ĕ/ breath includes about 1/3 of the words with 'ea'	**ee** /ē/ free, meet	**ay** ↧ /ā/ pay ends of words	**ai** /ā/ pail closed syllable
oo /ō͞o/=/ü/ loot /ŏo/ good book before 'd' and 'k'	**oy** ↧ /oi/ boy ends of words	**ei** /ē/ receive after 'c' /ā/ veil (rare)	**ie** /ē/ believe, cookie /ī/ pie (rare) frier where 'y' changes to 'i' before an '-ed', '-er', or '-est'
au /å/=/ŏ/ autograph	**ow** ↧ /ou/ town, owl brow before 'l' and 'n' if they are not in a blend and ends of words /ō/ blown, bowl, blow before 'l' and 'n' if they are not in a blend and ends of words	**oa** /ō/ boat	**ew** ↧ /ü/ /ū/ few end of words **ue** ↧ /ü/ /ū/ blue end of word
ough/augh 6 sounds and less than 30 words—memorize these words	**ou** /ou/ pout closed syllable	**oi** /oi/ boil closed syllable	**aw** ↧ /å/=/ŏ/ caw ends of words

ai ay ee ea

ie ei oy oo

ew
ue
oa ow au

aw oi ou ough
augh

"Tell-a-phone" Cards (4)

ur /ŭr/ curl (ur, ir, er, ear, and wor all say /ŭr/)	**ir** /ŭr/ girl (ur, ir, er, ear, and wor all say /ŭr/)	**er** /ŭr/ her (ur, ir, er, ear, and wor all say /ŭr/)	**ar** /år/ car /ŭr/ collar unaccented final syllable
th /th/ thing unvoiced **/th/ that** voiced **bathe** usually between vowels	**ear** /ēr/ ear /ŭr/ earth	**wor** /wŭr/ worm **war** /wōr/ warm	**or** /ōr/ corn medial /ŭr/ doctor final /ōr / core ends of words ↧ '-ore' at ends of words
ti /sh/ attention medial **tu** /ch/ picture medial (ti, si, ci, s(ure) all say /sh/ medially)	**ng** /ng/ singing ends of syllables	**igh** /ī/ light closed syllables **eigh** /ā/ eight	**wh** /hw/ what
ph /f/ photograph	**wr** /r/ write **kn** /n/ know	**ci** /sh/ physician medial (ti, si, ci, s(ure) all say /sh/ medially)	**si** /sh/ mission /zh/ vision **su** /sh/ insure /zh/ pleasure (ti, si, ci, s(ure) all say /sh/ medially)

ar er ir ur

or
ore

wor
war

ear

th

wh

igh
eigh

ng

ti
tu

si
su

ci

wr
kn

ph

Bibliography

Bishop, Margaret M., *The Complete Reference Book of Phonics and Spelling.* Milford, MI, 1986.

Bouldin, Mrs. Homer T., *An Acorn in my Hand.* Houston, TX, St. Thomas Press, 1964.

LA, CA, J.P. Tarcher, Inc., 1982

Dickson, Sue, *Sing, Spell, Read & Write.* Virginia Beach VA, CBNU Extended University, 1972.

Ekwall, Eldon E., *Locating and Correcting Reading Difficulty.* Columbus, Ohio, Charles E. Merrill Pub.Co., 1970.

Ellis, Kaethe, *The Word Book II.* Boston, Massachusetts, Houghton Mifflin Co., 1983.

Folsom, Franklin, *The Language Book.* New York, Grosset & Dunlap, 1963.

Games and Activities, by Teachers in the Duncanville Independent Schools, Duncanville, TX.

Keith, Joy L, *Word Attack Joy.* Naperville, Illinois, Reading Joy, 1974.

King, Fred M., *Palmer Method Transition to Cursive, Grade 2.* Schaumburg, IL, The A.N. Palmer Co., 1987.

Kottneyer, William, and Ware, Kay, *Basic Goals in Spelling, 2nd Ed.* St. Louis, Missouri, Webster Division, McGraw-Hill Book Co.,1964.

March, Francis A., *A List of Amended Spellings.* American Philological Association, Indianapolis, Indiana, 1897.

McCary, Margaret and Hicks, Laurel, *A Handbook for Reading: The New Blue-Backed Speller.* Pensacola, FL, A Beka Book, 1976.

McDonald, Blanche, et. all, *Methods That Teach.* Dubuque, IA, Wm. C. Brown Pub., 1972.

Platts, Mary E., *Spice.* Stevensville, Michigan, Educational Service, Inc., 1973

Raines, Bernice Jones, *Situation Learning: Alphabetic Phonics.* Cambridge, Mass., Educators Publishing Service, Inc., 1980.

Reader's Digest, Write Better, Speak Better. The Reader's Digest Association, Inc., Pleasantville, New York, 1972.

Rhyming Dictionary. Stein, Jess, (Ed.), New York, Random House, 1960.

Rico, Gabriele Lusser, *Writing the Natural Way.* Los Angeles, CA, J.P. Tarcher, Inc., 1983.

Spalding, Romalda Bishop with Spalding Walter T., *The Writing Road to Reading, 2nd Ed.* New York, William Morrow and Co., Inc., 1982.

Spelling Made Easy. Visual Education Corporation, Princeton, NJ, Gregg Division/McGraw-Hill Book Co., 1984.

The American Heritage Dictionary. Morris, William (Ed.), Boston, Houghton Mifflin Co., 1976,

The World Book Complete Word Power Library. World Book-Childcraft International, Inc., Chicago, Illinois, 1981.

Traub, Nina, with Bloom, Frances, *Recipe for Reading, 2nd Ed.* Cambridge, Massachusetts, Educators Publishing Service, Inc., 1975.

Young, Dr. Beverly S., *Reading Handbook, 3rd Ed.* Nacogdoches, TX, Stephen F. Austin State University.

Eagle's Wings
Educational Materials

Science

Considering God's Creation

"I bought 'Alphabet Island' and … 'Considering God's Creation.' I am so delighted with both that I tell everyone I can about them."
Portland, MI

2nd - 7th grades

"I can't say enough good things about your science program. My children think it is a reward to do it if they finish their other work.
Hesperia, CA

Easy to follow lesson plans!

"I love how easy your lesson plans are to follow. SIMPLE but challenging!" Bellevue, NE

"We have been using 'Considering God's Creation' this fall, and are loving it. I am enjoying the science part of homeschooling for the first time since we started four years ago.
Whitewater, KS

Exciting for students!

"I would like to commend you on the 'Considering God's Creation' science program. Besides my two second graders, I have a sixth grader and have never found a curriculum for science that is so easy and enjoyable to use. … My kids love it, too. They want to know, 'Is it science day?'" Canyon, TX

Designed for Multi-Level Teaching!

Phonics

Alphabet Island

Alphabet Island
Phonics

"As a reading specialist, … I say Alphabet Island Phonics is truly the best I have ever seen or used.
Duncanville, TX

My child loves the Alphabet Island characters, cares about them and is reading beautifully! ...I haven't found any other materials as clear and enjoyable. Thank you for a great Phonics program!"
Grand Rapids, MI

and more

Bible History

Remembering God's Awesome Acts

REMEMBERING
GOD'S AWESOME ACTS

Study history to understand the Bible!
Study the Bible to understand history!

Kinder-Math

Kinder-Math

A simple way to introduce your children to the world of math and it's practical application to the world in which they live.

To State It Simply
It's a Capital Game

A fun way to teach children the Capitals and States by turning this project into an exciting game!

A CAPITAL GAME

Adaptable to different learning styles
Easy to use, Hands-on Learning Approach
with the benefit of Workbooks!

Eagle's Wings
Alphabet Island Phonics 1 (Kindergarten)

Young students love this program. Don't be surprised if they enthusiastically beg for more! Each 15 minute lesson has a story, song, poem, game, blackboard and workbook activity, all geared toward optimum learning. The students master the phonetic sounds, alphabetic sequence, correct letter formation and the reading and spelling of more than 230 3-letter short-vowel words.

Alphabet Island Phonics 1 comes complete with step-by-step teacher's manual, student workbook, flash cards, games, and a cassette tape. Now includes laminated, four-color alphabet flash cards. **Price $69.95**

Order Alphabet Island Complete and get *Kinder-Math* **FREE** ($14.95 value)

Additional Alphabet Island 1 workbook **$9.95**

Formation poems teach proper direction, formation and placement of letters.

Alphabet Island

a, b, c, d, e, f, g
This alphabet is
easy for me.

Professional cassette tape teaches phonics sounds, stories, poems, and original songs.

READ ALOUD LESSONS are designed for the first time teacher. NO TEACHING EXPERIENCE NECESSARY.

Students **anticipate** rather than dread new rules. For the next rule is the next story on **Alphabet Island.**

Teacher's Manual—Sample Page

LESSON 20: Introducing Mutton 'M'

INTRODUCTION: *(Hold upthe Mutton 'M' card. Read the following story.)*

Mutton 'M'

Mutton 'M' is a wooly lamb. She likes to leap and play on the mountains. She sometimes gets lost among the cliffs, so her shepherd, Boy 'B' keeps his eye on her. She says /m/, as inmutton.

LETTER FORMATION: *(Have student practice forming the letter 'm' while saying following poem: 1. In the air with full arm movement. 2. Trace 12" letter on blackboard. 3. On workbook page 35.)*

Mutton 'M' likes the flower tops,
A short line down and she's off with two hops.

SONG: Let's sing along with the Alphabet Island Song (On cassette tape.)

AUDIO DISCRIMINATION Alphabetize the cards you have studied on the Alphabet Island Cardsboard. Get out the Mutton 'M' card. As I read each word, hold up the card showing the letter that the word begins with.

jelly	magnet	machine	loose	hook
lend	manners	market	investigate	maple

WORKBOOK: p. 35. Mutton 'M'. Trace the 'm' ten times on the character, then over the dotted letter on the guidelines. Say the poem to help you form it correctly and say the sound it makes. Then you may color the picture

p. 36. What starts with 'M'? Listen for the words that start with the sound /m/ "mutton". Write a large enough 'm' over the picture to fill the box.

1. **match**, office, **money**, nest, **mushroom**
2. ostrich, **monkey**, newspaper, **mouse**, **music**
3. **moose**, otter, **man**, nine, **mole**

Now at the bottom of the page color all the spaces with the upper and lower case of the new letter to see what picture it will be.

Alphabetizing and **reviewing the letter sounds** is easy in this game form.

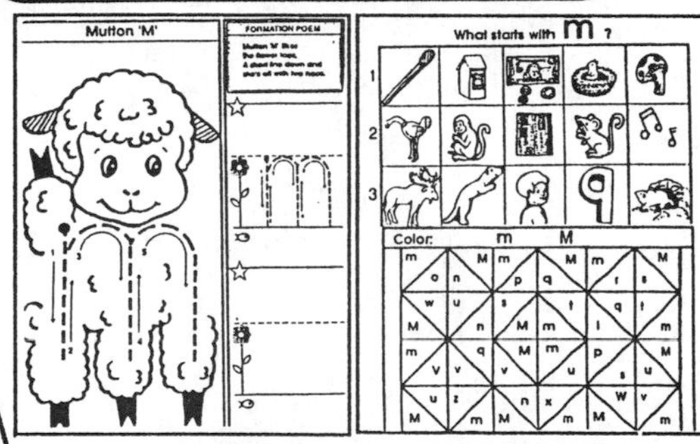
Mutton 'M'
What starts with m ?
Color: m M

Workbook pages reinforce lesson.

Your student will master reading and spelling 230 words with:

♦ Spelling words ♦ Workbooks
♦ Flash cards ♦ Songs ♦ Readers

pin
net
hat

♦ Flash cards— 5 fun reading games motivate your child to try harder and work longer

Write in the Number
Meet the "-ip" and "-in" Families
a b c
Circle the Word
I said, "I win."
I win."
I love Dad.
_in

♦ Workbooks—give more practice

Reading about
e
i
a
o
u

♦ Readers—Five take-home readers build reading confidence

*

cab	tin	pot
tab	ten	hot
tub	men	hop
rub	met	hip
run	set	sip
fun	sat	six
fin	pat	fix

♦ Spelling —teaches reasoning skills

The daily spelling words change only one letter at a time. This allows practice with a large number of words in a short time.

***A student who can spell these words is ready for Alphabet Island Phonics 2.**

Eagle's Wings
Alphabet Island Phonics 2 (1st to 9th grade)

Alphabet Island Phonics is the most thorough, **effective, and creative phonics and spelling program** available. Its strength lies in the fact that your students learn to **REASON** out the spelling of words and can account for every letter used. **Alphabet Island Phonics** gives your students what they need to be **competent readers and exceptional spellers**. Most importantly, **Alphabet Island Phonics** instills an **absolute love and enjoyment of reading and spelling.**

Alphabet Island Phonics 2 (Advanced) takes your child from short vowels into fluent reading. Even if your child has not been through **Alphabet Island Phonics1**, if he can spell three-letter short-vowel words, he is ready for **Alphabet Island Phonics 2**. In two workbooks, your student will learn to spell over four thousand words with **consonant blends, digraphs, silent 'e', doubled consonants, short vowels, long vowels, dipthongs and all other vowel combinations.** You will continue on through 9th grade with the in-depth coverage of the included ***Eagle's Wings Comprehensive Handbook of Phonics***. **Alphabet Island Phonics** 2 is a **MULTI-SENSORY** program that is excellent for **remedial** purposes as well as for the student progressing normally in reading. It is based on a **mastery approach** that systematically builds a solid foundation without missing any steps.

Alphabet Island Phonics 2 is all you need to cover spelling and phonics from 1st grade through 9th grade. Alphabet Island Phonics 2 comes complete with step-by-step teacher's manuals, student workbooks, flash cards, games, and a cassette tape. Includes *Eagle's Wings Handbook of Phonics.* **Price $84.95**

Additional Alphabet 2 wkbks $14.95

Q: How do Alphabet Island characters make rules easy to remember?

A: Few people can explain the two sounds of 'c'. With Alphabet Island you learn it the first time around and remember it for life. Vowels are divided into two groups—**'boys' ('a', 'o' and 'u')**, and **'girls' ('e', 'i' and 'y')**. **Clever 'C'** says **/s/**, "city", when in front of the "girls" ('e', 'i', 'y') and **/k/**, "cat", elsewhere. That makes the workbook page easy—color the boy vowels blue, the girls pink and write in the sound 'C' makes.

Clever 'C' Makes Two Sounds

k and s consonants

1 cat (k)	7 come	13 century
2 cent (s)	8 city	14 clip
3 cap	9 can	15 cop
4 cot	10 cope	16 cover
5 circus	11 cycle	17 cup
6 cut	12 coat	18 cave

Q: How is spelling taught in Alphabet Island Phonics?

A: Rules, often in the form of songs, give a concise and logical understanding of when and where to use a particular spelling for any given sound. This four-line poem covers all the options for the spelling of a long 'i'.

What makes a long 'i'?	Example:
To make a long 'i', use 'i' with silent 'e',	mine
But at ends of words, a 'y' will usually be.	sky
And then 'i' is long, with 'igh' or 'ind',	high/find
And again with 'ign' or 'ild'.	sign/child

Q: What is the procedure for teaching a new rule?

A: The rule is the "road map". Each aspect of the rule is studied in great detail, making sure the child can understand, hear and work with the rule. Letter cards and workbook pages reinforce the lesson and are followed by spelling lists **designed for each child to succeed.** Where there are only a few words with a unique pattern, such as these sixteen common words with 'igh', they are introduced at one time with a picture and poem.

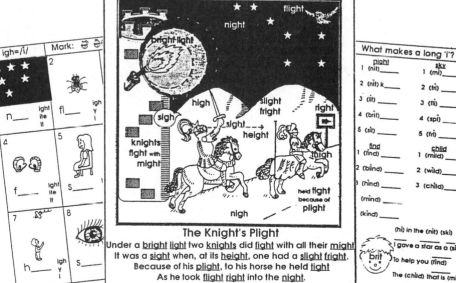

igh=/i/
Mark:
flight
night
bright light
high
sigh
slight fright
right
sight
height
knights fight with might
thigh
held tight because of plight
nigh
What makes a long 'i'?
night
sky
find
child

The Knight's Plight

Under a bright light two knights did fight with all their might
It was a sight when, at its height, one had a slight fright.
Because of his plight, to his horse he held tight
As he took flight right into the night.

Then riding his horse and sitting up high
His foe came nigh and giving a sigh,
He pulled out the sword that hung by his thigh,
Threw it down and waved good-bye.

With this **unique approach** of knowing the rule and the exceptions, your child **masters** the spelling of **hundreds of words** at a time. (See Chart on Long 'i' under *Eagle's Wings Comprehensive Handbook of Phonics.*) Most programs cover only 20-30 words in a week.

Susan Mortimer's **Create-a-Notebook Series**

Remembering God's Awesome Acts

Volume 1: Adam to Moses—a hands-on history/social studies course, with an introduction to linguistics, anthropology and archeology in light of God's hand in history. Enjoy the benefits of 'unit studies' with the ease of notebooks. Adaptable for Fifth grade and up.

Price $35.00—includes teacher's manual and one student notebook. Additional student notebooks (288 pages) $20.00 (Notebooks may NOT be reproduced.)

REMEMBERING GOD'S AWESOME ACTS is different from traditional textbooks which only teach one subject. Although the primary focus is Bible and Ancient History, the impressive student notebook includes a drawing course, a structured creative writing course, speech and drama. In addition, geography, anthropology, archeology and linguistics are studied. The ultimate purpose of each element is to give the student a better understanding of the Bible. The focus is not on the individual subjects, but on studying issues, playing with concepts and mastering skills while learning discernment and logic.

★ Study history to understand the Bible! Ur—Sumer—Egypt
★ Study the Bible to understand history! Adam (creation)—Noah (the flood)—Abraham—Isaac—Jacob—Joseph—Moses

The journey of learning is fascinating and life-changing as the Bible is presented not just as a historical document, but as a handbook for daily living. Jesus Christ is emphasized from beginning to end. Every story points to Him! (NIV version used.)

When studying the Tower of Babel and the dispersion of the nations, the student does a country study from each continent. This includes not only facts about a country, but also the nation's prayer needs, major religions and availability of scriptures. Art lessons help the student to appreciate the different facial features of other peoples. And language studies (using college-level techniques) help develop an awareness of the work of missionaries.

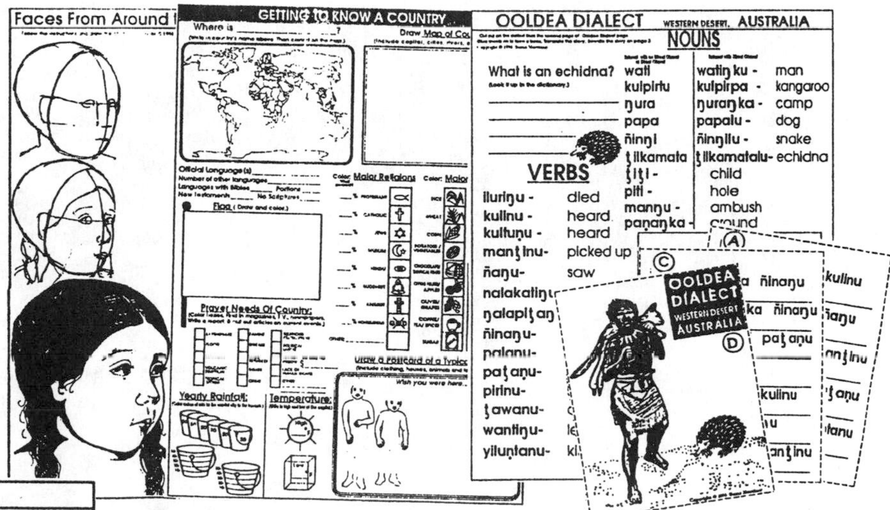
Faces From Around
GETTING TO KNOW A COUNTRY
Where is
Official Language(s)
Major Religions
Flag
Prayer Needs Of Country:
Yearly Rainfall:
Temperature:
OOLDEA DIALECT
WESTERN DESERT, AUSTRALIA
NOUNS
What is an echidna?
waṯi
kulpirtu
ŋura
papa
ñinŋl
ṯilkamata
watiŋ ku - man
kulpirpa - kangaroo
ŋuraŋka - camp
papalu - dog
ñinŋilu - snake
ṯilkamatalu- echidna
child
hole
ambush
ground
VERBS
iluriŋu - died
kulinu - heard
kulṯuŋu - heard
manṯinu- picked up
ñaŋu- saw
nalakatinu
ŋalapiṯaŋ
ñinaŋu-
palanu-
paṯaŋu-
pirinu-
ṯawanu-
wantiŋu-
yiluṉtanu-
OOLDEA DIALECT
WESTERN DESERT
AUSTRALIA

Moses and Jesus Compared

The verses listed below contain many similarities found in the lives of Moses and Jesus Christ. Read these verses and write eac... answer the detail questions in the grid below.

Similarities	Mos...
Born when Israel was dominated by an oppressive ruler	Exodus 1:8-14
Ruler was killing all the baby boys	Exodus 1:22
Rescued by parents	Hebrews 11:23
Ministry did not start until adulthood	Exodus 3:1-2
Spent 40 days/years in the wilderness	Deuteronomy 8:2 40 years
Was not received by his own people	Exodus 2:14
Was the savior of his people	Exodus 14:30-3...
Had a glorious mountaintop experience	Exodus 34:29
Gave commandments	Deuteronomy 31:...
Performed signs and wonders	Exodus 7:8-10
Blood of the 'Passover Lamb' saved others	Hebrews 11:28
Was sent by God	Exodus 3:13-14
Leaders hardened their hearts against him	Exodus 7:3
Said, "Man does not live on bread alone."	Deuteronomy 8:...

I Corinthians 5:7	Matthew 2:1
Exodus 1:22	Exodus 3:13-14
Matthew 4:1-2	Matthew 2:16-18
John 1:10-11	Exodus 7:3
Hebrews 11:23	Matthew 2:13
Exodus 3:1-2	Exodus 7:8-10
Deuteronomy 8:2	1 John 4:14

The God of Israel Challenges the 'gods' of Egypt

Color the plague or miracle. Where is the story of it found? Exodus________ © 1996 Susan Mortimer

snakes, water to blood, frogs, gnats, flies, livestock plague, boils, hail, locusts, darkness, death of 1st-born

WHO IS CHALLENGED: The Egyptians believed every person, animal, plant and all of nature had its own god or gods to rule and protect it. Who or what was affected and which gods were challenged?

☐ People	☐ Animals	☐ Plants	☐ Nature
☐ Pharaoh	☐ All animals	☐ All green plants	☐ Moon/stars
☐ Egyptian officials	☐ Fish	☐ Barley	☐ Nile
☐ Egyptian people	☐ Flies	☐ Flax	☐ Ponds/reservoirs
☐ Egyptian army	☐ Frogs	☐ Spelt	☐ Streams/canals
☐ Slaves	☐ Gnats	☐ Trees	☐ Sun
☐ Israelites	☐ Livestock	☐ Wheat	☐ Wind/weather

GODS: Isis, Osiris, Bu, Thoth, Hathor, The Eye of Horus, Khepera, Hapi

Did the Egyptians have time to beseech the gods of that specific day or time to prevent the plague?
☐ No time ☐ One day
☐ Until midnight ☐ Several days

The Egyptians had charms and amulets of protection for everything, but they didn't work for which of these things?
Locations: ☐ Palace ☐ House ☐ Bedroom ☐ Field
Belongings: ☐ Bread trough ☐ Wooden bucket ☐ Stone jar ☐ Oven

After the plague started, how long did the Egyptians gods have to show their power by ending the plague?
☐ Not told ☐ Three days
☐ Next day ☐ One week

The God of Israel was the only one who could offer any protection from the plagues. Whom did God protect?
☐ Israelites in Goshen
☐ Egyptians who followed God's instructions
☐ Israelites who followed God's instructions
☐ Does not apply

Leaders' Actions and Reactions:

Check any person a statement applies to	Pharaoh	Officials/Magicians	Aaron/Moses
Performed miracle by God's command			
By magical powers, imitated God's acts but only added to the problem			
Could not imitate what God had done			
Could not stop the plague			
Recognized God's power			
Heart was hardened			
Prayers to God caused plagues to end			

WHAT WAS THE RESULT:
Pharaoh's response to the Israelites:
☐ Would not let go
☐ Said could go with stipulations but changed his mind
☐ Told them to leave immediately

The God of Israel challenged and defeated:
☐ The gods of nature
☐ The gods of time, days and hours
☐ The 'magic' charms and amulets
☐ Pharaoh, the god of his people

Learn the answers to these questions and many more!

➤ What are twelve aspects of God revealed in the creation story?
➤ What five things did the serpent say in the Garden of Eden that are the basis of false religions today?
➤ What are the elements of Hebrew poetry and how can you recognize it in scripture?
➤ How many continents have pyramid structures and how do they compare to ziggarats?
➤ How many languages are found on each continent and how many groups of people do not have any portion of the Bible in their own language?
➤ In what ways do Adam, Abel, Abraham, Isaac, Jacob and Moses compare to and foretell of the life, death and salvation of Jesus Christ?
➤ How does studying the unique physical features of a camel give us a better understanding of Rebekah?
➤ Which of the dozens of titles and responsibilities given to the second in command, or Vizier of Egypt, can be demonstrated in the life of Joseph?
➤ What is it about hieroglyphics that make it possible for even young children to read the ancient Egyptian script without even knowing the language?
➤ How does turning the Nile River to blood show that God, and God alone, is the source of all creation, the sustainer of life on earth and the source of eternal life after death?

and more

Give your children a solid start in math with...

Kinder-Math

$14.95

Kinder-Math uses worksheets, flash cards and word problems to teach:

- ✓ Formation of numbers with poems
- ✓ Counting to 100 by 1's, 2's 5's and 10's
- ✓ > Greater than, < Less than, = Equal to
- ✓ Simple addition facts
- ✓ Simple geometry
- ✓ $ Money
- ✓ Telling Time
- ✓ Sequence

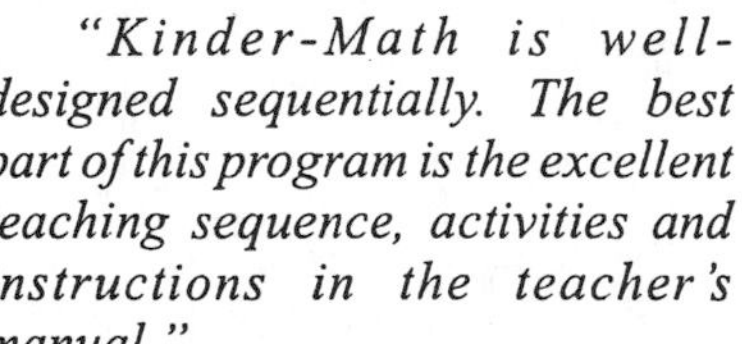

"Kinder-Math is well-designed sequentially. The best part of this program is the excellent teaching sequence, activities and instructions in the teacher's manual."

Mary Pride

To State It Simply It's a Capital Game

Only $4.95!

Learn the States and their Capitals

We will sail 'em even it the oar is gone.
What did Della wear when she dove her famous dive?

Your children will easily learn all 50 States and their Capitals with this fun game using captivating cartoons and clever puns. The game comes with a book with cut-apart flash cards that your children will love.

↖Flash Cards

Love conquered the new hampster.

Actual size 3 ¾ X 5"

Cut Here

Save $50.00
Buy Aphabet Island Complete

Order Today!

Name:

Street:

City: State:

Zip: Phone: ( )

Qty	Item	Price	Total
	Alphabet Island Phonics Complete Includes Alphabet Island Phonics 1 & 2 (free K-Math & Comprehensive Hdbk) Save $50.00	$ 119.95	
	Alphabet Island Phonics 1 (free Kinder-Math)	$ 69.95	
	Alphabet Island Phonics 2 (free Comprehensive Handbook)	$ 84.95	
	Comprehensive Handbook of Phonics	$ 19.95	
	Remembering God's Awesome Acts	$ 35.00	
	Considering God's Creation with tape	$ 29.95	
	Capital Game	$ 4.95	
	Kinder-Math	$ 14.95	
	Extra Workbooks & Tapes		
	Additional Alphabet Island 1 Wkbk	$ 9.95	
	Additional Alphabet Island 2 Wkbks	$ 14.95	
	Additional Kinder-Math Workbook	$ 4.95	
	Additional Awesome Acts Workbook	$ 20.00	
	Additional God's Creation Workbook	$ 13.95	
	Considering God's Creation Tape	$ 3.00	
	Alphabet Island Tape	$ 3.00	
	Alphabet Island Flash Cards	$ 3.00	
	New Supplemental Items!!!		
	21 Great Scientists Who Believed the Bible by Ann Lamont	$ 14.99	
	The Underground History of American Education by John Taylor Gatto	$ 30.00	
	Shipping & Handling (USA) $3 to $35 - add $3.50 $36 to $110 - add $5.50 $111 and up - add 5% Double above rates for UPS Please contact us for foreign rates		
	Subtotal		
	Tax (Oklahoma only) - 5.25%		
	Total		

Credit card orders accepted. Most orders are shipped the day they are received. Please send your check or money order (U.S. funds only) to address below:

Eagle's Wings
Educational Materials
P.O. Box 502
Duncan, OK 73534
Credit Cards Accepted (580) 252-1555
www.EaglesWingsED.com
E-mail: info@eagleswingsed.com

Satisfaction Guaranteed!

Money back guarantee when returned in good condition within 30 days (minus shipping and 10% restocking fee).

Please send _____ brochures for my friends.

I heard about you from:

- ❑ **M. Pride's** *The Big Book of Home Learning*
- ❑ **C. Duffy's** *The Christian Home Educator's Curriculum Manual*
- ❑ **Homeschool card deck**
- ❑ **Literature bag from book fair**
- ❑ **Friend**